THREE DANGEROUS MEN

ALSO BY SETH G. JONES

THREE DANGEROUS MEN

RUSSIA, CHINA, IRAN,
AND THE RISE OF
IRREGULAR WARFARE

SETH G. JONES

W. W. NORTON & COMPANY
Celebrating a Century of Independent Publishing

For information about permission to reproduce selections from this book,
write to Permissions, W. W. Norton & Company, Inc., 500 Fifth Avenue,
New York, NY 10110

For information about special discounts for bulk purchases, please contact
W. W. Norton Special Sales at specialsales@wwnorton.com or 800-233-4830

Manufacturing by Lakeside Book Company
Book design by Lovedog Studio
Production manager: Lauren Abbate

Library of Congress Cataloging-in-Publication Data

Names: Jones, Seth G., 1972– author.
Title: Three dangerous men : Russia, China, Iran, and the rise of irregular
warfare / Seth G. Jones.
Other titles: Russia, China, Iran, and the rise of irregular warfare
Description: First edition. | New York, NY : W. W. Norton & Company,
[2021] | Includes bibliographical references and index.
Identifiers: LCCN 2021025176 | ISBN 9781324006206 (hardcover) | ISBN
9781324006213 (epub)
Subjects: LCSH: United States—Foreign relations—Russia (Federation) |
United States—Foreign relations—Iran. | United States—Foreign
relations—China. | Russia (Federation)—Foreign relations—United
States. | Iran—Foreign relations—United States. | China—Foreign
relations—United States. | Hybrid warfare. | Cyberspace operations
(Military science) | Disinformation. | United States—Defenses.
Classification: LCC E895 .J66 2021 | DDC 327.73047086—dc23
LC record available at https://lccn.loc.gov/2021025176

ISBN 978-1-324-05056-8 pbk.

W. W. Norton & Company, Inc., 500 Fifth Avenue, New York, N.Y. 10110
www.wwnorton.com

W. W. Norton & Company Ltd., 15 Carlisle Street, London W1D 3BS

1 2 3 4 5 6 7 8 9 0

Asymmetric actions have come into widespread use, enabling the nullification of an enemy's advantages in armed conflict.

— Valery Gerasimov,
"Ценность науки в предвидении"
[The value of science is in the foresight]

CONTENTS

THREE DANGEROUS MEN

1: THE WRONG WAR

In mid-March 2020, cell phones across the United States lit up with alarming news. Citing a source in the US Department of Homeland Security, a series of apocalyptic texts warned that the Trump administration was deploying armed US soldiers onto the streets to enforce a lockdown in response to COVID-19. "They will announce this as soon as they have troops in place to help prevent looters and rioters," said one text. The anonymous sender noted that his friend "got the call last night and was told to pack and be prepared for the call today with his dispatch orders."[1] It urged recipients to spread the word. Similar messages warned of an imminent federal quarantine. "From a friend of a friend who works for Cleveland clinic," began another text, again citing unnamed sources. "Please be advised, within 48 to 72 Hours the president will evoke what is called the Stafford act.... Stock up on whatever you guys need to make sure you have a two week supply of everything."[2] It then implored people to forward the text to family and friends.

Back in Washington, the White House reacted quickly. "Text message rumors of a national #quarantine are FAKE," the National Security Council said in a tweet on March 15, just before midnight. "There is no national lockdown."[3] But it did little to stem the panic of some recipients, who frantically called their friends and family. As the US government explained, the texts were part of a disinformation campaign intended to sow disorder and confusion during the early stages of the COVID-19 crisis.

But who sent them? US intelligence agencies ultimately concluded that Chinese government operatives had forwarded texts to Americans on their cell phones and posted false information on social media platforms. Several US intelligence analysts I spoke to did not believe that Chinese agents had created the lockdown texts, but rather amplified existing texts. The messages were tailored to alarm people and drive recipients to share and spread the misinformation on their Twitter and Facebook feeds. China was weaponizing information by sending texts to cell phones on US soil.

For decades, Russia had conducted disinformation campaigns in the United States. The Soviets were famous for their propaganda. So were the Chinese—though largely outside the United States. Beginning in the 1940s, for example, China orchestrated a relentless propaganda and intelligence campaign against Taiwan. But China had never been this aggressive with operations targeting Americans in the US homeland. US officials were alarmed at how quickly China ramped up pro-Beijing and anti-Washington propaganda on social media platforms. "The Chinese have always had the capability to collect information, conduct espionage, and conduct a range of other activities against the United States," a former US intelligence agency leader told me. "But the Chinese have gone a step farther in conducting disinformation in the United States. And it is decidedly unneighborly."[4]

Even after American officials had discovered the source of the misinformation, Chinese government officials continued to pile on. Zhao Lijian, a Chinese spokesman for the Ministry of Foreign Affairs, wrote on Twitter in March that the US military might have spread COVID-19 in the Chinese city of Wuhan. "It might be US army who brought the epidemic to Wuhan," he wrote. "Be transparent! Make public your data! US owe us an explanation!"[5] The claim that the US Army had infected individuals in Wuhan was ridiculous and completely unsubstantiated. Undeterred, however, the Chinese government amplified the claim on the official Twitter accounts of Chinese embassies and consulates. The state-run

China Global Television Network Arabic channel produced an episode of *China View* that aired on March 17. Speaking in Arabic, the presenter falsely asserted that "some new facts" indicated that the pandemic might have originated from American participants in a military sports competition in October 2019 in Wuhan. The presenter further speculated that the virus might have originated out of US defense laboratories at Fort Detrick, Maryland, and raised "the possibility of the virus being transmitted to China from abroad during the period of the Military Olympic Games in Wuhan, which was attended by 109 countries, including the United States."[6]

Russian and Iranian government outlets soon joined the fray, aggressively promoting conspiracy theories that COVID-19 was a US-manufactured biological weapon targeting their countries. A news outlet funded by the Russian Ministry of Defense published an article titled "Coronavirus: American Biological Warfare against Russia and China."[7] It argued that Washington had unleashed COVID-19 against Russia and China to weaken their economies— an odd claim, since COVID-19 devastated the US economy as well. An article from RT, the state-run Russian news network, suggested that "the U.S. could be the prime culprit behind Covid-2019 outbreak that hit China and then Iran."[8] The head of Iran's Islamic Revolutionary Guard Corps said: "It is possible that this virus is a product of a biological attack by America which initially spread to China and then to Iran and the rest of the world."[9]

None of these claims were true, of course. But Chinese, Russian, and Iranian activity during the COVID-19 pandemic highlighted some of the major foreign policy instruments that those countries used to compete with the United States. Cyber campaigns, covert action, support to state and nonstate proxies, information and disinformation, espionage, and economic coercion—these are the tools of *irregular warfare*.

* * * *

WHILE CONVENTIONAL WARFARE—clashes between large military forces—defined twentieth-century power, irregular warfare will increasingly define international politics in the coming decades. Rising powers see an urgent need to globally compete for power and influence, and they are aggressively waging irregular warfare. Though the United States led the world after the Cold War as the only remaining superpower, supported by strong allies and a network of trading partners, the country is woefully unprepared for this type of competition today.

US government agencies and departments are focusing too much on planning for conventional and nuclear war with China, Russia, and other adversaries. Some policy makers are fixated on building a bigger navy with more than 350 ships, spending over $1 trillion on nuclear modernization, expanding the number of active duty and reserve soldiers to more than 1,040,000, and—perhaps most important—fighting conventional and nuclear wars against Russia in the Baltic states and China in the Taiwan Strait and South China Sea.[10] And they are giving too little attention to irregular warfare. Yet China, Russia, and Iran are daily—even hourly—targeting the United States at home and abroad, using irregular means. Their main tools are not fighter jets, battle tanks, or infantry soldiers, but hackers, spies, special operations forces, and private military companies with clandestine links to state security agencies. They are waging a war online and in the shadows—not primarily on conventional battlefields.

The United States does not need to choose *between* conventional and irregular competition. Both are important. Russia and China are developing conventional and nuclear military capabilities that pose a threat to the United States and its partners. The challenge is to find an equilibrium. As former secretary of defense Robert Gates said to me: "You have to be prepared for the full range of contingencies. One of the reasons that the Cold War, in many respects, was fought using nonmilitary instruments was because of the power of our conventional and nuclear forces to deter the Soviets."[11] But while the United States fought effective irregular campaigns during the global competition with the Soviet Union, today it has ceded that battlefield to others. The results are disturbing.

US adversaries have exploited polarization in American politics; taken advantage of a withdrawal of US forces from the Middle East, Africa, and South Asia; and targeted US universities, companies, and government agencies. These trends worsened under President Donald Trump. His hyperpartisan politics, isolationist tendencies, and disregard for allies made it easier for China, Russia, and Iran to exploit the United States' vulnerabilities and weaknesses at home and abroad. After Trump's refusal to accept the outcome of the November 2020 presidential election and his incitement of a mob that stormed the US Capitol Building on January 6, 2021, Chinese government officials and pundits excoriated the United States for lecturing the world about democracy and human rights.[12] Favorable views of the United States around the world plummeted, according to the nonpartisan Pew Research Center.[13] In some countries, the United States' unpopularity in the age of Trump was nearly on par with Kim Jong-un's North Korea, a regime run by a despot who butchered and starved his own population.

"We are not primed to compete against the Russians, the Chinese, and the Iranians. We are failing at it," former acting CIA director Mike Morell said to me. "I am fearful that when historians look back at this period, they will see it as the beginning of China overtaking the United States as a global power."[14] Charles Cleveland, former head of US Army Special Operations Command, bluntly warned: "The United States is facing death by a thousand cuts. We are not prepared for competition the way the Russians, Chinese, and Iranians see it. For these countries, competition is largely irregular— not conventional."[15]

The Chinese are engaging in economic and technological competition, the Russians are conducting aggressive covert action, and the

Iranians are leveraging partner forces and other assets in Lebanon, Syria, Iraq, Yemen, and other countries. All have aggressive cyber and espionage programs, and all view the United States as their main competitor. All three are also more active than most Americans recognize. "Competition is a daily occurrence," former CIA director Michael Hayden said to me. "It is happening all the time."[16] Irregular warfare is generally cheaper for these countries than building conventional and nuclear capabilities. Since they are authoritarian regimes with state-run economies, China, Russia, and Iran can also direct resources to irregular activities more quickly than the United States can and have few—or no—constraints in waging blatant disinformation campaigns and pilfering military and commercial secrets.

"The Chinese are not interested in a shooting war," said Admiral Bill McRaven, the former head of US Special Operations Command (SOCOM). "They are stealing our technology, they are trying to outpace us in artificial intelligence and other areas. While we can never discount the possibility of war with China, these issues concern me much more than conventional conflict."[17] In addition, US deputy secretary of defense Kathleen Hicks argued: "Today's competition of interests is often playing out in a place beyond diplomacy and short of conventional war, which some experts refer to as the gray zone. Too often, rivals are gaining an advantage at the expense of US interests."[18] Joseph Votel, former head of both SOCOM and US Central Command (CENTCOM), came to a similar conclusion. "We are way too focused on conventional war and deterrence," he told me. "I saw this when I was SOCOM and CENTCOM commander. Conventional war dominated our approach."[19]

There is still time to change course. But the United States needs to significantly alter how it thinks about—and engages in—competition before it is too late.

* * * *

THIS BOOK EXPLORES how Russia, Iran, and China each view competition with the United States. What are their respective objectives? What foreign policy instruments have they used to achieve their objectives? How are they attempting to weaken the United States? And what are the implications? This book views competition primarily *through their eyes*—through the perspectives of leaders in Moscow, Tehran, and Beijing. For these countries, competition is a means to an end, not an end in itself. This book does not focus on all adversaries. For example, North Korea has nuclear weapons, some cyber capabilities, and missiles, but it is an economic basket case with no meaningful power projection capabilities.

To understand irregular warfare by US rivals, I examined thousands of primary and secondary Chinese, Russian, and Iranian documents—from official white papers to defense journals and newspapers—in Mandarin, Russian, and Persian languages. I also interviewed Chinese, Russian, and Iranian subject matter experts and dozens of US military, diplomatic, and intelligence officials, from former secretary of defense Robert Gates to former CIA directors Michael Hayden and David Petraeus. Most were deeply concerned about where the United States is headed and how it is competing in international politics. Among them, there was virtual unanimity that the United States is unprepared for irregular competition with countries like Russia, Iran, and China—and is often far too risk averse, reactive, and slow to respond to threats.

The great British military strategist B. H. Liddell Hart once told a story of a conversation between the Irish statesman John Wilson Croker and Arthur Wellesley, 1st Duke of Wellington.[20] Walking on a country road in the early nineteenth century, they amused themselves by guessing what sort of country they might discover over the next rise. When Croker marveled at Wellington's accuracy, Wellington replied, matter-of-factly: "Why, I have spent all of my life in trying to guess what was at the other side of the hill." Wellington went on to explain, "All the business of war, and indeed all the business of life, is to endeavor to find out what you don't know by what you do."[21] For Wellington, a great general was defined by an ability to understand what was happening on the "other side of the hill"—behind the opposing lines and in the enemy's mind.

In an effort to better comprehend what is occurring on the "other side of the hill," this book examines Chinese, Russian, and Iranian sources and people. Far too many policy makers in the West read only Western and English-language sources. They do not read— or even translate—sources in Chinese, Russian, or Persian. That is tragic. The US bias for English-language sources leads to a danger-ous ignorance of its rivals' thinking.

This book also tracks the life and activities of an influential fig-ure in each country: General Valery Gerasimov, Russian chief of the general staff; Major General Qassem Soleimani, head of the Islamic Revolutionary Guard Corp-Quds Force in Iran; and General Zhang Youxia, vice chairman of China's Central Military Commission. By no means are these individuals the only important military lead-ers in their countries. But these three—Gerasimov, Soleimani, and Zhang—were critical in the development of their country's strategic thinking and policy implementation. Their lives provide an import-ant context for understanding competition with the United States. It is also telling that these individuals are all men, since there were few prominent women in senior positions within the Russian, Chi-nese, and Iranian militaries.

Gerasimov is one of the most influential Russian military leaders of our time and, along with President Vladimir Putin and a select group of Russian policy makers, helped Russia revitalize its foreign policy. "I'd be rich if I got a nickel for every time I've heard: 'Russia is a declining power,'" Tony Thomas, former head of SOCOM and Joint Special Operations Command (JSOC), told me. "If Putin and Gerasimov have a bad hand, they have played it awfully well."[22] Like-wise, Qassem Soleimani was instrumental in conceptualizing and implementing Iranian competition with the United States. Before he died in a US strike in 2020, Soleimani oversaw Tehran's irregular campaign in the Middle East, using Iran's paramilitary arm, the Islamic Revolutionary Guard Corps-Quds Force. Finally, Zhang Youxia's combat experience, political acumen, and—perhaps most important—childhood friendship with leader Xi Jinping shaped Chinese views of competition with the United States.

Among the United States' main competitors, China is by far the least transparent. China translates a limited amount of information into English, and Western countries—including the United States—have failed to translate and make publicly available some of China's most important military documents, speeches, and reports in English. Most Americans have to rely on what the Chinese Communist Party chooses to translate into English, using state-run media and propaganda outlets. A sea of domestic discourse, debate, and Communist Party documents remain hidden in plain sight. The US journalist John Pomfret astutely remarked that when it comes to keeping Americans in the dark about the Chinese political scene, "the Chinese language is the first level of encryption."[23] In addition, the Chinese system is structured in such a way that there is little personalization of national security decision-making and tremendous secrecy about the role that senior officials play. Nevertheless, during the tenure of Xi Jinping, Zhang Youxia was at the center of virtually every major national security discussion within China's Central Military Commission, the main national defense organization of the Communist Party.

All three of these men—Valery Gerasimov, Qassem Soleimani, and Zhang Youxia—carefully studied US successes and failures after the Cold War. Gerasimov was simultaneously impressed and alarmed as the United States conducted successful operations in the former Yugoslavia in the 1990s and then overthrew the governments in Afghanistan in 2001, Iraq in 2003, and Libya in 2011. "The war between NATO and Yugoslavia," Gerasimov remarked, "was proclaimed as a new-generation conflict, in which the goals were achieved without the active involvement of ground forces."[24] Soleimani closely observed the US military as it invaded Iraq, and then he attempted to exploit its vulnerabilities by aiding Shia militia groups in Iraq and across the Middle East. After watching the United States overthrow regimes in Afghanistan and Iraq in rapid succession, Zhang concluded that the future of warfare was rapidly evolving away "from taking cities through conventional operations and seizing land" and toward irregular activities like information operations.[25]

All three of these officials learned from the United States as they evolved their own irregular warfare campaigns. The irony of America's current weakness is that it set the example for how to compete in a post–Cold War world. Now the United States is being beaten at its own game.

✳ ✳ ✳ ✳

THE TOWERING US State Department diplomat and Cold War expert George Kennan once chided his fellow Americans for getting sucked into an unnecessarily narrow definition of warfare. He argued that warfare can involve political, economic, intelligence, information, military, and other means to achieve national objectives. The tools "range from such overt actions as political alliances, economic measures . . . and 'white' propaganda to such covert operations as clandestine support of 'friendly' foreign elements, 'black' psychological warfare and even encouragement of underground resistance in hostile states." While conventional and nuclear wars have a beginning and an end, irregular warfare is a persistent struggle. As Kennan noted, it is a reality of international politics—what he called "the perpetual rhythm of struggle, in and out of war."[26] General Sir Nick Carter, the UK's Chief of the Defence Staff, explained to me that Russia and China engage in irregular warfare daily—even hourly. "They regard the global context as being a *continuous struggle* where non-military and military means are used unconstrained," he said.[27]

For the purposes of this book, "irregular warfare" refers to activities short of conventional and nuclear warfare that are designed to expand a country's influence and legitimacy, as well as to weaken its adversaries.[28] It includes numerous tools of statecraft that governments can use to shift the balance of power in their favor: information operations (including psychological operations and propaganda), cyber operations, support to state and nonstate partners, covert action, espionage, and economic coercion.[29] Many of these tools, such as information and cyber operations, can be used for both irregular and conventional warfare. They are simply a means. In irregular warfare, however, a country designs and uses these tools to undermine its adversaries as part of balance-of-power competition without engaging in set-piece battles. Other government officials and scholars have used different terms—such as "political warfare," "hybrid warfare," "gray zone activity," "asymmetric warfare," and "the indirect approach"—to capture some or all of these activities.[30]

Irregular warfare is distinct from conventional warfare, which has sometimes been referred to as "traditional" or "regular" warfare. Conventional warfare involves the use of direct army, navy, air force, and other military capabilities to defeat an adversary's armed forces on a battlefield; control territory, populations, and forces; or annihilate an enemy's war-making capacity.[31] Irregular warfare is also different from nuclear warfare, which involves the use—or threat—of nuclear weapons against adversaries. Finally, irregular warfare is distinct from routine foreign policy, which can include diplomatic, humanitarian, intelligence, and other activities that have little or nothing to do with competition against adversaries.

Some might object to using the term "warfare" to describe nonviolent actions like economic coercion and information operations, but that is not how US rivals see it. They apply a broad view of warfare as "a struggle between competing entities."[32] China has used terms like *san zhong zhanfa* ("three warfares"), which includes public opinion, psychological, and legal warfare—none of which involve the direct use of violence.[33] As the Chinese general Sun Tzu remarked, the supreme art of war is to "subdue the enemy *without fighting*."[34] Iran has utilized terms such as *jang-e narm* ("soft war"), which includes activities like propaganda and disinformation to influence others. Finally, Russia has used *aktivnyye meropriyatiya* ("active measures") for decades as a tool of warfare against the United States and its partners. Gerasimov referred to actions in Syria as "asymmetric warfare" and argued that its effects can be as significant as conventional operations.[35] "The important point," writes US military historian Charles Bartles, "is that while the West considers these non-military measures as ways of avoiding war, *Russia considers these measures as war*."[36] In short, the concept of warfare used here is much closer to Sun Tzu than it is to the Prussian military theorist Carl von Clausewitz, who narrowly defined war as an "act of violence intended to compel our opponent to fulfill our will."[37]

Irregular warfare is as old as war itself, and these countries have rich histories of using it. During the Cold War, Russian services like the KGB waged aggressive irregular campaigns against the United States around the globe. Moscow used terms like *aktivnyye meropriyatiya* ("active measures"), *asimmetrichnym* ("asymmetrical"), *informatsionnoye protivoborstvo* ("information confrontation"), and *maskirovka* ("denial and deception"). Oleg Kalugin, the head of foreign counterintelligence for the KGB, described active measures as the "heart and soul of Soviet intelligence" that were used to "weaken the United States" and to "drive wedges in the Western community alliance of all sorts."[38]

Chinese strategists have written some of the most influential texts on irregular warfare. Sun Tzu argued in *The Art of War* that the most important factor in warfare is "moral influence," which includes swaying the views of a local population.[39] Chinese leaders have also tried to master the concepts of *douzheng* ("struggle"), *fei duicheng* ("asymmetric means"), and *san zhong zhanfa* ("three warfares"). While there are many similarities over time in how these countries have waged irregular warfare, there are also some differences in how it is used today. In particular, the internet and digital platforms have enabled adversaries to conduct propaganda, cyber warfare, and disinformation campaigns instantly around the globe—including in the US homeland—in ways they were never able to do in the past.

✳ ✳ ✳ ✳

DEPLOYING IRREGULAR TECHNIQUES and leveraging new technology, America's adversaries have made significant advances against the United States.

Take Russia. Under Vladimir Putin, Valery Gerasimov, and other officials, Russia has employed a mix of offensive cyber operations, espionage, covert action, and information and disinformation campaigns to weaken the United States and expand Moscow's influence. As former national security advisor and US secretary of state Condoleezza Rice argued, Putin adopted "an aggressive foreign policy abroad, aimed at redressing the 'tragedy,' as Putin called it, of the Soviet Union's demise" and expanding Russia's global influence.[40] But Russia isn't China. "While China is betting on getting stronger, Russia knows that it will never be economically or militarily stronger than the United States," said Mike Morell. "They can't close the gap by getting stronger. They can only close the gap by making us weaker."[41]

Russia has meddled in US elections and waged a disinformation campaign inside the United States, attempting to inflame social, racial, and political tensions through such issues as Black Lives Matter, COVID-19, the Me Too movement, gun control, white supremacy, abortion, and immigration. Russia has placed malware, such as Triton and BlackEnergy, in US critical infrastructure—threatening power plants, electricity grids, communications networks, and financial systems in the US homeland. These efforts have been led by cells like Military Unit 74455 within Russia's military intelligence agency, the Main Intelligence Directorate, commonly referred to as the GRU.[42] Other Russian intelligence agencies—particularly Russia's Foreign Intelligence Service, or SVR—have played an important role. In 2020, the SVR orchestrated a brazen attack against dozens of companies and US government agencies by attaching malware to a software update from SolarWinds, a company based in Austin, Texas, that makes network monitoring software. The DarkSide, a hacking group operating in part from Russian soil, conducted a ransomware attack in May 2021 against Colonial Pipeline, which led the company to shut down a major pipeline for several days and created fuel shortages across the southeastern United States. Russia also attempted to manipulate the 2020 US presidential election. A 2021 US intelligence assessment concluded that "Russian President Putin authorized, and a range of Russian government organizations conducted, influence operations aimed at . . . undermining public confidence in the electoral process, and exacerbating sociopolitical divisions in the US."[43]

With Gerasimov's involvement, Russian agencies have also leveraged shadowy organizations to help conduct information operations, cyber attacks, and combat operations, including private military companies like the Wagner Group, the Internet Research Agency (IRA), Kaspersky Lab, and networks and online personas with creative names like "Guccifer 2.0."[44] The IRA, a Russian organization funded by Yevgeny Prigozhin, who had close ties to Putin and Russian intelligence, created social media groups, accounts, and front companies that falsely claimed to be affiliated with US political and grassroots organizations in an attempt to influence US citizens.[45] According to FBI agents that I interviewed, Russian intelligence agencies have also funded white supremacist and other far-right networks in the United States and overseas—mostly through front groups—and have spread white supremacist and other far-right propaganda on the internet and social media through clandestine means.[46]

Overseas, Moscow has steadfastly worked to weaken the United States and undermine US relations with its allies. Russian intelligence agencies have conducted disinformation campaigns, falsely charging the United States with supporting the Islamic State and other terrorist organizations in countries like Syria and Afghanistan. Moscow has supported terrorist groups like Lebanese Hezbollah and nonstate organizations in Ukraine, Syria, Libya, and Afghanistan—including the Taliban. The GRU and SVR also have run extensive campaigns to support political leaders in Europe—including far-right organizations like Italy's Lega Party and Austria's Freedom Party. These efforts have partly paid off. Russia has expanded its influence in Europe, Central Asia, South Asia, North Africa, and the Middle East. As one Middle East leader told me: "The Russians are now a major power in the Middle East."[47]

Among the countries that have embraced Russia's new influence in the Middle East is Iran. With Qassem Soleimani and the Quds Force at the helm, Iran also possessed formidable irregular capabilities. Tehran adopted a strategy of "forward defense," which involves supporting terrorist groups and local militias across the Middle East. "Iran wants to be a hegemonic power—a Persian power—in the Middle East," said Mike Morell. "They want to reestablish a Persian empire. That means they want to get the US out of the region and end the state of Israel."[48] Thanks to Soleimani and his successor, Ismail Qaani, the number of Iran-linked militia fighters grew to over 200,000 by 2021 in Syria, Iraq, Yemen, Lebanon, and elsewhere—a 150 percent increase from 2013 levels.[49] In addition, Iran has maintained the largest ballistic and cruise missile force in the Middle East, courtesy of Russian, Chinese, and North Korean support. A ballistic missile based on Iran's Zoljanah space launch vehicle could carry a one-ton warhead as far as 5,000 kilometers, allowing Iran to strike every European capital.[50]

Iran has also improved its offensive cyber capabilities. As one US intelligence assessment summarized: "Iran uses increasingly sophisticated cyber techniques to conduct espionage; it is also attempting to deploy cyber attack capabilities that would enable attacks against critical infrastructure in the United States and allied countries."[51] Iran has targeted US casinos, dams, the power grid, and financial institutions like Bank of America, JPMorgan Chase, and the New York Stock Exchange. It has developed destructive malware through one of its state-sponsored hacking groups: APT33 (or Elfin). One example is Shamoon, a malware that deletes files from an infected computer and then wipes the computer's master boot record, making it unusable. Iran also has conducted aggressive cyber attacks against foreign parliaments, government agencies, and companies—including Saudi Aramco, the Saudi Arabian oil company. "Iran's malign cyber actions have been consequential, costly, damaging, and wide-ranging," said Norm Roule, former US national intelligence manager for Iran and a thirty-four-year CIA veteran.[52]

In addition, Iran has been involved in an aggressive disinformation campaign against the United States on digital platforms such as Facebook, Twitter, and YouTube. These campaigns frequently involve fake social media accounts run by individuals posing as Americans, which promote pro-Iranian issues. US companies like Google have taken down Iranian government-linked channels on YouTube and accounts on Google Plus, Blogger, and LinkedIn that have engaged in phishing and hacking attempts, influence operations, and digital attacks against political campaigns.

Not to be outdone, China has engaged in irregular activities to achieve its primary objectives of increasing influence, particularly in Asia; expanding its economic power with a mercantilist view of the world; and surpassing the United States as the dominant global technological, military, and economic power. "The rise of China is the single most important issue for US foreign policy," said General Petraeus.[53] Many will point to American military dominance as proof that China is still a long way from being a peer competitor with the United States. But as this book argues, Chinese military strategy generally aims to *avoid* a conventional war. China's goal is to weaken and surpass the United States without fighting. China is building conventional and nuclear capabilities to deter US action, but the vast majority of Chinese competition is through economic, technological, and other means. "For China, competition is 80 percent economic and 20 percent diplomatic and military," said Stanley McChrystal, former head of Joint Special Operations Command.[54]

Beijing has developed one of the most sophisticated cyber capabilities of any of the United States' adversaries, through such organizations as Unit 61398 of the People's Liberation Army. China's leaders have extended the country's global economic, political, military, and technological reach by using global development strategies like the Belt and Road Initiative. The Chinese government leveraged the telecom giant Huawei and other technology firms to expand 5G, the fifth-generation technology for cellular networks, and intelligence collection across the globe. Beijing also has utilized economic inducements and coercion, as well as covert support to foreign government officials, to expand its power and influence. It has used fleets of fishing vessels and created artificial islands by dumping millions of tons of sand and concrete onto reefs to assert its territorial and resource claims in the Pacific.

Chinese influence has even extended to the United States. Chinese political and intelligence agencies have conducted significant operations on US university campuses, including stealing sensitive technologies, collecting information, monitoring Chinese students, and pressuring publishers and researchers not to print negative portrayals of China.[55] Beijing's influence has reached into Hollywood, where approval by the Communist Party affects whether a major film can be distributed in China. There are sparingly few Chinese villains in Hollywood movies—a far cry from the Cold War, when movies like *The Hunt for Red October* and *Red Dawn* pitted the United States against an evil Soviet empire. As one study concluded, there is an epidemic of self-censorship in Hollywood to ensure access to the Chinese market.[56]

Given these troubling trends, China's attempt to manipulate the US population by using disinformation during the COVID-19 outbreak needs to be understood as the wave of the future—an intense global competition using conventional *and irregular* means.

* * * *

MOSCOW, TEHRAN, AND BEIJING have not chosen to wage irregular warfare against the United States out of some essential quality of national character. Instead, they have made a logical conclusion, based on three core tenets.

First, the United States remains the world's dominant conventional and nuclear power. Its defense budget is larger than the defense budgets of the next eleven countries in the world *combined*.[57] The United States' land, air, naval, space, and cyber capabilities are formidable. For Russia, Iran, and even China, choosing to fight a conventional war with the United States would be a risky and dangerous proposition.[58]

Second, the costs of conventional and nuclear war would be staggering. Over the past several years, the US government and think tanks have conducted numerous war games and analyses of conflicts with Russia in the Baltics, China in the Taiwan Strait and South China Sea, and Iran in the Middle East. I have participated in some of these war games. The results are bleak. Many conclude that war could lead to tens or hundreds of thousands of dead soldiers and civilians, domestic unrest, billions of dollars in economic damages, a global economic downturn, and the potential collapse of long-held alliances.

A US war with China could reduce China's gross domestic product (GDP) by between 25 and 35 percent and the United States' GDP by between 5 and 10 percent, according to a study by the RAND Corporation, a US-based research institution.[59] As that study concluded: "A long and severe war could ravage China's economy, stall its hard-earned development, and cause widespread hardship and dislocation. Such economic damage could in turn aggravate political turmoil and embolden separatists in China."[60] Both the United States and China would also likely suffer huge numbers of military and civilian deaths and risk large-scale destruction of their military forces. If war expanded to include their allies—as it did during World War I, World War II, and the Korean War—economic and casualty figures could skyrocket even further.

War games that involve a conflict between NATO and Russia, including scenarios with Russian forces invading one or more Baltic countries, often escalate to include the threat—or use—of nuclear weapons. Nuclear war could raise the number of deaths, both civilian and military, into the millions, creating far-reaching environmental destruction and triggering significant global financial costs. These costs and risks make conventional and nuclear war unlikely—and explain why America's adversaries have turned to irregular warfare.

Third, the United States is, to be blunt, *vulnerable* to irregular means. It is more dependent on financial, commercial, and government cyber networks than most of its adversaries, and its networks are open and exposed to attack. It has struggled to respond effectively to Russian, Chinese, and Iranian disinformation campaigns in the United States, especially in America's charged political climate. As former US undersecretary of defense for policy Michèle A. Flournoy remarked, the United States also has "no U.S. answer to Beijing's Belt and Road Initiative." She continued that "Chinese activities in the 'gray zone,' below the level of conflict—such as building militarized 'islands' and using coercive measures to enforce disputed sovereignty claims in the South China Sea—have gone largely unanswered by the United States."[61] Finally, the US military has struggled against poorly equipped terrorist and insurgent groups in Afghanistan, Iraq, and Somalia, to name just a few examples. The Biden administration's decision in 2021 to withdraw US forces from Afghanistan reinforced US vulnerability to an irregular warfare campaign. Pakistan's intelligence agency, the Inter-Services Intelligence (ISI) Directorate, ran one of the most successful irregular warfare campaigns against the US by providing sanctuary and aid to the Taliban after 9/11.

Acknowledging the realities of competition does not, of course, rule out cooperation. The Chinese market of 1.4 billion people is an attractive market for US companies, and trade between the United States and China is important for economic growth in both countries. Cooperation between the United States and China, Russia, and Iran is also important in arms control, climate change, trade, energy, and other sectors. But America's failure to develop and implement an effective strategy to compete with these countries— including using irregular means—has been calamitous. "I think the US is weaker internationally and has become weaker in recent years around the world," Robert Gates told me. "Without some kind of a change, our position internationally will simply continue to deteriorate."[62]

✳ ✳ ✳ ✳

IN HIS FAMOUS farewell address in January 1989, President Ronald Reagan referred to the United States as a city on a hill, which served as a beacon of light for freedom and democracy. "In my mind, it was a tall proud city built on rocks stronger than oceans, wind swept, God blessed, and teeming with people of all kinds living in harmony and peace—a city with free ports that hummed with commerce and creativity, and if there had to be city walls, the walls had doors, and the doors were open to anyone with the will and the heart to get here."[63]

This vision of America as a shining city has dimmed. Fewer people across the globe look to the United States as a beacon of freedom.[64] America's main adversaries—China, Russia, and Iran—are illiberal countries that seek to shape the international system in ways fundamentally distinct from the United States' approach. These countries view the United States and its Western partners—including their support of democracy, free speech, and free trade—as dangerous. These three US adversaries are undemocratic, and their populations have little or no say in choosing leaders. Their governments support state-run economies, not free markets. They control the media and abhor a free press.

The United States has been here before. In combating the Soviet Union, America pursued its own style of irregular warfare using information campaigns orchestrated by the US Information Agency (which the United States eliminated in 1999); military and diplomatic support to state and nonstate actors in Latin America, Europe, Asia, Africa, and the Middle East; covert action by the CIA; and economic pressure. These activities complemented the United States' conventional and nuclear buildup, which deterred a Soviet nuclear first strike and a conventional attack in Europe. The United States' actions were not always pretty, but irregular warfare was essential to overwhelming the Soviet Union and, later, to maintaining *Pax Americana*. A contemporary history of the Cold War written by two Russian military officers concluded that "the complex application of non-military means by the U.S. in a 'cold war' against the Soviet Union yielded more significant results than the use of [conventional] military force . . . [M]ethods of information-psychological influence have allowed the Americans to destroy the Soviet Union."[65]

Irregular warfare today is merely the newest variant of an age-old struggle between competitors. Doing it well, however, will require better understanding the nature of competition today and better implementing a strategy and policies aligned with US values. Perhaps the single most important step is to refashion US foreign policy on America's core principles, which have been in place since America's founding. Competition today is, to a great extent, a struggle between rival political, economic, and military *systems*—between authoritarian, state-controlled systems and democratic systems.

China, Russia, and Iran are vulnerable—much as the Soviet Union was vulnerable during the Cold War. Their authoritarian political systems and attempts to control access to information—including through state-run media—make them susceptible to a US and Western information campaign. The United States and its partners in Europe, Asia, and other regions should relentlessly expose China, Russia, and Iran's human rights abuses, oppression, and corruption. These adversaries have been involved in the arrest, torture, and assassination of defectors, political opponents, and individuals investigating or prosecuting bribery and fraud. China, for one, already has its hands full, from protesters in Hong Kong and Taiwan to Uyghurs in the Xinjiang autonomous region of China.

As Robert Gates said to me: "I frankly have been surprised—and it's a measure of how far we have fallen in the realm of strategic communications, for example—that we have not figured out ways to get past the firewalls in Iran, and Russia, and China." The primary US goal, Gates continued, should be to "expose the corruption—the vast corruption of the ayatollah and the clerics around him, and the revolutionary guard, or of Vladimir Putin and his henchmen, and how they're looting Russia and the consequence of that for the standard of living for most Russians, or the extent of corruption in China, including the leadership and so on."[66]

America's foreign policy—including in irregular warfare—needs to be aligned with US principles of democracy, freedom of the press, and free markets. These principles were essential in establishing the United States as a country. As Thomas Jefferson remarked, "Freedom of religion; freedom of press; and freedom of person. . . . These principles form the bright constellation, which has gone before us and guided our steps through an age of revolution and reformation."[67] They were critical in winning the Cold War against the Soviet Union, and they are just as important today.

This book thus begins, fittingly, with Russia—the country that emerged from the ruins of America's Cold War competition.

PART I

RUSSIA

VALERY GERASIMOV

2: ACTIVE MEASURES

IN MARCH 2020, THE US NATIONAL SECURITY
Council held a secret meeting to discuss an extraordinary US intelligence assessment. According to US spy agencies, the Russian military had provided money to Taliban-linked militants in Afghanistan to target foreign forces, including US troops. US intelligence agencies assessed that Russian activities were perpetrated by Unit 29155—a division of Russia's military intelligence agency known as the GRU, which fell under the command of Valery Gerasimov.[1] The unit was linked to the March 2018 nerve agent poisoning in the United Kingdom of Sergei Skripal, a former GRU officer who had worked for British intelligence and then defected, along with his daughter. Unit 29155 was also likely behind the September 2020 poisoning of Russian opposition politician Aleksei Navalny, a failed coup attempt in Montenegro in 2016, the poisoning of Bulgarian arms dealer Emilian Gebrev in 2015, and the 2014 attack against a Czech ammunition depot.

US spies had watched the Russians transfer money from a bank account controlled by the GRU to Taliban operatives through a complex *hawala* system—an informal method of transferring money outside of traditional banking systems. Earlier in the year, US and Afghan forces had raided a Taliban building in Afghanistan and seized approximately $500,000 in US currency and matériel that suggested Russian activity. In addition, the United States collected information from the interrogation of captured Afghan militants and criminals indicating possible Russian involvement in paying money to the Taliban for assassinations in Afghanistan. Around February 27, 2020, US intelligence analysts included some of this information in a President's Daily Brief provided to Donald Trump. The CIA and National Counterterrorism Center also concluded with "medium confidence" in July 2020 that Unit 29155 had provided money to Taliban militants to target foreign—including likely US—soldiers.[2]

Russia's actions were an escalation in the country's global competition with the United States, and a clear example of Moscow's embrace of irregular warfare.[3] In this case, Russia was targeting the United States not directly, but rather indirectly through partner forces. Yet Russia's activity was not entirely out of the blue. For several years, US and European intelligence agencies had watched with growing alarm as Russian military and intelligence agencies seized Crimea through irregular means, started a war in eastern Ukraine by aiding separatists, worked with Lebanese Hezbollah and other forces in Syria, conducted hacking-and-dumping operations against a US presidential election, and deployed private military companies to roughly thirty countries on four continents. On February 7, 2018, a force of several hundred well-armed contractors from Russia's Wagner Group, the 5th Assault Corps from the Syrian army, and foreign Shia militia conducted an assault in Syria on the Conoco gas field east of Dayr az Zawr. The gas facility was held by a small contingent of US special operations forces and their partners from the Syrian Democratic Forces. After repeated warnings to the Russian military, the United States attacked the assault force with air and artillery strikes, killing as many as 300 Russian private military contractors.[4]

"We let the dogs loose," General Tony Thomas, the head of US Special Operations Command, told me. "The score was US: 0 killed; Russian proxies: 300."[5]

It was now Russia's turn to return the favor. The GRU unit behind Russia's activities in Afghanistan was ultimately subordinate to one of Moscow's most influential leaders: General Valery Gerasimov, chief of the General Staff of the Armed Forces.

* * * *

VALERY VASILYOVICH GERASIMOV was born on September 8, 1955, in the Russian city of Kazan. Situated at a great bend in the Volga River, 450 miles east of Moscow along the M7 trunk road, Kazan displays a patchwork architecture of ancient palaces and industrial plants. It has long been an important trading hub because of its strategic location as the capital of Tatarstan, a majority-Muslim and oil-producing region. During the late Middle Ages, Kazan was one of the economic hubs of the Golden Horde, at the western edge of the Mongol Empire. In 1552, Russian tsar Ivan IV—whom Sir Jerome Horsey, an English visitor to Ivan IV's court, described as "cruel, bloody," and "merciless"—laid waste to Kazan and absorbed it into the Russian empire.[6] Following Hitler's invasion of the Soviet Union in June 1941, Stalin relocated industrial plants and factories to Kazan to escape the German war machine. The city transformed into a working-class military-industrial hub during the war, producing a slew of war material from battle tanks to airplanes.

Gerasimov was born here, only a decade after the end of World War II. His uncle, who had commanded a tank company during the war, told glorious—if slightly embellished—tales from the battlefield, catalyzing Gerasimov's interest in the military. For Gerasimov, the lead nation in defeating the Nazis in World War II—or the "Great Patriotic War," as he referred to it—was not the United States, United Kingdom, or any of the other Allied powers. It was the Soviet Union. As Gerasimov explained, the Red Army defeated over 600 German and Axis divisions—three and a half times more than on all other fronts. What's more, he believed, "In the first, most difficult years of the war, the USSR alone opposed the aggressor" after Hitler's ill-fated June 1941 invasion of the Soviet Union.[7] He would go on to say that these Western countries were "undertaking large-scale efforts to rewrite the history of the twentieth century."[8]

During his childhood, Gerasimov devoured the writings of Konstantin Simonov, a Russian poet, playwright, and war correspondent.[9] Simonov's works combined two of Gerasimov's early passions: reading and military service. His poem "Wait for Me" was wildly popular among Russian front-line soldiers, or *frontoviki*. Some of them folded a copy of the poem and put it inside their uniform, pressed against their heart, as a protective totem.[10] For Gerasimov, the poem put a poignant, human face on war:

> *Wait for me and I'll come back,*
> *Dodging every fate!*
> *"What a bit of luck!" they'll say,*
> *Those that did not wait.*[11]

Supported by his father and inspired by Simonov, Gerasimov applied to Kazan Suvorov Military School, his local military boarding school, at the age of eleven.[12] But he was rejected. It was a huge psychological blow, though Gerasimov was undeterred. Four years later, he reapplied and—to his amazement—was accepted.[13] His former classmates, such as Gumer Ziganshin, remember him as studious—nearly always surrounded by neat stacks of military textbooks or arguing with teachers about military tactics. "Before giving us some task," Ziganshin recalled, teachers "would approach Valery and say to him, 'Valery please have a look at this. What do you think? Is this a good solution?' And only then would the teacher give it to the rest of the class."[14]

Like any teenager, Gerasimov occasionally slipped into bouts of playfulness—a stark contrast to the stiff and solemn general he would become later in life. One year on International Women's Day, Gerasimov sent a celebratory card to one of the school's most grueling teachers—a male.

"Good morning cadets!" the teacher began class the next day.

"Good morning, comrade major," the cadets quickly responded, standing at attention.

"Thank you very much for the congratulations I have received on the International Women's Day of March 8!" the teacher said.

The class erupted into laughter. After motioning the students to sit down, the teacher—visibly indignant—turned to Gerasimov, "Please come and see me later."

When Gerasimov stopped by after school, the teacher demanded an explanation—in writing.

"Why me?" Gerasimov retorted, feigning incredulousness. "I didn't do anything!"

"Why did you laugh then?" the teacher said.

"Well, wasn't the situation comical?" Gerasimov asked.[15]

The teacher was unimpressed with Gerasimov's impishness.

While Gerasimov could occasionally pull off a practical joke, he had found his calling at Suvorov. "I am going to become a general," he announced to his friends. He enjoyed the military's sense of order, traditions, and sense of purpose—even his spit-polished boots. "They issued us very good boots," Gerasimov later recalled. "I thought to myself, 'Don't they regret giving us such nice boots?' After fifteen days of parade drills, they won't look so nice at all. But that's all right."[16] After graduating from Suvorov in 1973, Gerasimov attended the Kazan Higher Tank Command School.[17] He was no intellectual, but he did enjoy reading. He devoured stacks of military books by Russian theorists—Alexander Svechin, Makhmut Gareev, Georgy Isserson, and Alexander Suvorov—that molded his views of warfare.

Svechin, a Soviet military leader and eminent theorist, was one of Gerasimov's favorites. Svechin's seminal book *Strategy* was a tour de force, vaulting him to the status of "Soviet Clausewitz" for some Russian military leaders.[18] Gerasimov was drawn to Svechin's emphasis on the political, technological, economic, ideological, and social aspects of war—not just conventional warfare.[19] Countries needed to wage war using *all* instruments of national power, not just guns and tanks. For Svechin, warfare was constantly evolving, and Russia needed to adapt itself to the habitual changes in society. In a March 2018 speech while serving as chief of the General Staff of the Armed Forces, Gerasimov cited Svechin in noting that "the spectrum of possible conflicts is extremely broad, and the armed forces must be ready for any of them."[20]

✳   ✳   ✳   ✳

IN 1977, Gerasimov graduated from the Kazan Higher Tank Command School. By this time, the prospects of a conventional and nuclear war with the United States had subsided because of the unbearable costs—including fears of a nuclear holocaust. Instead, the Soviet Union turned to "active measures" (*aktivnyye meropriyatiya*) to compete with its rival superpower.[21] According to an analysis by the KGB, the Soviet Union's premier spy agency, active measures were designed to influence external populations using covert and other means: "The main value of all active measures lies in the fact that it is difficult to check the veracity of the information conveyed and to identify the real source. Their effectiveness is expressed as a coefficient of utility, when minimum expenditure and effort achieves maximum end results."[22]

Active measures encompassed a range of activities, such as disinformation (*dezinformatsiya*), forgeries, front groups, agents of influence, and covert broadcasting.[23] The primary Soviet actor was not the military, but Service A of the KGB. Active measures were different from routine espionage and counterespionage activities, such as stealing US and Allied secrets.[24] Instead, active measures intended to *influence* populations and were designed to be an offensive instrument of Soviet foreign policy.[25] Soviet active measures focused primarily on the United States, which the Soviet Union referred to as its "main enemy" (*glavniy protivnik*).[26] While Gerasimov's army was

still attempting to deter the United States in areas like the Fulda
Gap, the gently sloping lowlands northeast of Frankfurt along the
border of East and West Germany, the KGB was engaged in an
aggressive information war. As one former Warsaw Pact intelligence
operative noted:

> Target No. 1 was the United States.... The objective was to
> hurt the United States wherever and whenever it was possible, to
> weaken the positions of the United States and Western Europe,
> to create new rifts within the NATO Alliance, to weaken the
> position of the United States in developing countries, to cause
> new rifts between the United States and developing countries,
> to disinform the United States and the Western allies about the
> military strength of the Soviet bloc countries.[27]

As Gerasimov would discover firsthand, the United States could
also play this game—and spy agencies like the CIA were pretty good
in countries like Poland.

✳   ✳   ✳   ✳

IN 1977, the Red Army sent Gerasimov to the Northern Group of
Forces in Poland. He commanded a tank platoon and company, and
served as chief of staff of a tank battalion in the 80th Tank Regiment
of the 90th Guards Tank Division. In a grainy black-and-white photograph taken while serving in Poland, Gerasimov stands at attention with three other Red Army soldiers dressed in neatly pressed
uniforms. He has the distinct appearance of a steeled boxer preparing to enter the ring, with a flat nose, full lips, angular cheekbones,
and slightly protruding jawbone. His shoulders are squared, and he
stares confidently at the camera. His left hand grasps a saber, and his
right hand comfortably rests by his side. He exudes self-confidence
and solemnness—traits he will carry with him the rest of his life.[28]

Poland during Gerasimov's deployment was locked in the throes of crisis—thanks, in part, to the United States. It was Gerasimov's first taste of the East-West struggle from the front lines. By this time, the CIA had recruited a well-placed source in the Polish General Staff, Ryszard Kuklinski, whom the CIA code-named GULL because of his passion for the sea.[29] Over the next decade, Kuklinski became a wildly productive asset, providing over 40,000 Polish, Soviet, and Warsaw Pact pages of documents to the CIA.[30] The classified documents revealed Soviet plans to attack NATO, the location of Soviet command-and-control bunkers, and Soviet techniques to foil detection from US spy satellites. As CIA director William Casey later remarked: "In the last forty years, no one has done more damage to communism than that Pole."[31]

In mid-1981, Kuklinski alerted the CIA that the 90th Guards Tank Division, where Gerasimov served, had reorganized and received an increase in heavy weapons. As Kuklinski reported to his CIA handlers, Gerasimov's division had likely been reorganized "to ensure that they were more suitably configured for strikebreaking, internal policing, and administrative functions."[32] These forces might be needed to crush Solidarity, the labor union led by the charismatic former shipyard electrician, Lech Wałęsa. Soviet leaders had grown increasingly concerned that Solidarity's movement for greater self-government might trigger a wave of democracy across Eastern Europe.

Although the Soviets debated using Red Army forces—including Gerasimov's 90th Guards Tank Division—to crush Solidarity, they settled on pressuring Poland to do it instead. Late in the evening on December 12, 1981, Polish special motorized security forces set up roadblocks and checkpoints in the streets of cities like Warsaw as Polish leader Wojciech Jaruzelski proclaimed martial law and a state of emergency. Polish forces rounded up members of Solidarity, raided their offices, and seized radio and television buildings.[33] Over the next few days, Polish security services imprisoned approximately 6,000 Solidarity activists in twenty-four internment centers, including most of its leadership.[34] Soviet military and KGB officials had been deeply involved in the planning efforts.[35]

In response, US president Ronald Reagan authorized a CIA covert action program to aid the democratic opposition movement in Poland. Code-named QRHELPFUL, the CIA action provided nearly $20 million in aid to Solidarity to help wage an information campaign against the Soviet-backed government. Unlike the more controversial US programs in Afghanistan and Central America, this covert action program succeeded *without* providing weapons or participating in military action. Instead, CIA funds bankrolled many components essential to running an underground media enterprise: leaflets, posters, offset presses, Xerox machines, duplicators, typewriters, paper, and technical help in running clandestine radio broadcasts and breaking into television programs.[36] The CIA ran assets in places like Sweden, West Germany, Norway, France, Italy, and other European countries. As one CIA official remarked: "By the 1980s the Agency had accumulated a great deal of experience, stretching back to the 1950s, in smuggling things into and out of Poland."[37]

By the end of the 1980s, the CIA had outmaneuvered the KGB and severely undermined the Soviet Union's grip on the country. Aided, in part, by the United States, Solidarity swept the Polish elections in 1989, winning 99 of 100 seats in the Senate and 160 of 161 contested seats in the Sejm. The following year, Poles elected Solidarity's leader, Lech Wałęsa, as president—making him the first freely elected president of Poland in over six decades.

Gerasimov had been in Poland when the first cracks appeared in the Soviet-backed government. In a speech more than two decades later, he lamented that "asymmetric actions have come into widespread use, enabling the nullification of an enemy's advantages in armed conflict. Among such actions are the use of special operations forces and internal opposition to create a permanently operating front through the entire territory of the enemy state, as well as informational actions, devices, and means that are constantly being perfected."[38] Poland was a textbook case of US irregular warfare.

✳ ✳ ✳ ✳

AFTER POLAND, Gerasimov's next post was in the Far Eastern Military District, headquartered in Khabarovsk. Located on the outer rim of the Soviet empire, 400 miles from the Japanese island of Sapporo and over 5,000 miles from Moscow, Gerasimov could have been on the moon. He then attended the Malinovsky Military Armored Forces Academy in 1984, which trained Soviet and Warsaw Pact soldiers to command armored and mechanized units. Russian officers like Gerasimov went through a three-year program, while engineers attended for four years.

After he graduated in 1987, the Red Army sent Gerasimov to Estonia. It was a sobering experience, and Gerasimov watched in horror as the Soviet empire collapsed. By the time Gerasimov arrived in the region, the Baltic states of Lithuania, Latvia, and Estonia were in the midst of monumental change. Gerasimov served as the chief of headquarters in the 144th Guards Motorized Rifle Division in the Baltic Military District.

In March 1990, Lithuania—which had been a Soviet republic—declared independence. In response, Soviet airborne troops occupied buildings in Lithuania's capital, Vilnius. Over the next several months, the Soviet military attempted—and failed—to squash protests in Vilnius and reestablish a pro-Kremlin government. But they killed fourteen civilians and injured hundreds more in a clash with protesters on January 13, 1991, which became known as "Bloody Sunday." Most of those killed and wounded were either shot or run over by Soviet tanks. A similar democratic wave hit Latvia. In May 1990, the Latvian Supreme Soviet declared independence from the Soviet Union. In January 1991, the Soviets tried to restore order in Latvia. Soviet federal police seized the Press House and the telephone exchange. Pro-independence Latvians set up barricades around Riga, Latvia's capital, to keep out Soviet tanks. In the ensuing clashes, six people were killed and ten wounded. As Soviet ambassador to the United States Alexander Bessmertynykh confessed to US deputy secretary of state Lawrence Eagleburger: "The situation is almost out of control."[39]

Later that year, the chaos spilled into Estonia, where Gerasimov was stationed. On August 20, 1991, Estonian politicians declared independence, which Russia formally recognized in September. But Russian troops—including Gerasimov's 144th Guards Motorized Rifle Division—remained in the country in an effort to preserve Moscow's waning influence. In 1993, Gerasimov was promoted to commander of the entire division.[40] By the end of the year, Russian forces were gone from Estonia. In a humiliating setback for Gerasimov, he oversaw their withdrawal. Some of his equipment was seized by Lithuanians during the withdrawal, and his new base in Smolensk, Russia, was—at least initially—nothing more than an empty field.[41]

The great Russian bear had been declawed. Moscow lost *all* of the fourteen Soviet republics except for Russia itself, half of its population, and one quarter of its territory.[42] Its military alliance, the Warsaw Pact, ceased to exist. Even worse, most Warsaw Pact countries—which had pledged allegiance to Moscow and prepared to fight the United States and its allies—did a volte-face and joined their mortal enemy, NATO. And US forces had not even fired a shot. Russian lieutenant general Vladimir Serebryanikov and diplomat Alexander Kapko wrote: "Without direct use of military force, but as a result of the integrated use of political, diplomatic, economic, informational, ideological-psychological, intelligence, covert and other non-military means, the West destroyed the Soviet Union, the Warsaw Pact, Yugoslavia, and Czechoslovakia."[43]

For Gerasimov, the United States had won the Cold War not through a fair fight on the North German Plain, but by playing dirty. It had used covert action and subversion to manipulate Eastern European governments and their populations, and had provided Stinger missiles and other weapons to the mujahideen in Afghanistan to fight Soviet troops.[44] It was a lesson that Russia would have to learn if it ever wanted to regain its greatness.

✳   ✳   ✳   ✳

WITH HIS COUNTRY in shambles, Gerasimov was sent to the breakaway republic of Chechnya, which was in the midst of a violent war of independence from Russia.[45] Chechnya was Gerasimov's first combat tour. While he had been spared deployment to the Soviet Union's disastrous war in Afghanistan in the 1980s, the prospects in Chechnya were equally grim when he arrived. After Chechnya declared independence, the tattered Russian army suffered a series of embarrassing setbacks between 1994 and 1996. The Russian military faced Chechen guerrillas intimately familiar with the terrain and proficient in ambushes, raids, and targeted assassinations. Chechnya had deteriorated into near anarchy. Warlordism, organized criminal activity, hostage-taking, and gruesome attacks on humanitarian aid workers were rampant.[46] To make matters worse, Russian generals conducted wildly optimistic planning, soldiers were not trained for urban combat, operational command had broken down, and troop morale had cratered. Alcoholism and drug abuse among soldiers were widespread.[47] As Gerasimov admitted: "Our personnel in the field, including commanders," were "sometimes woefully unprepared" because of a "lack of combat training; personnel being distracted from their training programs by other tasks; and failure to implement our combat training plans."[48]

Much like his tour in Estonia, Gerasimov's time in Chechnya likely had a profound impact on his views of warfare. Chechnya in the 1990s played host to an odious war marked by ambushes, raids, and targeted assassinations—nothing like what Russian soldiers such as Gerasimov had spent their entire careers training to fight. Yet Gerasimov had an epiphany: he discovered that he could fight effectively against insurgents. He also emerged with a reputation for integrity.

As chief of staff of the 58th Army of the North Caucasus Military District, Gerasimov served under Vladimir Shamanov, a stocky, larger-than-life general with a volcanic temper who was known as the "butcher" and a "one-man curse on the Chechen people."[49] When the Russian journalist Anna Politkovskaya asked Shamanov whether he was offended by his brutish reputation, he brushed it off. "No," he said proudly, "for me it's praise."[50] Shamanov lived up to his reputation; he was investigated for multiple war crimes during his combat tour in Chechnya. One was the Baku–Rostov highway bombing, in which two Su-25 Russian attack aircraft repeatedly struck a convoy of refugees attempting to enter the neighboring Russian republic of Ingushetia.[51] In another incident, Russian forces seized the village of Alkhan-Yurt from Chechen fighters in December 1999, and then carried out extensive looting and massacred civilians. According to a Human Rights Watch investigation, Shamanov's soldiers expelled "hundreds of civilians from Alkhan-Yurt, and then began systematically looting and burning the village, killing anyone in their way."[52]

Despite his brutality, Shamanov embraced the limelight, encouraging journalists to produce television documentaries on his daring escapades against bloodthirsty Chechen guerrillas. It was no surprise when Shamanov ran for governor of the Ulyanovsk Oblast region while serving as commander of the 58th Army—and won.

Gerasimov took command from Shamanov in 2000 just as the second phase of the Chechen war began. Gerasimov and Shamanov were polar opposites. Shamanov was short and stocky, with a fleshy face and a neck as thick as a Siberian lumberjack's. Gerasimov was tall, with deep-set eyes and a large, protruding nose.[53] Shamanov wanted his every breath documented, photographed, or filmed. Gerasimov eschewed media attention and preferred to operate in the shadows. There are few mentions of Gerasimov in Russian- or English-language media, and he gave almost no interviews. One of his few media appearances was in the Russian war documentary *Real War*, which followed Russian troops on daring operations in Chechnya and described Gerasimov as "a general from the tips of his fingers to the buttons on his coat."[54] Gerasimov appears visibly uncomfortable in the documentary, quickly ducking out of the frame in one shot.[55]

Gerasimov preferred to quietly immerse himself in the minutiae of combat operations. Chechnya was his first opportunity to put into practice everything he had read from the great Russian military theorists—Konstantin Simonov, Alexander Svechin, Georgy Isserson, and Alexander Suvorov. "I spent a lot of time in the field," he later recalled. "I knew in great detail what was happening on the administrative border with Chechnya. . . . No one had any illusions; we all knew that the Chechen boil would have to be punctured sooner or later."[56] Gerasimov experienced the war up close, with all of its unvarnished, raw violence. Militants ambushed his armored convoy in the Bamut area of Chechnya, near the border with Ingushetia, firing at point-blank range with small arms and grenade launchers. Gerasimov and his soldiers put up fierce resistance until reinforcements came, including attack helicopters. Gerasimov quickly made the Chechens pay. A week later, his force lured a band of Chechen guerrillas into a trap and ambushed them, killing a dozen militants and seizing a large cache of weapons.[57]

One of Gerasimov's major achievements in Chechnya was the capture of Komsomolskoye, a village on the southern edge of Grozny, the capital of Chechnya.[58] Gerasimov's forces used massive artillery and air strikes against fixed Chechen positions, and then deployed dismounted troops supported by fire from artillery, tanks, surface-to-surface missiles, attack helicopters, Su-24 bombers, Su-25 ground-attack aircraft, and the thermobaric weapon TOS-1 (which used oxygen from the surrounding air to generate a high-temperature explosion). Although Russian forces retook Komsomolskoye, the village was almost completely destroyed. Several hundred Chechen rebel fighters and civilians, along with more than fifty Russian servicemen, were killed during more than two weeks of siege warfare.[59] True to form, Gerasimov received virtually no public attention, despite his pivotal role in the battle. He is barely named, let alone profiled, in most accounts of the battle.

Gerasimov also evolved into a principled commander. In March 2000, Russian colonel Yuri Budanov—who was serving under Gerasimov—abducted, raped, and murdered an eighteen-year-old Chechen woman named Elza Kungaeva.[60] Budanov violently beat Kungaeva, then grabbed her by the neck and strangled her with his bare hands until her face turned blue.[61] When Gerasimov confronted the thirty-seven-year-old Russian colonel, Budanov exploded in anger, waving a pistol at Gerasimov.[62] The case attracted international attention and was followed widely within Russia, where many viewed Budanov as an unjustly vilified hero. As the journalist Anna Politkovskaya wrote, it was a small miracle that Budanov's actions even came to light thanks to Gerasimov:

> There is a rule in the Russian armed forces that serving personnel can be arrested only with the permission of their superior officers. For Budanov, only General Gerasimov had this status. Accordingly, we are obliged to Gerasimov for the fact that there ever was a Budanov case. The majority of commanding officers in Chechnya do not give the prosecutor's office permission to arrest those under their command who have committed war crimes and go to great lengths to protect them. Given the situation in the Zone of Antiterrorist Operations, Gerasimov's act must be regarded as very courageous. It could well have cost him his career. Perhaps because the affair became a major focus of public attention, the general was not punished.[63]

At the trial, Gerasimov testified that he had heard from other officers that a girl had been abducted during the night and his soldiers were suspects. Gerasimov had then driven to the town where Kungaeva had been taken, and the villagers identified Budanov as the culprit. By the time Gerasimov returned to the regiment, Budanov had run off, and Gerasimov ordered his arrest.[64] According to one account of the arrest, Gerasimov confronted Budanov coming out of a bathhouse, and when he tried to arrest the colonel, "Budanov's men trained their weapons on Gerasimov and his soldiers."[65] But they quickly backed down. Gerasimov's actions put him at odds with his old commanding officer, Vladimir Shamanov, who publicly came to Budanov's defense. Still craving the spotlight, Shamanov remarked, in a self-serving media interview—his trademark—that Budanov "was one of my best commanders." In a direct challenge to Gerasimov, Shamanov then warned: "To [Budanov's] enemies I say: Don't put your paws on the image of a Russian soldier and officer."[66]

But Gerasimov was unmoved. A Russian military court charged and convicted Budanov for the murder of Eliza Kungaeva, sentenced him to ten years in a labor camp, and stripped him of his rank and state awards.[67] Budanov was later assassinated by Chechen extremists after being released from prison. Roza Kungaeva, the murdered girl's mother, was overwhelmed with gratitude. "This is not a unique case," she said. "There are thousands like us. But Allah helped us. We were lucky that morning. Gerasimov proved to be a decent person."[68]

✳︎ ✳︎ ✳︎ ✳︎

BY THE END OF Gerasimov's tour in Chechnya, he had come full circle from his time at the Kazan Suvorov Military School. He was well-read, battle hardened, principled, and adored by his soldiers. During the Chechen war, he spent a month and a half in the mountains during one operation melting snow for drinking water, eating dry rations, taking cover from enemy bullets, and—perhaps most important—earning the undying loyalty of his soldiers. "They can bear all the hardship life throws at them," Gerasimov explained, beaming with pride. "They don't whine, and they do their job well."[69]

With these qualities, Gerasimov helped Russia turn the tide of the second phase of the Chechen war. Moscow beat back Chechen guerrillas, though not without turning Chechnya—and especially Grozny—into a pile of rubble.[70]

Despite Russia's eventual success in Chechnya, Gerasimov's world was crumbling—thanks, in part, to the United States. He was incensed that US leaders had taken advantage of Moscow's weakness and expanded NATO to Russia's borders. As Gerasimov remarked, war itself was also changing. "The role of nonmilitary means of achieving political and strategic goals has grown, and, in many cases, they have exceeded the power of force of weapons in their effectiveness," he said.[71] Gerasimov was determined not to let the United States get the better of his country again.

3: THE MAIN ENEMY

AS GERASIMOV BATTLED CHECHEN INSURGENTS, the United States scored one of its most impressive military victories since the end of the Cold War: the overthrow of the Taliban regime in Afghanistan. A CIA team code-named JAWBREAKER and led by Gary Schroen landed in the Panjshir Valley in northeastern Afghanistan on September 26, 2001, just two weeks after the September 11 attacks. Schroen's team was part of the agency's Special Activities Division, the paramilitary arm of the CIA. The team was soon joined on the ground by US special operations forces and worked with local Afghan commanders, provided arms and equipment, and coordinated US air strikes against Taliban and al-Qaeda positions. CIA and special operations forces also provided money to buy—or at least rent—the loyalty of local commanders and their militia forces. "Money is the lubricant that makes things happen in Afghanistan," Schroen explained.[1]

As Gerasimov surely would have recognized, the American campaign was remarkably effective—at least initially. Roughly 100 CIA officers and 350 US special operations soldiers, supported by as many as 100 combat sorties per day from US combat aircraft, defeated a Taliban army estimated at 50,000 to 60,000—along with several thousand al-Qaeda fighters.[2] Instead of fighting a conventional war, the United States fought an irregular one by leveraging Northern Alliance forces and Pashtun tribes. It was a remarkable achievement. The United States overthrew the Taliban in less than three months while suffering only a dozen US fatalities.[3]

Afghanistan was not America's first foray into precision operations. In 1995, US and other NATO forces conducted an air campaign against Yugoslav forces called OPERATION DELIBERATE FORCE, which culminated in the Dayton Agreement brokered by US ambassador Richard Holbrooke. The result was the formal breakup of Yugoslavia and the eventual inclusion of several of its fledgling countries—such as Albania and Croatia—into NATO and the European Union. The United States repeated this strategy in 1999 in Kosovo during OPERATION ALLIED FORCE. After nearly three months of bombing, the United States and its NATO allies secured Kosovo's independence.

For Gerasimov, these military operations—especially Kosovo—highlighted the United States' creeping influence eastward.[4] Russian leaders and military analysts had, of course, long been wary of the United States. Former foreign minister and prime minister Yevgeny Primakov established what became known as the "Primakov Doctrine," which held that Russia would oppose a world with a single global center of power—the United States.[5] Now, with the collapse of the Soviet empire, Gerasimov believed that the United States was becoming increasingly aggressive.[6] "A determining influence on the development of the military-political situation in the world is the United States' striving to prevent losing its 'global leadership' and to maintain a unipolar world by any means, including military," he remarked.[7]

Washington's power grab, as Russian leaders saw it, made it the "main enemy," or *glavnyy protivnik*.

* * * *

FOR GERASIMOV and other Russian leaders, there were several additional concerns about the US invasion of Afghanistan. Among the most worrisome was that US soldiers, spies, and military might—fighter jets, armed drones, and Black Hawk helicopters—were now parked on Russia's southern flank. For Moscow, the United States and its partners were slowly encircling Russia by co-opting its former partners and encroaching on its spheres of influence.

After all, Afghanistan came on the heels of NATO enlargement. As Gerasimov argued, the goal of NATO expansion was to undermine Russian power.[8] The first round of enlargement had occurred in 1999, when Moscow's former satellites—Hungary, Poland, and the Czech Republic—joined NATO. The second round followed five years later and included additional countries behind the Iron Curtain: Bulgaria, Estonia, Latvia, Lithuania, Romania, Slovakia, and Slovenia. Russian leaders viewed NATO expansion with alarm. "The new members of the alliance are almost all former parties to the Warsaw Pact and the post-Soviet republics," wrote Gerasimov. "In other words, since the 1990s, NATO has been expanding strictly to the East, toward the Russian borders."[9]

For Gerasimov, US actions were part of an effort to take advantage of the Soviet Union's collapse and the end of a bipolar international system by expanding US power at Moscow's expense. "Considering itself to be the 'winners' in the Cold War," Gerasimov remarked, "the United States decided to redraw the world exclusively for itself" in "striving for absolute dominance."[10] The year after the invasion of Afghanistan, the Bush administration pulled out of the Anti-Ballistic Missile (ABM) Treaty, which barred Washington and Moscow from deploying nationwide defenses against strategic ballistic missiles. In the preamble, the two countries had agreed that effective limits on antimissile systems would be a "substantial factor in curbing the race in strategic offensive arms and would lead to a decrease in the risk of outbreak of war involving nuclear weapons."[11] Gerasimov now worried that the United States intended to undermine Russia's nuclear deterrent by building up America's ballistic missile defense and starting an arms race.[12]

From Gerasimov's perspective, the United States was now on a roll. Over the next decade, Gerasimov watched—with growing unease—as the United States overthrew successive governments. The next nation to fall would be Iraq.

* * * *

ON MARCH 19, 2003, the US Army's V Corps, the 1st Marine Division, and the British 1st Armoured Division rapidly advanced through Iraq on parallel axes and began the next US experiment in regime change, dubbed OPERATION IRAQI FREEDOM.[13] Iraq's geography—with its flat, arid deserts in the south—allowed US ground forces to push easily into the country and then make mincemeat of Saddam Hussein's overmatched Republican Guard divisions and regular army units. It took just over a month for the United States to overthrow Saddam Hussein's regime—even less time than Afghanistan. Major combat operations ended on April 14. On the flight deck of the USS *Abraham Lincoln*, US president George W. Bush announced that "the tyrant has fallen and Iraq is free."[14]

US leaders explained that the purpose of regime change in Iraq was to unseat Saddam Hussein—who had gassed his own population, invaded neighboring Kuwait, started (though then dismantled) a nuclear weapons program, and repeatedly thumbed his nose at the United States and international community. But Gerasimov and other Russian leaders were unconvinced. In Gerasimov's view, Iraq was a textbook example of the "traditional" approach to war.[15] The US had deployed well-trained and well-equipped conventional forces; initiated military operations against the enemy in set-piece battles; employed ground, air, and naval forces; and achieved the eventual destruction of the enemy.[16] Gerasimov assessed the American justifications for Iraq and other military operations over the previous decade. They were different each time: "threat to peace and stability," "genocide by the Belgrade authorities," "fight against international terrorism," and "prevention of the proliferation of chemical weapons."[17] But he was convinced these rationalizations were fig leaves. The US approach was generally the same: decide to overthrow a government, search for a pretext to launch military operations, and then conduct military operations to install a friendly regime.[18]

By this time, Gerasimov had completed his time as commander of the 58th Army in Chechnya and was chief of staff of the Far Eastern Military District. Gerasimov was one of Russia's bright new generation of army leaders that might help the once great Russian military—the legacy of imperial Russian leaders like Peter the Great and Catherine II—rise like a phoenix from the ashes at the end of the Cold War.

In many ways, Gerasimov was impressed by the advances in US strategy, tactics, and technology used to conduct the war in Iraq. US special operations forces and intelligence units infiltrated the country to find and destroy Saddam's suspected long-range ballistic missiles and launch sites, link up with Iraqi tribes and resistance groups, and secure Iraq's southern gas and oil platforms. The US military also conducted psychological operations against the Iraqi military, including dropping leaflets urging soldiers to capitulate and making tape-recorded phone calls to Iraqi military leaders encouraging them to surrender.[19] Over the course of the campaign, US and coalition aircraft flew more than 41,000 sorties against Iraqi integrated air defenses, leadership targets, surface-to-air missile forces, ballistic missiles, airfields, and Iraqi ground forces.[20] Against this onslaught, the entire Iraqi military structure quickly collapsed. US military leaders heralded this revolution in military affairs. Secretary of Defense Donald Rumsfeld bragged that the US military used "an unprecedented combination of speed, precision, surprise, and flexibility."[21]

Yet much like with Afghanistan, Gerasimov believed there was something more sinister at work. The United States was perfecting its military capabilities to, in his words, "eliminate the statehood of unwanted countries, to undermine sovereignty, and to change lawfully elected bodies of state power" in ways that benefited the United

States.[22] Gerasimov saw the war as being much bigger than Iraq—or even the Middle East. It was another example, Gerasimov concluded, of the "U.S. aspiration toward global domination."[23] In 2007, Russian president Vladimir Putin railed against the United States to a packed audience at the Munich Security Conference. He described a "world of one master, one sovereign" and accused the United States of adopting "an almost uncontained hyper use of force" that was "plunging the world into an abyss of permanent conflicts."[24]

✳ ✳ ✳

GERASIMOV AND PUTIN were not entirely wrong that the United States was attempting to expand its influence across the Middle East and Asia. Yet the United States was not invincible. Quick victories were followed by protracted insurgencies in which the United States deployed over 100,000 soldiers in both Afghanistan and Iraq—yet failed to win.

Gerasimov saw a fundamental flaw in the US approach. "Attempts to transfer the values of Western democracy to countries with their own mentality, spiritual values and traditions lead to the opposite result," he remarked. "The occupation of Iraq, the elimination of the next leader and the 'democratization' of the country at gunpoint led to the fact that most of the dispersed armed forces and the remaining political elite formed the backbone of ISIS and established their power in a significant part of this country."[25] Washington failed to stabilize both countries and instead faced growing chaos, where terrorist groups like al-Qaeda and eventually the Islamic State filled the vacuum. Not only did the US fail to ensure peace, Gerasimov lectured, but the wars "led to an escalation of tension, the exacerbation of contradictions, the growth of armed violence and civil wars, the death of civilians."[26]

Take Afghanistan, where, Gerasimov noted, the "United States and its allies spent more than $800 billion on Operation Enduring Freedom in Afghanistan." Rather than peace, however, Afghan forces failed to defeat the Taliban and "most of the state's territory is still under the control of various armed groups."[27] In an inflammatory speech titled "ISIS Began with the 'Taliban,'" Gerasimov argued that the US war in Afghanistan led to a growing number of terrorists, an escalating drug trade, and a proliferation of refugees.[28] The Americans could argue otherwise. Most indicators—though not violence levels—showed dramatic improvements since the Taliban years. Gross domestic product per capita in Afghanistan rose over 180 percent from 2001 to 2019, and foreign direct investment skyrocketed during the same time period. Health metrics improved from appalling conditions during the Taliban years. The infant mortality rate declined from 90 per 1,000 live births in 2000 to 47 per 1,000 live births in 2019, and life expectancy rose from fifty-six to sixty-four years during the same time period. Education also improved, as a growing number of male and, especially, female Afghans went to school.[29] Afghans were richer, healthier, and better educated than under the Taliban regime.

But as Gerasimov recognized, the United States had failed to pacify the country, and the US military now looked vulnerable.

✳   ✳   ✳   ✳

OVER THE NEXT several years, Russian leaders believed that the United States had moved away from the "traditional" approach to warfare. Instead, the United States had developed a "new," more clandestine approach to overthrowing governments and maximizing influence, which Gerasimov termed a "concealed use of force."[30] Rather than using large numbers of conventional military forces to achieve political objectives, as it had eventually done in Afghanistan and Iraq, the United States would focus on irregular methods.

These types of operations might begin with an aggressive information campaign dedicated to undermining the legitimacy of the target government. According to Gerasimov, the United States tended to use what he considered state-sanctioned television propaganda such as CNN, the internet, social media, and nongovernmental organizations to create or fuel political dissent.[31] As the security situation deteriorated, the United States would then leverage special operations forces, intelligence units, local militias, and private military corporations as the main ground forces—but, to limit the shedding of US blood, not large numbers of US military forces.[32] US air force and naval power was still important in this new way of warfare to strike targets.[33] But the more insidious and clandestine approach enabled the United States to overthrow regimes using local forces.[34]

Gerasimov's analysis would be borne out in the next conflict—in Libya. It was an operation that the American media covered and then quickly forgot, but it made an enduring impression on Russia and other regional powers.

✳ ✳ ✳ ✳

ON AUGUST 23, 2011, Libyan insurgents in Tripoli overran the fortified perimeter of Muammar al-Qaddafi's headquarters, the sprawling Bab al-Aziziya compound. "It's over! Qaddafi is finished!" announced one fighter over the clamor of celebratory gunfire, as rebels raised their red, green, and black flag over the building.[35] Libyan insurgents, or *thuwwar*, then proceeded to shatter a gilded statue of Qaddafi, tear up a portrait of the Libyan leader, and raze parts of the building. The same day, *thuwwar* also seized control of the Tripoli airport and key neighborhoods of the city, as rebel supporters danced in Tripoli's Green Square. The insurgent victory was startling in its speed and lethality, overthrowing Qaddafi's government in only six months.

Gerasimov saw something much more sinister at work. The United States overthrew a Libyan regime that had been a major ally of Moscow by using local—not US—forces. However, Gerasimov noticed that NATO allies provided a great deal of firepower. Beginning in March 2011, American, French, and British aircraft began targeting Qaddafi's air defense systems. On the first day of the operation, US-guided missile destroyers and submarines fired more than 120 Tomahawk missiles that struck Libyan radar, missile, and command-and-control sites.[36] The United States flew B-2 stealth bombers from Whiteman Air Force Base in Missouri, which dropped forty-five precision-guided bombs on the regime's aircraft shelters near Sirte. Additional cruise missile strikes destroyed Qaddafi's command-and-control facility in Tripoli. NATO aircraft conducted a total of 26,300 sorties against the regime's armored vehicles, artillery, and other targets, and provided rebels with an opportunity for victory in Libya.[37] The main ground force was composed not of US or other irregular soldiers, but of Libyan militias.

NATO allies supported the rebels in other irregular ways as well. Intelligence agencies from NATO countries provided matériel, money, information, and other assistance to Libyan rebels. In addition, US, French, British, and other special operations forces and intelligence operatives conducted direct-action operations; collected intelligence; trained, advised, and assisted insurgent forces; and provided money, arms, and nonlethal equipment.[38]

By the time the Qaddafi regime fell in 2011, Gerasimov had risen to become deputy chief of the General Staff of the Armed Forces after stints at prestigious leadership positions in the Leningrad and Moscow Military Districts. He used his strategic position to consider what the United States—Russia's "main enemy"— had accomplished.

From a purely military perspective, Gerasimov was impressed by US actions. He wrote that in Libya "a no-fly zone was created, a sea blockade imposed, and private military contractors were widely used in close interaction with armed formations of the opposition."[39] Gerasimov was also fascinated by the United States' use of information operations. He noticed that the United States clandestinely "mobilized capabilities of the social networks Facebook, Twitter, and other information-technical effects . . . for the first time."[40]

Ever the military student, Gerasimov concluded that war was now conducted by a roughly 4:1 ratio of nonmilitary and military tools. These nonmilitary measures include economic sanctions, disruption of diplomatic ties, and political and diplomatic pressure.[41]

Much like in Afghanistan and Iraq, the United States stumbled after the regime change in Libya. As Gerasimov remarked, "Libya, where President Gaddafi was ousted by military intervention, has virtually ceased to exist as a centralized state, becoming the basis for the growth of ISIS and other terrorist groups."[42] Gerasimov described the results in Libya as destabilizing—a "division of the country into the spheres of influence by military tribe formations and their confrontation," "uncontrolled migration," "spread of terrorism to other regions," "safety threat to foreign citizens," "legalization of illegal armed formations," "increase in extremism and crime," and "uncontrolled weapons proliferation."[43] It was a categorical failure. Gerasimov and other Russian leaders believed Libya was in a much worse position *after* the overthrow than before.

The war in Libya had a profound impact on Russia's understanding of future wars—one that largely escaped the attention of Western analysts.[44] Russians saw Libya as indicative of how big powers can "erode the morale of citizens and collapse its support for the national government," in the words of one senior Russian military official.[45] And Libya was only the tip of the iceberg in the United States' new way of warfare. When the Arab Spring and the "color revolutions" spread like wildfire throughout North Africa and the Middle East, Gerasimov and others saw the hidden hand of the United States across the globe, including in Russia itself.[46]

Beginning in 2011, protests erupted in Russian cities like Moscow—and continued through 2013—against fraudulent elections, corruption, and poor economic conditions in Russia. In December 2011, former Soviet leader Mikhail Gorbachev, speaking on Moscow Echo radio, even called for Vladimir Putin to resign.[47] For Russian leaders, covert US activity was hitting too close to home.

✳ ✳ ✳ ✳

IN 2011, Mohamed Bouazizi, a twenty-six-year-old fruit vendor, set himself on fire in the rural town of Sidi Bouzid, Tunisia, helping to trigger the Arab Spring. Over the next several years, popular movements erupted across the Arab world to overthrow authoritarian regimes—from Tunisia to Egypt, Syria, Yemen, and Algeria. Outside of the Arab world, Gerasimov and other Russian leaders were concerned about the proliferation of these "color revolutions."[48] The color revolutions included movements across regions like Eastern Europe and Central Asia where participants used mostly nonviolent resistance, such as demonstrations and strikes, to protest government incompetence and push for democratic reforms. Some of these movements adopted a specific color or flower as their symbol, such as Georgia's Rose Revolution and Ukraine's Orange Revolution.

Russian leaders, however, saw the Arab Spring and color revolutions as part of the United States' new way of warfare: an attempt to increase US influence indirectly and discreetly through clandestine means.[49] As Gerasimov explained, a color revolution was "a form of non-violent change of power in a country *by outside manipulation* of the protest potential of the population in conjunction with political, economic, humanitarian, and other non-military measures."[50] What particularly concerned Gerasimov was the speed of state collapse that the United States, in his view, could engineer.[51]

By this time, Putin had elevated Gerasimov to chief of the General Staff of the Russian Armed Forces, while allowing him to retain day-to-day control of Russia's main military intelligence agency, the GRU. There was no equivalent position in the United States, since Gerasimov had far more power than any flag officer in the US military. He was now something of a celebrity overseas, frequently photographed in a stiff, forest-green uniform and with a perpetually sagging frown. Gerasimov struck many US officials as thoughtful and rational—though hopelessly crusty. He lacked warmth and rarely cracked a smile. But he appreciated when Americans recognized Russian accomplishments—for example, cheering Russian hockey players in the National Hockey League, such as superstar Alexander Ovechkin of the Washington Capitals.

Gerasimov stooped when he walked into a room and relentlessly smoked, often asking—practically begging—for smoke breaks during meetings. He worked long hours and had virtually no time for hobbies, though he still voraciously read military books.[52] "He is neither a Clausewitzian intellectual, nor a knuckle-dragging soldier—but somewhere in the middle," said one senior US defense official that met with him routinely. "And he is also a very good diplomat."[53] But he could light a fire when he wanted.

In an influential speech in May 2014 at the Russian Ministry of Defense's Moscow Conference on International Security, a gruff Gerasimov ripped into the United States. Pointing to a map of so-called color revolutions, he accused the United States of grossly irresponsible behavior by attempting to manipulate foreign governments and destabilize parts of the Middle East, Africa, Europe, and Asia. The result, Gerasimov concluded, was that "forces were brought to power having mainly a pro-Western and anti-Russian orientation."[54]

American analysts felt this claim was unfounded. Outside of a few cases like Libya in 2011, the United States played little or no meaningful role in the Arab Spring or the color revolutions.[55] In fact, US policy makers and US intelligence agencies were repeatedly blindsided by the rapid developments in the countries highlighted by Gerasimov. As acting CIA director Mike Morell lamented, US intelligence agencies and diplomats failed to fully anticipate the Arab Spring, in part because they had become too dependent on their counterparts in Middle Eastern governments for insights. "We were lax in creating our own windows into what was happening,"

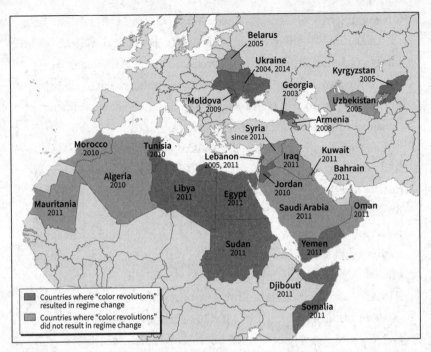

GERASIMOV'S ILLUSTRATION OF
US-MANIPULATED COLOR REVOLUTIONS[56]

Morell acknowledged, "and the leadership we were relying on was isolated and unaware of the tidal wave that was about to hit."[57]

But Moscow did not see the Arab Spring or color revolutions this way.[58] Much like in Afghanistan and Iraq, Gerasimov argued that US actions contributed to growing instability and terrorism in Africa, the Middle East, and other regions.[59] So, too, did Russian minister of defense Sergey Shoigu, who concluded that the "phenomenon of 'color revolutions' is becoming a significant factor in destabilizing many regions of the world."[60]

Russian leaders were concerned about developments in North Africa and the Middle East. But Gerasimov and others were most alarmed at recent developments in Ukraine.

＊ ＊ ＊ ＊

IN LATE 2013, protests erupted in Ukraine after President Viktor Yanukovych refused to sign a political association and free trade agreement with the European Union, preferring to establish closer relations with Moscow. In early 2014, the protests expanded into a revolution that overthrew the government. On February 22, Yanukovych fled to Russia and, in a 328–0 vote, the Ukrainian parliament (Rada), voted to remove Yanukovych from office. The Maidan Revolution, as the uprising became known, was a stunning development. Ukraine—a neighbor of Russia and a former Soviet republic—quickly transitioned from a pro-Russian to a pro-Western government.

Russian leaders saw a hidden US hand at work again, calling Ukraine a US and European "coup d'état."[61] "In February 2014, radicals and Russophobes who came to power in Ukraine legitimized the activities of neo-fascist and nationalist organizations in the country," Gerasimov remarked.[62] In reality, much like with the Arab Spring, the United States had done little to inflame tensions in Ukraine. Rather than pushing for Yanukovych's overthrow, US diplomats were encouraging a deal between Yanukovych and the protesters.[63] Russia's attempt to cast the United States as a boogeyman masked the key issue for Ukrainians. They wanted a better economy and political reforms. In short, they wanted what the West—not Russia—had to offer.

But Yanukovych's overthrow was devastating for Russia—and for Russians living in Ukraine. Putin, Gerasimov, and other Russian leaders now had to respond.

4: RUSSIAN CHESS

AS RUSSIAN LEADERS CONTEMPLATED THEIR options to counter US influence, Putin told a joke that circulated throughout Russian government circles. Gerasimov found it particularly apropos.

"A retired military officer asks his son if he has seen his dagger," Putin began. "The son replies that he exchanged the dagger for watches."

"Show me the watch, yes, good," says the father. "And if bandits come to us tomorrow to kill me, your mother, and brothers—and rape your sister—what do you tell them? 'Good evening, it is 12:30 Moscow time'?"

Putin then paused and said, "We do not want such a development."[1]

For Gerasimov, Russia needed to use the dagger to protect its interests—including from the United States. "It was a very relevant, good joke, with a deep meaning," Gerasimov reflected.[2]

In considering Russia's next steps, Gerasimov turned to one of his favorite writers: a Russian military theorist named Georgy Isserson, whom he called a "prophet of the Fatherland."[3] Isserson argued in his book *New Forms of Combat* that "war in general is not declared. It simply begins with already developed military forces." Isserson saw World War I—in which war was declared and then armies were raised—as an anomaly. "Mobilization and concentration are not part of the period after the onset of the state of war as was the case in 1914 but rather, unnoticed, proceed long before that."[4] In other words, wars were fought and often won long before the start of formal hostilities. Gerasimov believed that Russia paid a heavy price in ignoring Isserson.[5] He felt it was now time for Russia to respond—to embrace a new form of warfare that the United States had already adopted.

✳ ✳ ✳ ✳

ON THE NIGHT OF February 22, 2014, the same day that Ukrainian President Viktor Yanukovych fled to Russia, President Vladimir Putin convened an all-night meeting with senior Russian security chiefs to discuss the escalating situation. Around 7:00 a.m. on February 23, just before they wrapped up, Putin addressed the group. "We *must* start working on the return of Crimea to Russia," Putin said. "We cannot leave the territory and the people who live there to their fate."[6] Putin, Gerasimov, and other leaders considered Crimea low-hanging fruit. Most of the Crimean population was Russian and, they hoped, would ultimately be supportive of Russian annexation.[7] After all, some opinion polls in 2013 had indicated that over half of Russian citizens believed Crimea was part of Russia—not Ukraine.[8]

Senior Russian officials then began to furiously implement efforts to retake Crimea. Plans for a *coup de main* had already been forming for months. Invading Crimea, Russian leaders concluded, would require taking a page out of the US playbook and include a heavy dose of irregular forces—primarily intelligence and special operations forces. A year earlier, Gerasimov had announced the creation of Russia's own Special Operations Forces Command (KSSO).[9] With a nod toward the United States, his main enemy, Gerasimov explained: "Having studied the practice of the formation, training, and application of special operations by the leading foreign powers, the leadership of the Ministry of Defense has also begun to create such forces."[10]

To retake Crimea, Gerasimov and other Russian military leaders relied on special operations forces—not conventional units—

making it a quintessential irregular warfare campaign. On February 23, 2014, Russia airlifted units—especially battalions of *spetsnaz* (special operations forces) and Russian Airborne Forces, or VDV— to the area. The next day, with help from Moscow, the city council in Sevastopol installed a Russian citizen as mayor.[11] The Russian military also airlifted the 45th Airborne Spetsnaz Unit from Kubinka to Sevastopol, and several units from the 810th Naval Infantry Brigade, which were already stationed in Crimea, drove to the city square in armored personnel carriers.[12] On February 25, the *Nikolai Filchenkov*, an Alligator-class landing ship carrying 200 Russian special operations forces, arrived in Sevastopol. On February 26, roughly forty Russian Ilyushin Il-76 military transport aircraft left Ulyanovsk Air Base in Russia, with many of them moving VDV and *spetsnaz* troops to Anapa, a staging area just east of Crimea.[13]

US intelligence agencies picked up highly sensitive signals and human intelligence that Russian leaders had reached out to China for help. "In return for supporting the Russian bid in Ukraine, Russian leaders told China that they would support China's attempt to gain control of territory in the South China Sea," said one senior US official. "It was a quid pro quo. China mulled it over for a bit and then agreed."[14] The Russians then moved with lightning speed. On February 27, fifty special operations forces from the KSSO, disguised as local self-defense militia, seized the Crimean parliament and raised a Russian flag over the building. Later that night, Russian soldiers without markings surrounded Belbek Air Base, Ukraine's main military airport in Crimea. The next morning, a convoy of three Mi-8 transport helicopters and eight Mi-35M attack helicopters crossed into Ukraine, giving Russia the ability to neutralize Ukrainian armor and operate at night. On February 28, Russian forces also seized Simferopol's civilian airport, canceled all flights, and began airlifting VDV units into Crimea. On March 1 and 2, Russia brought reinforcements by heavy landing ships, which quickly seized bases and military facilities.[15]

The takeover of Crimea was a spectacular success for Russia. In roughly two weeks—even faster than the US operations in Afghanistan and Iraq—Russia had used clandestine special operations and intelligence units to annex part of Ukraine, a sovereign country. There were no clashes between Russian and Ukrainian conventional forces. It was a textbook example of Sun Tzu's axiom: "To subdue the enemy without fighting is the acme of skill."[16]

Perhaps most surprising of all, the Obama administration did little in response except for issuing a hollow protest of Russian actions and enacting limited sanctions. The United States did not provide military or international assistance to the Ukrainian government to help it retake territory, as some US politicians, such as Senator John McCain, suggested.[17] "We left a big fat piece of meat with Ukraine," said General Tony Thomas, who was serving at CIA headquarters as the associate director for military affairs. "What did we do?" he asked rhetorically. "Very little beyond slapping sanctions."[18] The head of US Special Operations Command, Admiral Bill McRaven, concurred. "The Russians outmaneuvered us in Ukraine, plain and simple."[19]

* * * *

RUSSIA WAS NOW on the offensive, retaking territory and increasing its influence. Military force—particularly through irregular means—was central to Russian operations. During the Cold War, the Russians had been adept at utilizing active measures, and Russian military thinkers had long appreciated the importance of irregular operations.[20]

Russia had committed to rebuild its military capabilities in 2007 as part of a "new era" in Russian military strategy. Now—in 2014—Moscow was flexing its muscles. Citing another of his favorite military theorists, Alexander Svechin, Gerasimov emphasized that Russia needed flexibility in how it reasserted Russian greatness through military means. "It is extraordinarily hard to predict the conditions of war," Gerasimov quoted Svechin. "For each war it is necessary to work out a particular line for its strategic conduct. Each war is a unique case, demanding the establishment of a particular logic and not the application of some template."[21] While each war might be different, Gerasimov and other Russian officials concluded that the primary tools of Russia's "new generation war" would include a heavy dose of intelligence efforts, special operations, and information activities.[22] It was irregular warfare.

US officials would not have to wait long to see where Moscow moved next.

✳   ✳   ✳   ✳

IN MARCH 2014, as the Russian government was in the midst of its Crimea operation, Russian intelligence and special operations stoked a wave of popular unrest—and then war—in eastern Ukraine. Six different *spetsnaz* brigades were involved in the Ukrainian operation in its early stages.[23] In describing the conflict, Putin rekindled the term *Novorossiya* ("New Russia"), referring to a historical area of the Russian empire that stretched across southern and eastern Ukraine.[24] The symbolism was clear. Much like with Crimea, Putin considered eastern Ukraine a historical part of Russia.

On March 1, pro-Russian protesters seized the regional administration buildings in Kharkiv and Donetsk, Ukraine. On March 9, protesters took over the regional administration building in Luhansk and demanded that a referendum be held to annex the Luhansk Oblast to Russia. The violence continued into April. Separatists seized the main administrative building in Donetsk on April 6, overran a Ministry of Interior rapid response force at the Luhansk administration complex on April 11, and raided the city halls in Slovyansk, Kramatorsk, and Krasny Liman on April 12. From late April to late May, the Ukrainian army mounted an intense campaign to contain the pro-Russian rebellion by securing key terrain around Donbas cities held by the separatists. Over the summer of

2014, fighting continued around Ukrainian cities and towns like Luhansk, Semenivka, Stepanivka, Yampil, and Slovyansk. In September 2014 and February 2015, Russia and Ukraine agreed to respective cease-fires in Minsk, Belarus, with help from France, Germany, and the Organization for Security and Co-operation in Europe. Although neither agreement ended the war in eastern Ukraine, the fighting temporarily subsided by late 2015.[25]

The role of Russian special operations forces—or "little green men," as they were subsequently called because they wore unmarked green army uniforms—was unmistakable in eastern Ukraine. Russian *spetsnaz* and other special operations forces under the GRU—and ultimately under Gerasimov—provided training, weapons, money, and other assistance to separatists.[26] They helped create, sustain, and fund separatist political parties and unions; established and aided paramilitary groups such as the Russian Orthodox Army and the Night Wolves; and recruited Cossack, Chechen, Serbian, and Russian paramilitaries.[27] Ukraine also became a training ground for white supremacists from Europe and other regions, who came to train with rebels (with some Russian government aid) and progovernment volunteer battalions.[28]

In addition, Russia established an aggressive cyber campaign. Russia had conducted a limited cyber operation against the country of Georgia during the August 2008 war in the separatist region of South Ossetia. But Russian actions in Ukraine were a major escalation. GRU units—including the Russian hacker group known as "Sandworm," which the US and UK governments identified as GRU Military Unit 74455—orchestrated one of the world's most brazen offensive cyber campaigns by taking down multiple parts of Ukraine's critical infrastructure, including its electricity grid. Russian operatives planted several types of malware—including "BlackEnergy," "KillDisk," and "Industroyer"—against companies that supported Ukraine's electric power grid and against the Ukrainian government's State Treasury Service and

Ministry of Finance.[29] They then used the malware to open every circuit breaker in a transmission station north of Kiev, systematically disconnect circuits, delete backup systems, and shut down substations. The result was a blackout across a wide swath of Ukraine's capital. Two years later, Russian intelligence operatives in Military Unit 74455—such as Yuriy Andrienko, Pavel Frolov, Sergey Detistov, and Petr Pliskin—conducted another massive cyber attack with malware called "NotPetya," which froze up to 30 percent of Ukraine's computers.[30] The impact of NotPetya rippled across the globe. Victims in the United States suffered nearly $1 billion in damage from the attacks and included Heritage Valley Health System in Pennsylvania, a FedEx Corporation subsidary called TNT Express BV, and a major US pharmaceutical company.[31]

As a US Army Special Operations Command assessment concluded, Russian efforts also included aggressive propaganda that targeted Ukrainian "television, radio, and social media through the use of highly trained operatives, including 'hacktivists' and seemingly independent bloggers; use of Russia Today television as a highly effective propaganda tool; use of professional actors who portray themselves as pro-Russian Ukrainians."[32]

"Once again, the US did virtually nothing in response," former CIA and NSA director Michael Hayden told me. "The Obama administration stopped short of providing the Ukrainian government with defensive arms, though they did respond with some sanctions."[33] The United States had considered sending arms such as Javelin anti-tank missiles to Ukraine. As former CIA director John Brennan acknowledged, however, the administration ultimately rejected this course of action "because of fear that the Russians would get access to Javelin's sensitive technology."[34] In addition, European governments slapped sanctions on Russia—but did little else in response.

Russia used irregular warfare methods to destabilize eastern Ukraine and deter closer relations between the Kiev government and the West—while maintaining deniability of direct Russian military involvement. The campaign was certainly not a clear victory like Crimea. But it was effective in creating a frozen conflict in eastern Ukraine, in which Moscow could dial up—or down—the intensity of war, depending on political calculations.[35] Russian leaders also believed that their actions in Ukraine and other countries would deter US action in Russia's periphery, such as Belarus, Moldova, and Georgia.[36]

Perhaps most surprising for Moscow's leaders, the United States barely pushed back against Russian aggression. While President Obama might have reacted differently if Putin and Gerasimov had sent conventional forces into Ukraine, Russia faced only muted criticism by spearheading an irregular campaign. Putin and Gerasimov were emboldened, and they would not have to wait long for another opportunity. It came in Syria.

✳   ✳   ✳   ✳

BY 2015, Putin, Gerasimov, and other Russian officials were alarmed at the deteriorating situation in Syria. The war, which began in 2011, had dramatically escalated over the previous four years. According to Russian intelligence assessments briefed to Gerasimov, there were up to 4,500 citizens from Russia and Central Asia in the ranks of the Islamic State and other terrorist groups in the Middle East—particularly Syria—and a grand total of 60,000 terrorists.[37] Russian intelligence also concluded that Syrian government forces controlled only 10 percent of Syrian territory.[38] In northern Syria, Kurdish forces had seized growing swaths of territory at the expense of the Assad regime. In southern and central Syria, the Islamic State enlarged its area of control and conducted brutal attacks in the north and west. Finally, the rebel group Jabhat al-Nusrah, which had links with al-Qaeda, expanded its presence in northwestern and southwestern Syria, driving back Syrian government forces and threatening major population centers.[39]

The situation seemed hopeless as cities like Hasaka, Raqqa, Aleppo, and even areas around Damascus fell to rebels. "It was a very difficult situation," recalled Gerasimov. "There was low morale and high fatigue, as well as a lack of ammunition, matériel, and other types of support," he said.[40] In some cases, the Russian military was forced to repair the Syrian military's "broken equipment on the spot," Gerasimov acknowledged.[41]

For Moscow, Syria was not just any country. It had long been an important Russian partner, and its warm-water port at Tartus was helpful for Russia's regional ambitions and power projection. In 1946, the Soviet Union supported Syrian independence and provided military aid to the newly formed Syrian Arab Army. This cooperation continued throughout the Cold War. Successive Soviet and then Russian leaders developed an important relationship with Hafiz al-Assad, who ruled Syria from 1970 until his death in 2000.[42] But now Russian leaders were concerned that Washington was attempting to overthrow the Assad regime and replace it with a friendly government, much like the United States had done in Afghanistan, Iraq, and Libya—among other countries.[43] Gerasimov blamed the United States for destabilizing Syria and creating a terrorist safe haven in the country. "The development of events in Syria according to the Libyan scenario would lead to the fact that a recently prosperous country would become a source of the spread of terrorist danger for the entire region," he said.[44]

In February 2015, US president Barack Obama repeated his call for Assad to step down, which he had been urging since 2011, and he vowed to aid rebel groups. "We'll continue to support the moderate opposition there and continue to believe that it will not be possible to fully stabilize that country until Mr. Assad, who has lost legitimacy in the country, is transitioned out," Obama remarked.[45] In early 2015, a delegation of US senators led by John McCain had visited Saudi Arabia and Qatar to discuss increasing support to Syrian rebels.[46] McCain had secretly visited rebel leaders inside Syria

and discussed the possibility of providing heavy weapons and establishing a no-fly zone in Syria to help topple Assad.[47] As McCain
observed: "We need a strategy that can force Assad to leave power
and defeat ISIS in both Syria and Iraq, and that strategy should
start with greater support to these Syrian opposition forces, especially vital military training and assistance."[48] Near the end of 2015,
McCain and US senator Lindsey Graham publicly supported the
deployment of 10,000 troops to Syria.[49] Gerasimov had seen enough,
and he blamed the United States for supporting Syrian rebels and
fomenting terrorism.[50]

In late 2015, Putin finally put his foot down.

* * * *

IN A SPEECH at the United Nations in September 2015, Putin
vowed to support the Assad regime. "We think it is an enormous
mistake to refuse to cooperate with the Syrian government and
its armed forces who are valiantly fighting terrorism face-to-face,"
he said.[51] Over the summer of 2015, Gerasimov helped spearhead
efforts involving Russian, Iranian, and Syrian leaders to ramp up
military operations. Russia and Syria signed a treaty stipulating
the terms and conditions for Russia's use of Hmeimim Air Base,
southeast of the city of Latakia.[52] Russia then began to position air,
naval, and ground forces in and near Syria in preparation for military operations.[53]

Compared with Moscow's approach in Afghanistan in the 1980s,
which involved a heavy footprint of 115,000 Soviet forces to fight
the Afghan mujahideen, the approach adopted by Russian leaders
in Syria beginning in 2015 was vastly different.[54] On the basis of his
assessment of recent wars—including the US campaigns in Afghanistan, Iraq, and Libya—Gerasimov helped craft a light footprint strategy that included a mix of airpower and maneuver elements. Syrian
armed forces, not the Russian army, served as the main maneuver
element to take back territory. With Russian aid, Syrian forces were

supported by militia forces like Lebanese Hezbollah (which received support from Iran's Quds Force, led by Qassem Soleimani), and private military contractors like the Wagner Group (which received training and other aid from the Russian military).[55] These forces did most of the fighting and held territory once it was cleared, with help from Russian special operations forces on the ground.[56]

At the end of September 2015, Russia conducted its first air strikes in support of Syrian forces around the cities of Homs and Hama.[57] The Russian air force then conducted 1,292 combat missions against 1,623 targets in October 2015 alone, from its fleet of thirty-two combat aircraft.[58] Many of these strikes were of low accuracy, and Russian aircraft used unguided weapons to hit targets in urban areas, causing substantial collateral damage. Russian aircraft lacked significant numbers of targeting pods and high-precision weapons to conduct accurate strikes early in the conflict, though Russian precision-strike capabilities improved over the course of the war.[59] Russia also benefited from forward air controllers deployed with Syrian and other ground units, who helped call in air strikes.[60]

✳   ✳   ✳   ✳

SOME US OFFICIALS in the Middle East were aghast at the lack of a US response. Lieutenant General Michael Nagata, who was serving as head of US Special Operations Command Central, the special operations component of US Central Command, had kept a wary eye on Russia's growing presence in Syria and the Middle East more broadly. "The expansion of Russian activities and personnel had begun in at least 2014," he told me. "The United States neither fully recognized the extent of the problem nor did anything about it."[61] US intelligence agencies failed to fully understand that Moscow would become deeply engaged in Syria, which Gerasimov described as "asymmetric warfare."[62] Russia also began to ramp up a disinformation and propaganda campaign designed to distract the Syrian population and discredit Americans. "The Russians repeatedly pushed the line that the United States was aiding the Islamic State," said a senior US Department of Defense official. "I mean really?" he said. "That was clearly ludicrous. But the Obama administration did not adequately push back."[63]

The US and European failure to counter Russia's growing military, diplomatic, and intelligence presence in the Middle East was particularly perplexing for US partners in the region. During a 2015 meeting with General Lloyd Austin, head of US Central Command and future US secretary of defense, King Abdullah of Jordan opened with a concern that took much of the US delegation by surprise. "Before we begin," King Abdullah said, "I wanted to raise one issue. I am starting to worry about the presence of Russia in the region. I wish to discuss with you how we are going to deal with this."[64] US officials were entirely unprepared for the question and did not have a reassuring response. By this time, most Middle East leaders were raising the same issue. "Never once," said one US official, "did we have a satisfactory answer."[65]

Over time, however, the tone of many Middle Eastern leaders changed. With a limited response from Washington, a growing regional perception that the United States was unwilling to support its traditional partners, and a steady stream of Russian officials and activity in the region, Middle Eastern leaders had to make peace with Moscow. "You are my preferred partner, and my dedication to the U.S.-Jordanian relationship is strong," said King Abdullah to another delegation of US officials. "But I have to reach my accommodation with the Russians."[66]

✳　✳　✳　✳

AS THE RUSSIAN PRESENCE grew in the Middle East, Moscow simultaneously turned its attention to the United States, seeking to undermine the 2016 presidential election. As US intelligence agencies concluded, Putin directly ordered the Russian influence campaign to damage public trust in the US democratic system and ultimately weaken the United States at home and abroad.[67] The GRU was the lead agency. Its base of operations was the "Tower," a twenty-story behemoth complex cased in oversized windows that dwarfed nearby brick and concrete apartments. Because of its low-key location at 22 Kirova Street in the Moscow suburb of Khimki, few outsiders—except intelligence agencies—knew that Moscow was mounting one of its boldest irregular warfare campaigns yet.[68]

This was not Moscow's first foray into cyber operations against the United States. In 2008, Russian intelligence hacked into the Pentagon's classified SIPRNet (Secret Internet Protocol Router Network) system.[69] Over the next decade, the Russians implanted malware in US critical infrastructure—including in power plants, industrial systems, and communications networks. The malware took numerous forms, such as BlackEnergy.

By 2016, covert Russian activity against the US elections included two main parts.[70] The first was a hacking-and-dumping operation led by two groups within the GRU: Military Unit 26165, a cyber unit dedicated to conducting operations against military, political, and other targets outside of Russia, including the United States; and Military Unit 74455, a separate GRU unit that engaged in cyber operations.[71] Key GRU officers included Viktor Netyksho, who headed Unit 26165, and Alexander Osadchuk, a GRU colonel who was the commanding officer of Unit 74455.[72]

Around April 12, 2016, the GRU hacked into the Democratic Congressional Campaign Committee (DCCC) computer network by using credentials stolen from an employee who had fallen for a spear-phishing attack the week before. Over the next several weeks, the GRU traversed the committee's computer network and, on April 18, gained access to the Democratic National Committee (DNC) computer network through a virtual private network (VPN) between the DCCC and DNC networks. GRU Military Unit 26165 then implanted malware in both networks and began to exfiltrate stolen data—including thousands of strategy documents, fundraising data, opposition research, and emails—from their computers.[73] In addition, the GRU hacked into email accounts of individuals affiliated with the Hillary Clinton campaign.

GRU officers then publicly leaked the material through two fictitious online personas: "DCLeaks" (using the website dcleaks.com and supported by Facebook, Twitter, and Gmail accounts) and "Guccifer 2.0" (using blog posts and direct releases to reporters and other individuals). The information eventually came out in WikiLeaks. Officers of GRU Military Unit 74455 also hacked into computers belonging to state boards of elections, secretaries of state, county governments, and US companies that provided other support related to the administration of US elections.[74]

The second component of Russia's irregular warfare campaign was a social media campaign implemented by the Internet Research Agency (IRA). It was housed in a nondescript four-story building on Savushkina Street in Saint Petersburg, with heavy drapes pulled tight over the windows to keep out prying eyes. The IRA was funded by Yevgeny Prigozhin—a Russian oligarch and confidant of Vladimir Putin who earned the nickname "Putin's chef"—and companies he operated.[75] As part of its clandestine operations, the IRA hired individuals and deployed some to the United States who were specialists focusing on Facebook, YouTube, Twitter, Tumblr, and Instagram. These individuals created social media accounts that pretended to be the personal accounts of US citizens. IRA Facebook groups included fictitious conservative groups with names like "Being Patriotic," "Secured Borders," and "Tea Party News"; fake African American social justice groups like "Black Matters" and "Blacktivist"; and purported religious groups like "United Muslims of America."[76]

For Russian leaders like Gerasimov, it did not matter *that much* who won the election—Donald Trump or Hillary Clinton—though Putin later acknowledged that he preferred Trump.[77] Much more important was that Russian activities exploited an already polarized domestic political climate in the United States that exploded between 2016 and 2020 during Trump's presidency. It was a cost-effective strategy. For a paltry amount of money, Russia helped catapult the United States into four years of social and political turmoil that culminated in two impeachment proceedings against President Trump. And, even better, Moscow did not have to create anything. Russian leaders simply exploited US weaknesses.

"The Russians are *still* laughing about the 2016 election," Mark Kelton, former head of counterintelligence and counterespionage at the CIA told me, "as they sip their vodka."[78]

✳ ✳ ✳ ✳

BACK IN SYRIA in 2016 with Russian help, the Syrian army and allied forces retook successive Syrian cities, such as Aleppo, Homs, Palmyra, and Deir ez-Zor. The Russians conducted sixty to seventy air strikes per day on rebels and their infrastructure.[79] While Russia's mix of airpower and maneuver was similar in some ways to the US model in Kosovo, Afghanistan, and Libya, it was different in one critical respect.[80] Russia adopted a punishment strategy, not a population-centric strategy characterized by winning local hearts and minds.[81] Russian and allied military forces inflicted civilian harm on opposition-controlled areas by using artillery and indiscriminate weapons, such as thermobaric, incendiary, and cluster munitions.[82] As the Russians demonstrated in Grozny during Gerasimov's time in Chechnya, a punishment strategy is designed to raise the societal costs of continued resistance and coerce rebels to give up.[83]

Russia committed human rights abuses, triggered the displacement of millions of refugees and internally displaced persons, caused large-scale destruction of infrastructure, and conducted wanton killings of civilians. As one Human Rights Watch report concluded: "Russia continued to play a key military role alongside the Syrian government in offensives on anti-government-held areas, indiscriminately attacking schools, hospitals, and civilian infrastructure."[84] Moscow also provided diplomatic cover when Syrian forces used chemical weapons against its own population. In August 2013, the Syrian government used sarin against rebel positions around Ghouta, killing more than 1,400 people.[85] In April 2017, Syrian aircraft operating in rebel-held Idlib province conducted several air strikes using sarin. The strikes, which occurred in the town of Khan Sheikhoun, killed an estimated 80–100 people.[86] In April 2018, Syrian government forces launched a chlorine attack in the southwestern city of Douma.[87] Russia provided diplomatic cover for these atrocities by vetoing more than a dozen international attempts to condemn Assad's actions at the United Nations, as well as conducting a wide-ranging disinformation campaign.[88]

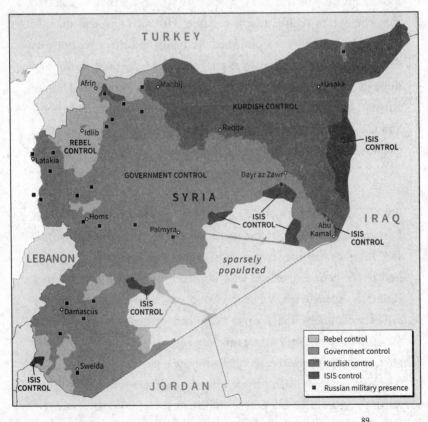

RUSSIAN MILITARY PRESENCE IN SYRIA, 2018[89]

Other units were also involved in ground operations. The Iranian leader Qassem Soleimani and his Islamic Revolutionary Guard Corps-Quds Force helped organize, train, and fund over 100,000 Shia fighters.[90] Up to 3,000 Quds Force troops helped plan and execute campaigns such as OPERATION DAWN OF VICTORY in Aleppo.[91] Lebanese Hezbollah deployed up to 8,000 fighters to Syria and amassed a substantial arsenal of rockets and missiles.[92] Hezbollah also trained, advised, and assisted Shia militias in areas like southwestern Syria.[93]

By 2021, the Syrian government—with Russian and Iranian support—controlled most of Syria's major cities and had retaken bases in Manbij and Kobani abandoned by US forces. None of this looked possible in late 2015, when Russian policy makers assessed that the Syrian regime might collapse without rapid and decisive assistance. Moscow accomplished its main objectives without its forces becoming engaged in a quagmire, like the Red Army had done in Afghanistan in the 1980s. Yet there were problems. Despite Russian support, Assad still was not popular among many Syrians, and the economy was in shambles. Some in Russia complained that the war in Syria was a drain on Russia's fragile economy.[94]

❋ ❋ ❋ ❋

RUSSIA'S GROWING irregular operations did not stop with Ukraine and Syria. Moscow methodically expanded its use of private military companies like the Wagner Group across the globe. Led by Yevgeny Prigozhin, who was also involved in the Internet Research Agency, the Wagner Group was Russia's largest private military company. The Wagner Group conducted a variety of military and information warfare missions overseas, such as combat support, training, protective services, and site security.[95]

Russia's strategy with private military companies was straightforward: to undermine US power and increase Moscow's influence by using low-profile, deniable forces that could do everything from providing foreign leaders with security to training, advising, and assisting partner security forces. As Admiral McRaven told me: "The Russians are using small paramilitary forces and contractor forces. They did much of this during the Cold War. And they are doing it now. It gives them plausible deniability but allows them to build a presence in multiple countries."[96] The Russians were not always successful. In Libya, for example, Moscow used the Wagner Group to provide training, intelligence, and combat support to General Khalifa Haftar, Haftar's Libyan National Army (LNA), and the government in Tobruk. Despite this aid, however, the LNA failed to seize Tripoli.

Nevertheless, Moscow significantly expanded its use of private military companies like the Wagner Group as part of its irregular warfare campaign. Between 2015 and 2021, there was a seven-fold increase in the number of countries where Russian private military companies operated, from 4 countries in 2015 to 27 in 2021.[97] Russian military companies were active in Africa, the Middle East, Europe, Asia, and Latin America—including in such countries as the Central African Republic, Iraq, Libya, Sudan, Syria, Ukraine, and Venezuela. The Kremlin and Russian security agencies— including the GRU, the Foreign Intelligence Service (SVR), and the Federal Security Service (FSB)—provided guidance and aid to companies like the Wagner Group.

✳ ✳ ✳ ✳

BEGINNING WITH the Crimea operation in 2014, Gerasimov helped engineer a stunning reversal in Russia's fortunes with a mix of clandestine activity and cyber operations. Moscow annexed Crimea, spearheaded an irregular war (complete with cyber attacks) in Ukraine that undercut Ukraine's sovereignty, saved the Assad regime by using a heavy dose of *spetsnaz* and air strikes, undermined a US presidential election, fomented schisms in an already polarized US political system, and expanded its power and influence in Europe, the Middle East, Africa, Asia, and even Latin America.[98]

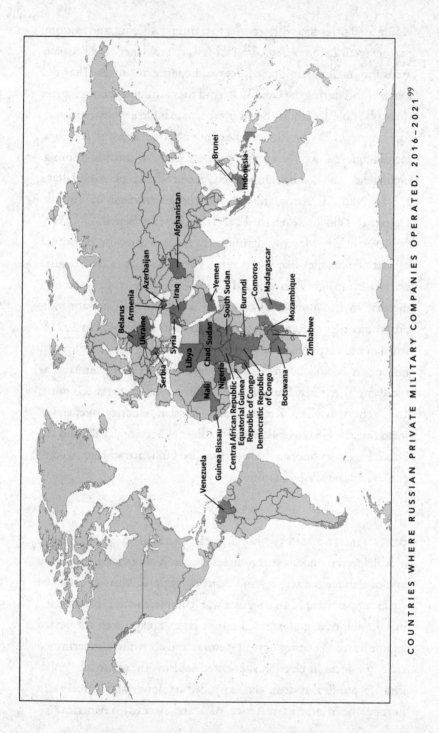

COUNTRIES WHERE RUSSIAN PRIVATE MILITARY COMPANIES OPERATED, 2016–2021[99]

To be clear, Russia is not a global superpower. Its economy is stagnant, with low gross domestic product growth, blatant corruption, and stifling bureaucracy. Yet Russia punched above its weight, thanks to the strategy and helmsmanship of individuals like Putin and Gerasimov. "The Russian use of special operations forces, private military companies, and intelligence has been pretty innovative," said former CIA director General David Petraeus. "Moscow is having some success."[100] Instead of expanding Russian power and influence through brute conventional force, Moscow became nimble, covert, and well versed in deception. As Gerasimov argued, Moscow was now able to wage war using asymmetric methods.[101]

Russia was aggressive in expanding its influence and undermining the United States through a combination of cyber operations, espionage propaganda, hacktivists, bots, and trolls. And the Russians were adaptive. The trolls at the Internet Research Agency ditched email accounts that were being tracked by US and other Western intelligence agencies and moved to encrypted communication platforms that were harder to trace. Russia's Foreign Intelligence Service, or SVR, orchestrated a massive cyber attack in the United States that affected several hundred federal agencies and businesses.[102] Russian intelligence agencies also successfully recruited some Americans, such as Peter Rafael Dzibinski Debbins, a former US Green Beret, who passed classified information to Moscow.[103] As Putin reminded the US in 2021, "Russia's response will be asymmetrical, swift and tough" to any threats, emphasizing the word *asimmetrichnym* ("asymmetrical").[104]

Gerasimov had long preached that there were no clear boundaries between war and peace in international politics. "In the twenty-first century," he wrote, "we have seen a tendency toward blurring the lines between the states of war and peace."[105] Countries fight during peacetime, he said, and they use political, economic, and information means during wartime. The graduate of Kazan Suvorov Military School, who had dreamed as a child of serving in the military, had now helped energize a newly proud and emboldened nation.

"The Russians are a relatively weak actor, but they are playing chess," said Lieutenant General Michael Nagata. "The United States is a strong actor, but we are playing checkers. The Russians are out-thinking us, not outfighting us."[106] Moscow had also chosen its allies well. Another country effectively competing with the United States by using irregular warfare was Russia's partner in Syria: Iran.

PART II
IRAN

QASSEM SOLEIMANI

5: GUARDIAN OF THE REVOLUTION

QASSEM SOLEIMANI WAS RUNNING LATE TO HIS own funeral. Cham Wings Airlines Flight 6Q501, which was transporting the head of Iran's Islamic Revolutionary Guard Corps-Quds Force (IRGC-QF) to Baghdad, was delayed at Damascus International Airport. The flight had been scheduled to depart at 7:30 p.m. on January 2, 2020. But a spy at the airport in Damascus reported that the burly Soleimani, with his snow-white beard and broad smile, was nearly three hours behind schedule. He had been in Beirut to see Hezbollah leader Hassan Nasrallah and was now supposed to be heading to Iraq. As the hours dragged on, some US officials wondered whether they should call off the operation. But then—suddenly—the headlights from a convoy appeared out of the darkness. The vehicles pulled up to the waiting Cham Wings flight. Soleimani, who was accompanied by two aides, stepped out, shuffled up the passenger stairs, and disappeared into the aircraft. The plan was back on.[1]

Soleimani settled into his seat for the short, hour-and-a-half flight to Baghdad. US and Israeli intelligence had monitored Soleimani's travel patterns, including his frequent flights around the region, where he bounced between Lebanon, Syria, and Iraq in a bid to expand Iranian influence. They knew that Iran sometimes bought him tickets for multiple flights to throw off surveillance, and once on board, they knew, Soleimani preferred sitting in the first row of business class so that he could exit the plane first.[2] The plane landed at 12:36 a.m. in Baghdad on January 3, way behind schedule. Soleimani and his entourage were the first to disembark. They were greeted on the tarmac by Abu Mahdi al-Muhandis, a tall figure with thick glasses and a neatly combed mane of gray hair who was decked out in a sports coat and button-down shirt. US special operations forces had al-Muhandis on their target list, referring to him as OBJECTIVE MORGAN. He looked more like a university professor than head of the Iraqi militia Kataib Hezbollah, which received aid from Soleimani's Quds Force. The week before, al-Muhandis's supporters had laid siege to the US embassy in Baghdad in retaliation for US air strikes that killed twenty-five of his militia fighters.[3]

Soleimani, al-Muhandis, and their security guards climbed into two armored SUVs and headed into the night. But they were not alone. US special operations soldiers in vehicles were waiting for Soleimani. So were US MQ-9 drones, which were circling above the airport. Dubbed the "Reaper," the MQ-9 is the United States' cutting-edge killing machine. Its large, 66-foot wingspan and hulking 4,900-pound frame hide its two most lethal attributes: it is nearly silent in flight, and it can be armed with laser-guided Hellfire air-to-surface missiles designed to destroy tanks. But these MQ-9s had a special Hellfire variant, the R9X "Ninja," which has a warhead with pop-out blades intended to gash their targets and reduce collateral damage. The vehicle carrying Soleimani skirted down an access road past rows of palm trees at the far end of the runway. US special operations forces followed a half mile behind.[4]

US president Donald Trump, flanked by key members of his national security team, watched video footage of the strike from the Situation Room at the White House.

"Sir, they have two minutes and 11 seconds," a soldier briefed the president by secure video. "Two minutes and 11 seconds to live, sir."

Soleimani's convoy turned toward the airport's low perimeter wall, which was topped with barbed wire. Trump sat in suspense.

"They're in the car, they're in the armored vehicle," the briefer continued.

"Sir, they have approximately one minute to live, sir. Thirty seconds. Ten, 9, 8 . . ." and then BOOM! "They're gone, sir."[5]

At 12:47 a.m., the R9X missiles slammed into the car carrying Soleimani and al-Muhandis, buckling the metal and setting it on fire. Another missile struck the second car, carrying the bodyguards. The strike engulfed the vehicles in flames and left ten charred bodies inside. While al-Muhandis was instantly vaporized, Soleimani's body lay in flames next to the car, grossly disfigured. His severed hand, covered in gray ash, dangled through a window, identifiable by his trademark flashy ruby ring. US special operators raced to the wreckage to conduct a "bomb damage assessment." They dragged Soleimani's body from the burning debris and snapped pictures of Soleimani and his possessions—poetry books, pistol, assault rifle, and wads of cash.[6]

The United States was quick to announce the strike. "General Soleimani was actively developing plans to attack American diplomats and service members in Iraq and throughout the region," Secretary of Defense Mark Esper declared. "This strike was aimed at deterring future Iranian attack plans."[7] In his typical bluster, President Trump confirmed the strike by tweet: "General Qassem Soleimani has killed or badly wounded thousands of Americans over an extended period of time, and was plotting to kill many more . . . but got caught!"[8]

It was not the first time that the Trump administration had weighed targeting Soleimani. One senior US government official had parked his airplane not once—but twice—next to Soleimani's on the tarmac at Erbil International Airport in Iraq. On one of those occasions, the official reached out to Michael Rogers, the head of the US National Security Agency.

"Mike," he said, "what can I do to help out?"

"Thanks for the offer," Rogers responded. "But we know where Soleimani is virtually every second of every day. The problem is that no one has any guts to do anything about it."[9]

On another occasion during the Obama administration, Soleimani sent a message to the United States through intermediaries, protesting that the Americans had fired a drone at him. "It wasn't us," Obama officials replied, indicating that they had no intention of killing Soleimani.[10] He was off-limits. Most senior US officials assessed that the benefits of killing Soleimani were outweighed by the risks, especially the possibility of a significant escalation in tensions with Tehran and Iranian retaliation.

But in 2020, Soleimani's luck finally ran out. Senior Trump officials concluded that the benefits of killing him now outweighed any risks, since Soleimani was dangerously expanding Iran's power and influence by using a network of militias in Lebanon, Syria, Iraq, Yemen, and other countries. Understanding the significance of Soleimani's death requires recognizing just how dangerous his irregular warfare campaign had become. His death was a major blow to Iran, to be sure. But thanks to Soleimani and his Quds Force, Iran posed a serious threat to the United States and many of its regional partners, such as Israel, Saudi Arabia, and Jordan. And this threat was unlikely to end with his death. Soleimani's project had been years in the making—going back to his childhood dream of becoming a great warrior, or *javanmard*, for his country and a guardian of the Iranian Revolution.

✳ ✳ ✳ ✳

QASSEM SOLEIMANI—often described with the honorific "Hajj Qassem"—was born in Rabor, a mountain village in Kerman province in southeastern Iran, on March 11, 1957. His family was poor and, as their last name indicates, came from the Soleimani tribe.[11] Soleimani was the middle child in a family of five.[12] His father took out a 900-toman agricultural loan—over $100 at the time—from the government of Mohammad Reza Pahlavi.[13] But he couldn't pay it back. In an effort to help, Soleimani left school around the age of thirteen with a relative, Ahmad.

"Come promise, Qassem," said Ahmad, "that we will not return to the village until we have collected the right amount of money."

"Let's shake hands," responded Soleimani.[14]

And so they went. They hopped on a bus to the city of Kerman and looked for work to pay off the debts. "It was almost noon when the minibus entered Kerman and parked next to the square," recalled Soleimani. "The driver quickly jumped onto the luggage compartment and dumped our luggage from above. Among the heap of yogurt containers, sacks of whey, and other goods, there were two packs of bed clothes for us." That was it. Soleimani and Ahmad were now broke and alone. "We felt those heavy and long moments with all of our being," said Soleimani. "Really, we were left behind and didn't know what to do." Homesickness and despair quickly set in. "At night, we couldn't sleep because of the grief that one day the government would come and arrest our fathers, and they would go to prison," remembered Soleimani. "The thought of such a day broke our hearts."[15]

But they eventually found work. Soleimani secured a job at the Kerman Water Organization and spent most of his leisure time at the Atai and Jahan *zourkhanehs* ("athletic clubs").[16] The clubs were more than workout facilities and were designed to instill Iranian youth with a warrior (*javanmard*) ethos. Soleimani became proficient at karate and even worked as a fitness coach.[17] He attended sermons by a firebrand preacher named Hojjat Kamyab—a protégé of Ali Khamenei, Iran's future supreme leader.[18] Soleimani became inspired by the prospects of a Shia revolution and helped organize marches and strikes in Kerman.[19] In 1979, Iran experienced a dramatic revolution that overthrew Pahlavi and installed Grand Ayatollah Ruhollah Khomeini in his place. The new Iran centered around the doctrine of *velayat-e faqih*, the Islamic system of clerical rule. The country would be run as an Islamic republic led by Shia clergy, who enforced conservative social values.

Swept up in the excitement but with no military experience, Soleimani joined the newly established Islamic Revolutionary Guard Corps (IRGC), or *sepah-e pasdaran-e enqelab-e eslami*, with a desire to be a guardian of the revolution. He recalled: "We were all young and wanted to serve the revolution in a way. This is how I joined the Guards."[20] The IRGC was founded in 1979 shortly after the Islamic revolution. Ayatollah Khomeini was suspicious of the loyalty of some officers in Iran's regular military, or Artesh, and worried that they retained ties with Pahlavi. Proclerical militants had been helpful in bringing down the Pahlavi regime, and Khomeini pulled them together under a single banner. The IRGC would defend Iran from more powerful countries, such as the United States, and— more important—safeguard Iran's theocratic system from within.[21] As Khomeini remarked, these individuals were expected to be "the guardians of the revolution and the fighting sons of Islam."[22]

The IRGC's proximity and devotion to Khomeini gave it immense power and legitimacy, enabling it to eclipse Iran's traditional military.[23]

* * * *

SOLEIMANI'S CAREER with the IRGC began in earnest when, after roughly six weeks of training, he was sent to Mahabad in Iran's West Azerbaijan province, where there was a Kurdish separatist uprising.[24] The Kurdish rebellion erupted in March 1979 and became one of the largest nationwide uprisings against the new Iranian state. In 1980, the IRGC initiated a sustained and bloody offensive against Kurdish rebels, which successfully cleared most Kurdish militants from their strongholds by the end of the year.[25]

When Soleimani returned from Mahabad, he was appointed head of the Kerman IRGC Quds Garrison.[26] By then, Iran and Iraq had become embroiled in a decade-long war that Iranians frequently refer to as the *jang-e tahmili* ("imposed war").[27] It began when Saddam Hussein's forces invaded Iran's Khuzestan province on September 22, 1980.[28] Although Soleimani had limited military experience, he trained several units from Kerman, which eventually deployed to the southern front against Iraq, along with tens of thousands of other Iranians. Over the course of the war, Soleimani participated in a number of operations, eventually commanding the 41st Division. It was nicknamed "Tharallah," or "Vengeance of God."[29]

In about 1982, he befriended Ismail Qaani, a native of Mashhad in northeastern Iran. Qaani would become Soleimani's Quds Force deputy and eventually take over after Soleimani's death at the hands of the Americans in 2020.[30] In commenting on his friendship with Soleimani, Qaani, who accepted the honorific title "Hajj Ismail," emphasized that fighting together created impenetrable bonds:

> For us kids of the war, the point of connection, relation, and camaraderie is not our geography, territory or city. . . . We became friends on the battlefield, and people who become friends in hardships have stronger and more stable relationships than those who meet and become friends in the city or a neighborhood.[31]

Soleimani and Qaani experienced the war's brutality up close. In November and December 1981, for example, Soleimani helped liberate the Iranian city of Bostan from Iraqi forces, in what was dubbed OPERATION TARIQ AL-QODS.[32] The Iranians used "human wave" attacks in the war, which involved frontal assaults by masses of Iranian soldiers against Iraqi lines. While Iran lost more than twice as many soldiers as Iraq because of these suicide missions, the operation was successful in enabling Iran to retake Bostan—which was 10 miles from the Iraqi border—and significantly interrupt one of Iraq's most important supply routes. But Soleimani lost numerous friends during the brutal fighting. For the rest of his life, Soleimani memorialized these and other Iranian soldiers in speeches as martyrs for the nation.[33]

War is the great test of a soldier's mettle. Soleimani emerged from the "imposed war" with a reputation for valor and élan.[34] He took risks and conducted cross-border operations into Iraq that earned him the nickname "goat thief."[35] On July 2, 1986, Soleimani was nearly taken prisoner by Iraqi forces during OPERATION KARBALA 1, when Iranian forces recaptured the strategically important Iranian city of Mehran.[36] Soleimani also developed a deft appreciation of irregular warfare skills like clandestine operations. While preparing for the battle at Shalamcheh on October 5, 1981, he remarked: "Our training of the expedited forces reveals our maneuvers. We must instruct the forces in various fields so no one finds out what our maneuver is and where our operational area will be."[37] Secrecy was imperative.

Soleimani took care of his soldiers and inspired confidence. "Soleimani dressed simply, he ate humbly with his soldiers, and he grieved with his soldiers," said one Afghan official I spoke to who knew him. "This is one reason why they loved him so much. He was a soldier's soldier."[38]

Soleimani was also unafraid to provide his unvarnished opinion. He was unapologetic in excoriating military deficiencies and encouraging changes. In October 1987, he pressed the IRGC leadership to improve its planning and demanded that the IRGC establish lessons-learned units to examine battlefield performance, analyze mistakes, and highlight ways to improve. He also complained about the paucity of soldiers available to train conscripts, as well as about poor cooperation between IRGC headquarters and frontline IRGC regiments.[39]

Footage of Soleimani's speeches during the war shows him motivating men under his command by praising martyred comrades, weeping, and begging forgiveness for not having been killed himself.[40] Soleimani frequently embraced his men and bid them farewell before each offensive. He was also committed to taking care of the families of fallen soldiers. On August 2, 1986, on a visit to his native Kerman, Soleimani blasted local health care officials for not doing enough to treat his wounded soldiers.[41] His brother Sohrab, who fought with Soleimani in the Iran-Iraq War, recalled: "Hajj Qassem loves the children of martyrs so much that sometimes his own children become jealous of them. He has a very close relationship with the children of martyrs."[42]

In a well-publicized photograph taken during the Iran-Iraq War, Soleimani sits humbly with the future supreme leader, Ali Khamenei, as they share a meal with other fighters. Soleimani has a dark-black beard and thick, bushy eyebrows, and he looks much like the *javanmard* of his childhood dreams.[43] This close relationship with the supreme leader would continue for the rest of Soleimani's life.

✳ ✳ ✳ ✳

THE IRAN-IRAQ WAR had a profound impact on Soleimani in two ways. First, he concluded that Iran was surrounded by enemies. Many Iranians like Soleimani believed the conflict was a Western— particularly a US-driven—invasion. As an official IRGC history of the war claimed: "The war was financed and engineered by the U.S." because of "the severe threat that [the Iranian Revolution] posed to the predatory interests of world imperialism."[44] The United States had imposed economic sanctions on Iran and provided weapons, equipment, money, and intelligence to Iraq.[45] Soleimani viewed Iraq as a mere proxy of the United States that tried—and ultimately failed—to crush the Iranian Revolution.[46]

Second, Soleimani realized that Iran was not—and would likely never be—a conventional power. Its comparative advantage would have to be irregular operations. Iranian conventional units did not perform particularly well on the battlefield against Iraq's better-trained and better-equipped forces, and they were forced to use vastly inferior military equipment.[47] The war cost Tehran as much as $645 billion and left its economy and infrastructure in shambles.[48] But Soleimani began to appreciate the importance of irregular warfare—what Iranians called *jang-e gheir-e kelasik* ("nonclassic war").[49] Iran adopted a military doctrine, "Complete Regulations of the Islamic Republic of Iran Armed Forces," that emphasized the importance of irregular activity.[50]

The IRGC had also started to develop some irregular capabilities during the war when it provided aid to Shia militant groups in Iraq. Among the most important was the Badr Corps, the armed wing of Ayatollah Mohammad Baqir al-Hakim's Supreme Council for the Islamic Revolution in Iraq, or SCIRI. Overall, nearly 5,000 foreign Shia militia fighters were killed during the war.[51] Outside of Iraq, the IRGC established a relationship with the Amal Movement in Lebanon and then Lebanese Hezbollah, to which it provided money, equipment, training, and strategic guidance.[52] Iran sent as many as 1,500 IRGC advisers to the Bekaa Valley in Lebanon to build and run training camps that prepared Hezbollah fighters for war with Israel.[53]

To expand and improve Iran's irregular warfare capabilities in countries like Lebanon and Iraq, Ayatollah Khomeini then approved in 1988 the establishment of the Quds Force (*sepah-e quds*)—which Soleimani eventually headed—under Brigadier General Ahmad Vahidi. The Quds Force (*Quds* is the Farsi word for "Jerusalem") would become Iran's elite paramilitary arm, roughly equivalent to a mix of US special operations forces and the CIA's paramilitary Special Activities Center.[54] It gathered intelligence, trained and equipped partner forces, and conducted assassinations and bombings outside of Iranian territory.[55] Ali Khamenei perhaps said it best: the Quds Force's mission was to "establish popular Hezbollah cells all over the world."[56]

After the Iran-Iraq War ended in 1988, Soleimani and his 41st Tharallah Division returned to Kerman. The IRGC then deployed Soleimani to southeastern Iran to conduct counter–drug operations against cartels, most of whom were involved in the cultivation, production, and transit of Afghan poppies.[57] His friend and future deputy, Ismail Qaani, also deployed to the Iran-Afghanistan border to fight drug cartels.[58] The southeast was a challenging space for the IRGC, with a robust tribal structure and a Sunni majority in a Shia state. Soleimani's division was successful in disrupting the cartels and improving border security. His time along the Iran-Afghanistan border also provided him an opportunity to observe CIA support to the mujahideen in neighboring Afghanistan. As one report summarized: Locals "still consider the era of the presence of Qassem Soleimani in the eastern and southeastern parts of the country among the securest eras."[59]

In 1998, Soleimani got his next big break. IRGC chief Sayyid Yahya "Rahim" Safavi appointed Soleimani as chief of the Quds Force.[60] From his perch as Quds Force commander, Soleimani would eventually become the most influential—and certainly the most active—military commander in Iran. Soleimani appointed Qaani as his deputy and began reorganizing the Quds Force, building from the foundation laid down by Brigadier General Vahidi. "Soleimani's personality and connections to the Iranian supreme leader made the Quds Force what it was," said General Joseph Votel, head of US Special Operations Command and US Central Command. "He was smart and charismatic. You have to respect your adversary. But make no mistake about it: he was an enemy."[61]

As a guardian of the revolution, Soleimani set off to build Iran's irregular warfare capabilities and expand Iran's influence in the region. He just needed an opportunity. It came quickly in neighboring Afghanistan. In the late 1990s the Taliban, an extremist Sunni militant group whose ideology was deeply rooted in the Hanafi school of Islamic jurisprudence, was rapidly overrunning northern Afghanistan in a series of blitzkrieg operations. Its goal of establishing an Islamic emirate in Afghanistan raised alarm bells in Tehran, and some Iranian political leaders called for an invasion of Afghanistan.

How would the newly minted Quds Force commander respond in his first serious test?

6: THE "SOLEIMANI STRUT"

THE TALIBAN WAS A THROWBACK MOVEMENT that had seemingly emerged from the Dark Ages. Its leaders were dedicated to implementing an extreme and unorthodox version of Sunni Islam.[1] The Taliban banned music, movies, television, and most sports in Afghanistan. Its leaders also prevented girls from attending schools, prohibited most women from working, required men to grow beards, and banned Western clothing.

The Taliban was now Qassem Soleimani's problem. Beginning in late 1994, Taliban forces had advanced through southern and eastern Afghanistan, capturing nine out of thirty provinces by February 1995. In September 1995, the Taliban seized the western Afghan city of Herat—only 75 miles from the Iranian border—causing alarm in Iran.[2] In 1996, the Taliban captured Kabul and, despite temporary setbacks, conquered the northern Afghan cities of Kunduz, Taloqan, and Mazar-e-Sharif in 1998.[3] The Taliban then turned on Iran.

On August 8, Taliban forces executed nine Iranian diplomats and one Islamic Republic News Agency journalist in Mazar-e-Sharif. Some in the Iranian government advocated invading Afghanistan.[4] In October 1998, nearly 200,000 regular Iranian troops massed along the border with Afghanistan, and the Taliban mobilized thousands of fighters to thwart an expected Iranian incursion. But Soleimani strongly opposed an Iranian invasion, arguing that the Soviets had lost roughly 15,000 soldiers during their war in Afghanistan, which was barely a decade old. "Did anyone seriously think that Iran could do better?" Soleimani asked.[5] The new Quds Force commander argued that it made more sense for Iran to adopt an irregular strategy through his Quds Force and support Afghan resistance groups, particularly those under the vaunted Northern Alliance commander Ahmad Shah Massoud.

Using Tajikistan as a base of operation, Soleimani and his Quds Force ramped up assistance to Massoud and his Jamiat-e Islami militia force.[6] A picture taken around this time shows a proud Massoud, dressed in a tan jacket, combat boots, and his iconic *pakol*—a soft, round-topped woolen hat. Soleimani stands to Massoud's left, just off-center, with his hands folded comfortably in front.[7] Soleimani's dark hair has started to turn gray, giving him a salt-and-pepper beard, and he flashes a confident smile.[8] While Soleimani had developed a menacing reputation in the West, he was nothing of the sort for many Iranians.[9] He was "very kind and emotional," recalled his brother Sohrab. "Hajj Qassem was born in our family, but he belongs to the country and the Shia."[10]

As Soleimani became involved in Afghanistan, US government agencies were watching closely. One US State Department assessment concluded that "officials from Iran's Ministry of Intelligence and Security (MOIS) and the Revolutionary Guards (IRGC) were stationed in Massoud's key base in the town of Khenj in the Panjshir Valley, where they participated in the off-loading of the supplies."[11] But Soleimani and his Quds Force failed to prevent the Taliban's takeover. By the summer of 2001, the Taliban controlled virtually all of Afghanistan. The only exception was a small sliver of land northeast of Kabul in the Panjshir Valley, where Massoud and his Northern Alliance forces had retreated. Just when it looked like the Taliban would control the entire country, Soleimani got a huge break—9/11.

* * * *

ON SEPTEMBER 12, 2001, Soleimani hopped on an airplane and secretly flew to the northern Afghan province of Takhar, near the border with Tajikistan, to meet with Northern Alliance leaders. The world had turned upside down. The United States had just been attacked in New York and Washington, and Soleimani's Afghan colleague, Ahmad Shah Massoud, had been assassinated by al-Qaeda operatives two days before 9/11. Soleimani addressed the small gathering of Afghans. He spoke softly and humbly, but with authority.

"God has given you an opportunity," Soleimani said.

"You need to take advantage of these events and overthrow the Taliban regime," he implored them. "Now is the time!"

Rumors were rife about who was responsible for Massoud's death. Some blamed Pakistan. Others blamed the Taliban. According to Iranian intelligence, however, the signs pointed elsewhere. "I believe he was killed by individuals associated with Osama bin Laden," Soleimani said, confidently.[12] He was right.

That same month, Ryan Crocker, who was deputy assistant secretary of state for Near Eastern affairs, became the lead US diplomat to negotiate directly with the Iranians as part of the Geneva initiative. The group included Iran, the United States, Italy, and Germany, with the United Nations as the convener. The discussion focused on the future of Afghanistan. "I flew to Geneva on Friday nights," Crocker told me, "and returned on Sundays, so almost no one even knew that I was gone." His main conduit was Ambassador Mohammad Ebrahim Taherian-Fard, one of Iran's leading experts on Central Asia, with close ties to the IRGC. The Iranians sometimes used IRGC officials—including Quds Force officers—as ambassadors, including Hassan Kazemi-Qomi, who served as Iran's ambassador to Iraq. "At the first coffee break," said Crocker about his initial meeting with Iranian officials in September 2001, "Taherian came over to me and said, 'Let's grab a cup of tea.' That's the way the Iranians liked to operate—informally." Taherian and the Iranian delegation also told Crocker that they kept Qassem Soleimani regularly informed about negotiations.[13]

As conversations about the future of Afghanistan intensified in early October, the Iranians became impatient with US foot-dragging. At one of the Geneva meetings, Taherian fell quiet, though his anger appeared to be building. "He finally stood up," remembered Crocker, "and screamed at us that we were living in fairyland. Until we were ready to do something in Afghanistan, Taherian said, this talk was all b******t. Taherian then walked out of the meeting."[14] On October 7, the US bombing campaign finally began.

Later in October, at another Geneva meeting, Taherian brought along Soleimani, who was using a pseudonym. As Taherian later told Crocker, who was not present at that meeting, "I took great pleasure in introducing Qassem Soleimani to all of your guys. They had no idea who they were shaking hands with."[15] It is a wonder that Soleimani had time to attend, since his Quds Force was active in Afghanistan at the time. They had clandestinely entered the city of Herat with Hazara militia forces and helped engineer an insurrection against the Taliban, whose government and control of territory across the country were crumbling.[16]

In December, Iran participated in the Bonn negotiations that put together a temporary Afghan government. James Dobbins, the US ambassador who led the US delegation to Bonn, recalled that US-Iranian cooperation was surprisingly good. "The Iranians were very interested in cooperating on Afghanistan and other areas," he told me. In 2002, Ambassador Dobbins met with a Quds Force general under Soleimani who offered to help train the Afghan National Army under US leadership. "Condoleezza Rice organized a Principles Committee meeting at the White House to discuss the offer," said Dobbins, "But there was little interest. We never even responded to Iran."[17] Still, for a brief moment, the United States and Iran cooperated. They shared a common enemy in the Taliban. "I went to Paris in December to meet with Iranian officials," said Crocker, "and they were in a good mood. They were happy about Hamid Karzai becoming the interim Afghan leader and Abdullah Abdullah as the foreign minister."[18] In January 2002, Crocker took over as the US ambassador to Afghanistan. On the way to Kabul, he stopped off in Geneva and again met with Taherian and two other Iranian officials. "Somewhere in the bowels of the US State Department," Crocker said, "is a voucher for several bottles of wine between an American and three Iranians."[19]

In late 2001, Soleimani supported providing intelligence to US officials on Taliban military positions. In return, the United States gave Iran information on an al-Qaeda facilitator in eastern Iran.[20] US government officials held face-to-face discussions with Iran about the growing number of al-Qaeda operatives on Iranian soil, though the meetings produced nothing meaningful.[21]

In early 2002, tensions between the United States and Iran significantly deteriorated for at least two reasons. The first was the decision by US president George W. Bush in January 2002 to finger Iran—along with North Korea and Iraq—as states that sponsored terrorism *and* produced weapons of mass destruction.[22] Iran was part of this "axis of evil." As Bush explained to a packed Congress at his January 29 State of the Union address: "Iran aggressively pursues these weapons and exports terror, while an unelected few repress the Iranian people's hope for freedom." He also made a veiled threat at regime change, noting that "America will do what is necessary to ensure our nation's security."[23] By this time, US policy toward Iran was deeply contradictory. As Ambassador Dobbins negotiated with Iranian officials about Afghanistan, Bill Luti, a senior Defense Department official who briefly served on Dobbins's staff, met with Iranian opposition groups in Rome about potentially supplying them funding. "The United States was two-faced on Iran," Dobbins sighed. "We had senior officials like me cooperating with the Iranians and Luti trying to overthrow them."[24]

The "axis of evil" speech had one interesting unintended consequence. Iran had captured Gulbuddin Hekmatyar, the former Afghan mujahideen leader who had worked with Osama bin

Laden and publicly declared his opposition to the US campaign in Afghanistan, and were holding him under house arrest in Tehran. As Crocker explained: "They were willing to hand him over to the AIA as part of a rendition operation, since [the Iranians] wanted to keep a low profile."[25] Crocker was referring to the newly established Afghan government, which was called the Afghan Interim Administration, or AIA. At that point, it would have been possible for the United States to seize Hekmatyar. After the speech, however, Iran took the option off the table. Nevertheless, Taherian told Crocker that they had brought Hekmatyar from Tehran and dropped him in Rabat, Pakistan—located in the Lower Dir District of Pakistan's Federally Administered Tribal Areas. The CIA moved quickly to grab Hekmatyar, but just missed him.[26] The Americans would regret the failure to seize Hekmatyar, since his Hezb-e-Islami organization waged a lethal campaign against US forces in Afghanistan along with the Taliban.

A second reason for the collapse of US-Iranian relations centered on al-Qaeda. Around October 2001, the Iranian government—led by Soleimani's Quds Force—dispatched a delegation to Afghanistan to guarantee the safe travel to Iran of several hundred fleeing al-Qaeda members and their families.[27] Sa'ad bin Laden (Osama's third son) and Abu Mus'ab al-Zarqawi (the future leader of al-Qaeda in Iraq) fled to Iran, as did a handful of others.[28]

By 2002, Osama bin Laden had established al-Qaeda's "Management Council" in Iran, which served as a backup body in case the United States captured or killed al-Qaeda's leaders in Pakistan. Key members of the Management Council included Abu al-Khayr al-Masri, Abu Muhammad al-Masri, Saif al-Adel, Sulayman Abu Ghayth, and Abu Hafs al-Mauritani. All five remained influential over the next several years and retained close links with Osama bin Laden and other senior leaders.[29] Over time, however, many of them were killed or captured. Sulayman Abu Ghayth was initially captured by Turkey in early 2013 and eventually handed over to the United States. He was convicted in 2014 of conspiring to kill Americans and other terrorism charges.[30] The United States killed Abu al-Khayr al-Masri in a drone strike in Syria in February 2017. And Israel's spy agency, the Mossad, assassinated Abu Muhammad al-Masri in Tehran in August 2020, in cooperation with the United States.[31]

For some US intelligence analysts, Iran's willingness to allow al-Qaeda on its soil was a puzzle: Why would Shia Iran establish *any* relations with Sunni al-Qaeda? Iran and al-Qaeda did not have compatible ideological views, but they shared a common enemy: the United States. Iran was likely willing to allow some al-Qaeda leaders on its soil under tight monitoring as a wild card. If the United States attacked Iran, al-Qaeda could be helpful in responding. Once again, under Soleimani's guidance, Iran had employed an asymmetric approach, choosing to work with an enemy in order to balance the greater threat: the United States. British prime minister Winston Churchill once said to his secretary, John Colville: "If Hitler invaded Hell, I would make at least a favorable reference to the devil in the House of Commons."[32] Al-Qaeda made the same calculation. Al-Qaeda leaders did not support Shia-led Iran. But although US targeting of al-Qaeda leaders in Pakistan, Yemen, Iraq, and other countries had been effective, the United States had almost no operational reach in Iran.

With a growing contingent of al-Qaeda leaders in Iran, the United States then handed Iran a gift: it invaded Iraq. More than almost any single event since 9/11, the 2003 US invasion of Iraq shifted the balance of power in the region in favor of Iran and Soleimani. It gave Soleimani a chance to support Iraq's majority Shia population, influence a government in Baghdad that had shed so much Iranian blood during the Iran-Iraq War, and target vulnerable US forces. Iran would capitalize on the US miscalculation not through conventional means, but by developing a sophisticated irregular warfare campaign.

※ ※ ※ ※

SOLEIMANI AND HIS Quds Force were well placed to take advantage of the chaos in Iraq. Not long after the US invasion, Soleimani crossed the border from Iran and helped oversee the training of some Iraqi Shia militia forces, such as the Badr Corps.[33] In the late spring of 2003, US officials began to worry about Soleimani's growing activism in the country. In a May 29 briefing to President George W. Bush, Ambassador Paul "Jerry" Bremer, the head of the US-led Coalition Provisional Authority that was temporarily governing Iraq, noted that the United States faced an increasing threat from Soleimani's Quds Force and "Iranian-sponsored Islamic extremism."[34] CIA operatives tracked the movement of Iranian intelligence and Quds Force officials into and out of Iraq.[35] US officials like Ryan Crocker frequently conveyed their concerns to some of Iraq's Shia groups, which had close relations with Soleimani and his Quds Force.[36]

British ambassador John Sawers also told one Iraqi Shia leader that the British and Americans were concerned that his militia forces "were receiving weapons from Iran and crossing the Iranian border on a regular basis."[37] Sawers traveled to Tehran and expressed British concerns about Iranian activism in meetings with senior Iranian officials from Soleimani's Quds Force and Iran's Ministry of Intelligence and Security (MOIS). In a sensitive memo to US ambassador Bremer, Sawers said that he gave "clear messages on the IRGC's presence" and "the hostile MOIS activity."[38] But US and British démarches to curb Soleimani and the Quds Force largely failed.

To expand Iranian influence, Soleimani developed a two-pronged approach: increase attacks against US forces from Iran-aided militia groups, and become more deeply enmeshed in Iraq's formal security institutions.[39] This approach was classic irregular warfare, since Iran was operating against the United States indirectly through Iraqi partner forces—rather than directly through Iranian conventional forces. Soleimani, who would eventually develop a swagger that the CIA's Norm Roule referred to as the "Soleimani strut," succeeded on both fronts.[40]

Over the next several years, US military casualties spiked following a lethal campaign of improvised explosive devices (IEDs) from the Badr Corps and at least two other militias established with the help of the Quds Force: Kataib Hezbollah, led by Abu Mahdi al-Muhandis; and Asaib Ahl al-Haq, led by Qais al-Khazali. Al-Muhandis was the same individual, dubbed OBJECTIVE MORGAN by US special operations forces, that the United States killed along with Soleimani in January 2020. The situation became so serious for US forces that President Bush complained in a press conference in 2007 that "the Quds Force was instrumental in providing these deadly IEDs to networks inside of Iraq."[41]

Among the most lethal Iranian IEDs were the explosively formed penetrators, or EFPs. They were shaped charges with a concave end, which sent a molten copper slug through targets such as armored vehicles, and then created a deadly spray of hot metal. "EFPs are really bad," recalled Brian Castner, the head of a US explosive ordnance disposal unit in Iraq. "They take off legs and heads, put holes in armor and engine blocks, and our bosses in Baghdad and Washington want every one we find."[42] Between July 2005 and December 2011, a startling 1,534 EFPs killed 196 US and coalition troops and wounded another 861.[43] Soleimani and the Quds Force were instrumental in transporting EFP components from Iran into Iraq. The Quds Force built EFP components like infrared triggers and explosive circuits in secret laboratories in Iran, and smuggled them across the border to safe houses in locations like An Numaniyah and Basra, concealed in oil drums, food containers, and other items.[44]

Although Soleimani was an enemy of the United States, US officials recognized his adeptness. "I was impressed by Qassem Soleimani's ability to influence the sweet spot of intelligence and covert action—what the CIA and US special operations forces do in the United States—to conduct activity," said Lieutenant General Charles Cleveland, who headed US Army Special Operations Command.[45] Militias linked to the Quds Force also became more influential within Iraq and developed close ties with Iraqi politicians.

Yet Soleimani did not get along with all Shia militias. One example was Jaysh al-Mahdi, led by the fiery upstart Muqtada al-Sadr. Al-Sadr's father was a fervent Shia Arab activist, and his beliefs on Arab nationalism ran counter to Ayatollah Khomeini's pan-Shia ideology. Al-Sadr also did not support Khomeini's *velayat-e faqih* (the Islamic system of clerical rule) over all Shias—including Iraqi Shias.[46] Al-Sadr remained a thorn in the side of Soleimani and continued to criticize Iran for its outsized influence in Iraq. Despite these issues, Soleimani's influence ran deep in Iraq's Shia community. As an official US Army history of the Iraq War concluded, "The Quds Force and its Iraqi surrogates were the primary instruments employed by the Iranian regime to wage a proxy war against the United States at minimal cost."[47]

With the Quds Force ramping up operations in Afghanistan and Iraq, Soleimani decided to increase Quds Force operations in one of his organization's most important fronts: Lebanon.

✳   ✳   ✳   ✳

IN JULY 2006, as war raged between Israel and Hezbollah in Lebanon, a calm Qassem Soleimani sat in Hezbollah's main operations room in the heart of Dahieh, a Shia suburb of Beirut, and Hezbollah's main stronghold in the city. Thanks to Soleimani and his Quds Force, Hezbollah had a secure communications facility to run military operations. Soleimani's personnel were also providing Hezbollah with money, weapons, intelligence, and other matériel.

The war had begun on July 12, 2006, when Hezbollah fighters abducted two Israeli soldiers patrolling near the Israel-Lebanon border and dragged them across the border into Lebanon. Soleimani and the Quds Force had been involved in the planning of Hezbollah's operation. In response, Israel launched a ground invasion into southern Lebanon, imposed an air and naval blockade, and conducted withering air strikes against Hezbollah targets across Lebanon. To keep Iranian leaders informed about the war, Soleimani provided daily updates to Tehran, using a Quds Force secure line in Hezbollah's operations room.[48]

Soleimani had spent nearly the entire duration of the war in Lebanon—an indication of how strategically important it was for him and for Iran. Lebanon had a large Shia population, which made up between 25 and 30 percent of the country, and it bordered Israel—Iran's enemy.[49] Lebanon was also home to Iran's most important partner force, Hezbollah, which Iran's Islamic Revolutionary Guard Corps had helped establish and fund in the 1980s.

Soleimani had entered Lebanese territory from Syria—a perilous journey. The war had already begun, and the Israeli Air Force was patrolling Lebanese airspace, hunting for targets. "So we contacted a friend through a safe line," Soleimani recalled, and a Hezbollah operative "came to pick me up to move me from Syria to Lebanon through a road where we walked a part of it and drove through the rest."[50]

Each night, Soleimani and senior Hezbollah officials—including Hezbollah leader Hassan Nasrallah, whom Soleimani referred to by the honorific title "Sayyid"—listened to Israeli aircraft scream past the operations center and strike targets. "One night in the operations room," Soleimani said, "almost all of those managing the war had gathered together." The Israeli Air Force had destroyed several nearby buildings in Dahieh. Around 11:00 p.m., Soleimani decided the situation was too precarious. "I felt there was real danger threatening Sayyid," he said. But transporting Nasrallah out of Dahieh made little sense, since the Israelis would almost certainly find and kill him. "Israeli drones were constantly flying over Dahieh in groups of three, tightly tracking every movement, even if it was a motorcycle," Soleimani said. As the explosions temporarily stopped and a tense quiet settled in around midnight, Soleimani moved. He and his small group—including Nasrallah—stepped outside, breathed in the cool night air, and then dashed to a nearby building.[51]

No sooner had they taken cover than the Israelis hit the building where they had just hidden. They could be next. "We were alone in the building," Soleimani recalled, fearing the worst. They decided to move again and, once outside, felt an eerie calm. "We left the building, we were on foot; we had no car," Soleimani said. "Dahieh was completely plunged in darkness and total silence. The only sound that broke the silence was the sound of the enemy's planes flying above Dahieh." Soleimani stripped down to his T-shirt, still wearing his olive-green military pants. The small group, with Hassan Nasrallah in tow, dashed to a tree that provided some cover, though Soleimani was acutely aware that Israel had thermal cameras on their aircraft that could see body heat. "It was impossible to hide from them," Soleimani thought.[52]

One member of the group disappeared for a few minutes and returned with a car. They jumped in, but they feared an Israeli drone might have locked onto the car. They quickly dashed to another car and then moved through multiple underground rooms to safety. "The important point here is that, usually, there is a lot of haste in a war," remarked Soleimani. "I understand this very well after forty years of military-security work."[53] Soleimani had survived once again.

By the end of the war, in August 2006, Hezbollah had managed a draw with Israel. The popularity of Hezbollah leader Nasrallah soared throughout Lebanon and the Arab world as he gloated in the "divine and strategic victory."[54] The Israeli population was split on the war, with 63 percent of Israelis in August 2006 demanding that Prime Minister Ehud Olmert resign.[55] An opinion piece in the *Jerusalem Post* concluded that "if you fail to win, you lose," and that "because Hezbollah survived, it won the war."[56]

Perhaps. But with his fingerprints all over the conflict, it was more likely *Qassem Soleimani* who deserved much of the credit. It was now time to turn back to Iraq. Soleimani wrote to US military commanders: "I hope you have been enjoying the peace and quiet in Baghdad. I've been busy in Beirut!"[57]

But would Soleimani be so fortunate again?

✳ ✳ ✳ ✳

ON A CRISP EVENING in January 2007, Soleimani was in a convoy of vehicles en route from Iran to northern Iraq. His Quds Force continued to inflict significant punishment on US forces—particularly with the EFPs used by its militias. Unbeknownst to Soleimani, he was being watched by the US military's elite Joint Special Operations Command (JSOC) and its commander, General Stanley McChrystal.

"There were good reasons to target Soleimani," McChrystal told me. Roadside bombs that had been deployed by the Quds Force—under Soleimani's command—had killed American soldiers in Iraq. But there were also risks with killing him, McChrystal recognized. At the time, there were nearly 150,000 US troops in Iraq, who would have been vulnerable to Iranian retaliation. McChrystal also worried that targeting Soleimani would significantly escalate conflict with Iran and would infuriate Iraqi politicians. After all, Soleimani was Iran's most important military leader. "I believed we shouldn't kill him," McChrystal told me. "In my view, that would have created more problems. It would have been a provocative step." McChrystal was also aware that Iranian leaders felt threatened because the United States had essentially surrounded them with forces in Iraq, Afghanistan, and in the Persian Gulf. "We were on their west, east, and south," he said. "We were virtually everywhere—almost omnipresent."[58] By the time the vehicles arrived in the northern Iraq city of Irbil, however, it was too late. Soleimani had slipped away into the night.

A year later, Soleimani survived another close call. The CIA and

Israel's intelligence agency, the Mossad, had tracked a Hezbollah leader, Imad Mughniyeh, to an apartment in the upscale Kfar Sousa district of Damascus. Mughniyeh was the head of Hezbollah's military and intelligence apparatus and had been wanted by the US and Israeli governments for his involvement in numerous terrorist attacks—including the 1983 bombings in Beirut that killed nearly 250 Americans and a 1992 attack at the Israeli embassy in Argentina that killed 29 people. On the evening of February 12, 2008, Mossad agents received word that Mughniyeh was en route to his Kfar Sousa apartment, and they parked an SUV fitted with explosives in position near the front door. On a large video screen in Israel's operation center, intelligence officers watched Mughniyeh's car pull up.[59]

But he was not alone. Israeli officials recognized two others who hopped out of the car. One was Qassem Soleimani. The other was Muhammad Suleiman, a Syrian military commander. "We just had to push a button and all three of them would disappear," said a former Israeli official. "That was an opportunity given to us on a silver platter."[60] But since the United States had authorized killing *only* Mughniyeh, Israel held off on the strike. The three figures slipped upstairs into the apartment. As Mossad officers monitored the video feed, Soleimani and Suleiman eventually emerged and disappeared into the night. Mughniyeh exited the building ten minutes later, and Israel detonated the car bomb, killing him instantly. "His body was thrown in the air—he was killed on the spot," said an Israeli official who had watched the video feed.[61]

For the United States, Soleimani was untouchable—at least for the moment—because of US concerns that killing him would trigger Iranian retaliation against US forces and escalate US-Iranian tensions. But his underlings were fair game. The year before, US troops from Joint Special Operations Command had captured General Mohsen Chizari—the Quds Force commander of Department 600, the operations staff.[62] JSOC referred to him as OBJECTIVE CLARKE IV and had been tracking his cell phone.[63] Over the next few days, however, senior Iraqi officials secured the release of Chizari and other Iranian officers captured in the raid, underscoring the depth of Iran's influence among Iraqi leaders.

In March 2008, the Iraqi government showed more backbone against Iran when it conducted an offensive against the Iran-linked Jaysh al-Mahdi, headed by the Shia cleric Muqtada al-Sadr in the southern city of Basra, that was termed OPERATION SAULAT AL-FURSAN (or OPERATION "CHARGE OF THE KNIGHTS"). With help from US and coalition forces, which collected intelligence and conducted air strikes, the Iraqi government successfully retook most of the city by April. The military offensive unnerved the Iranians, including Qassem Soleimani, who requested a meeting with Iraqi president Jalal Talabani and vice president Adel Abdul-Mahdi. "Soleimani wouldn't come into Iraq," Ryan Crocker, who was serving as US ambassador to Iraq at the time, told me. "He was worried we'd try to grab him. Those were the days when Soleimani was careful."[64] Talabani and Mahdi met with Soleimani in Iran, though little came of the meeting. "Iraqi prime minister Nouri al-Maliki concluded that nothing good was going to happen with the Iranians," recalled Crocker.[65]

But Soleimani was undeterred. Around the same time, he sent a message to General David Petraeus, the top US military commander in Iraq, through the Iraqi president: "You should know that I, Qassem Soleimani, control the policy for Iran when it comes to Iraq and also Syria, Lebanon, Gaza, and Afghanistan." The boast was extraordinary not just for the content of the message, but for who Soleimani was. "He wasn't just the equivalent of the heads of US Central Command, Joint Special Operations Command, and the director of the Central Intelligence Agency," General Petraeus told me. "He was also acting like the foreign minister." It reminded Petraeus of the story about Soleimani being asked whether he would run for president of Iran. "Why would I?" Soleimani allegedly responded with a grin, hinting that he was already more powerful than the president![66]

At the time, US forces under Petraeus were helping Iraqi soldiers target Shia militias in Iraq's second-largest city, Basra. As Petraeus understood it, Soleimani was signaling that any effort to deal with Shia militias needed to go through him.

"I told him to pound sand," Petraeus said.[67]

✳ ✳ ✳ ✳

OVER THE NEXT three years, the United States and Iran maintained their tug-of-war in Iraq. Rather than take the United States on directly, Soleimani and his Quds Force continued to use irregular methods by working through Shia militias and influencing Iraqi government officials. With chaos now gripping the region because of the Arab Spring, Soleimani chose Qom, a lively industrial Iranian city 90 miles south of Tehran and one of Shia Islam's holy sites, to outline his vision of the future.

On May 22, 2011, Soleimani stepped up to the podium at the Haqqani Seminary school in Qom. The warrior-statesman was now fifty-four years old, and the heavy toll of running Iran's elite paramilitary organization had aged him visibly. His thick, wavy hair had pronounced streaks of gray, and there were conspicuous creases on his forehead and charcoal circles under his eyes. "He gets up at four every morning, and he's in bed by nine-thirty every night," remarked an Iraqi politician who knew him well.[68]

Soleimani was in Qom to celebrate the anniversary of Iran's 1982 recapture of Khorramshahr, a port city on the Persian Gulf that Iraqi forces had seized in the fall of 1980 in the opening salvos of the Iran-Iraq War. Beginning in April 1982, Iranian soldiers from the 88th Armored Division and the Islamic Revolutionary Guard Corps inspired by deafening chants of *Allahu Akbar* ("God is great") blasting out of loudspeakers, laid siege to Khorramshahr during OPER-

ATION BAIT AL-MOQADDAS. After bitter fighting and heavy losses on both sides, Iranian forces liberated Khorramshahr on May 24.[69] It was a major victory for Iran that reached near-mythical proportions in Iranian film, books, and poetry, which lauded the bravery of Iranian soldiers and their commanders. Iranian forces claimed they had destroyed 361 tanks and killed 25,000 Iraqis.[70] An enraged Saddam Hussein executed several of his top generals—including the commander of Iraq's 9th Division, General Kamal Latif—because of their failure at Khorramshahr.[71]

During his speech, Soleimani paid fulsome tribute to those Iranians who died at Khorramshahr and other battlefields. In doing so, he tapped into the deep tradition of sacrifice at the heart of Iran's military culture that had prevailed since the 1979 revolution. But Soleimani wasn't in Qom just to pay tribute to the martyrs. He also had a vision for the future. The Arab Spring had recently erupted in North Africa and was sweeping across the Arab world, and Soleimani sensed the arrival of a historic moment.

"Social revolutions in the Middle East and North Africa have provided the best opportunities for our revolution," Soleimani remarked, his eyes panning across the audience.

"Today," Soleimani continued, "Iran's victory or defeat no longer takes place in Mehran and Khorramshahr. Our boundaries have expanded, and we must witness victory in Egypt, Iraq, Lebanon, and Syria."

He then paused and said emphatically, "*This* is the fruit of the Islamic revolution!"[72]

As Soleimani plotted ways to bring his vision to fruition, US president Barack Obama handed him an extraordinary opportunity. Less than a week before the Qom speech, Obama had slapped sanctions against Soleimani because of his escapades in Iraq.[73] But Obama's next step would essentially give Iraq to Soleimani: he withdrew all US military forces from Iraq.

* * * *

"As a candidate for President, I pledged to bring the war in Iraq to a responsible end—for the sake of our national security and to strengthen American leadership around the world," Obama remarked on October 21, 2011. "So today I can report that, as promised, the rest of our troops in Iraq will come home by the end of the year. After nearly nine years, America's war in Iraq will be over."[74] It was a fateful speech, which broadcast a message that played directly into Iran's hands. Obama was mistaken. The Iraq conflict continued to rage, and the United States' role in it was far from over.

No one knew this better than Soleimani. On a trip to Iraq in 2011, Soleimani reminded Iraqi leaders that US forces would soon leave Iraq, but Iran would always be their neighbor. Soleimani then began to exercise a newfound influence in Iraq. With Iraqi politics in flux, he lobbied to keep the embattled Nouri al-Maliki as prime minister and Jalal Talabani, the renowned Kurdish guerrilla leader, as president. Soleimani dangled cash payments to Iraqi officials who cooperated, and he warned those who didn't that they "would suffer the most dire of consequences."[75] US officials were frustrated by the inconsistent messaging. "Iran used the US hot-and-cold presence in Iraq—including the break after 2011—to spin these episodes into a persuasive argument for Iraqis: 'The US is at best a fair-weather friend, while we have never left you,'" recalled Lieutenant General Michael Nagata.[76]

On December 17, 2011, the last column of roughly 100 US mine-resistant ambush-protected armored vehicles, or MRAPs, headed south through the vast Iraqi desert on an empty highway toward the Kuwait border—just as Obama had promised. Soleimani and the Iranians pounced. They added former CIA informants—though most likely low-level sources—to the payroll of Iranian intelligence. One Iraqi that had spied for the CIA, who went by the nom de guerre "Donnie Brasco" after the FBI undercover agent played by Johnny Depp in the 1997 film, was a prized recruit for the Iranians. The CIA had been paying him $3,000 per month, plus a onetime bonus of $20,000 and a car, but he was now flat broke. The Iranians swooped in. "SOURCE 134992," as Iran would refer to him, provided a wealth of information on the location of CIA safe houses, the names of hotels where CIA case officers met their informants, and the names of other Iraqis who had been recruited by the CIA. "I will turn over to you all the documents and videos that I have from my training course," he promised to his new Iranian handlers, swearing on the Quran. "And pictures and identifying features of my fellow trainees and my subordinates."[77]

Soleimani quickly made inroads in Iraq. Leaked Iranian intelligence documents showed that Bayan Jabr, the Iraqi minister of transportation, was "very close" to Iran and a strong ally.[78] Although US officials had repeatedly asked the Iraqi government to stop allowing Iranian weapons shipments through their airspace en route to Syria, US influence had plummeted.

As Jabr explained, Soleimani "came to me and requested that we permit Iranian airplanes to use Iraqi air space to pass on to Syria." Jabr relented.

"I put my hands on my eyes," Jabr recalled, "and said, 'On my eyes! As you wish!'"

Soleimani then "got up and approached me and kissed my forehead."[79]

Iranian influence continued to grow. Over the next several years, Soleimani and his Quds Force ramped up assistance to some Iraqi militia groups—the *Hashd al-Shaabi*, or Popular Mobilization Forces—such as the Badr Corps, Asaib Ahl al-Haq, and Kataib Hezbollah. Iran provided these groups with EFPs, short-range ballistic missiles, anti-tank guided missiles, tanks, armored personnel carriers, artillery, unmanned aerial vehicles, and man-portable air defense systems—a whole suite of weapons.[80] Soleimani did not exert his influence directly, but rather indirectly through militia forces. A US Army lessons-learned study summed up the result of the US withdrawal. "An emboldened and expansionist Iran appears to be the only victor," it concluded.[81]

With the United States out of the way in Iraq, Soleimani turned his attention west. The next domino to fall was Syria. President Bashar al-Assad, who had replaced his father as president of Syria in 2000, faced a burgeoning insurgency that provided Soleimani and his Quds Force yet another opportunity to wage irregular warfare.

7: THE MARTYR

IN JULY 2015, QASSEM SOLEIMANI FLEW TO MOS-
cow to discuss plans for Russian-Iranian military operations in
Syria. The unflappable, self-confident Soleimani—with his neatly
trimmed beard—boarded a Russian Aeroflot flight in Tehran,
landed in Moscow, and was quickly whisked away to the Kremlin.[1]
After exchanging pleasantries with senior Russian officials, Soleimani placed a map of Syria on the table. The color-coded map highlighted Syrian government and rebel positions on the battlefield, as
well as their respective control of territory.[2] It was a grim picture.
Iran had failed to save Syrian president Bashar al-Assad and needed
Russian support. The Islamic State, the al-Qaeda-linked group
Jabhat al-Nusrah, and other rebel forces were gaining momentum.
The Islamic State had recently seized the ancient city of Palmyra and
massacred local tribal leaders.[3]

Despite these negative developments, Soleimani was undeterred.
He confidently told Russian leaders that it was still possible to salvage the situation and prevent the collapse of the regime. "Defeat
can be turned into victory," Soleimani promised. But they would
need to act quickly.[4] Russian leaders were nervous. By 2015, President Putin, Minister of Defense Sergey Shoigu, and General Gerasimov (the chief of the General Staff of the Armed Forces) had
become deeply concerned that the Syrian regime would collapse
without rapid outside assistance. As Gerasimov had warned, "a per-
fectly thriving state can, *in a matter of months and even days*, be
transformed into an arena of fierce armed conflict, become a victim

of foreign intervention, and sink into a web of chaos, humanitarian catastrophe, and civil war."[5]

But Syria did not have to suffer the same fate, Soleimani suggested. The tide of the war could be turned with decisive support from Iran and Russia, operating together. Unlike Russia's war in Afghanistan in the 1980s, which involved a heavy footprint of 115,000 Red Army forces, Syria would have to be different. Moscow and Tehran would need to fight a war in the shadows using proxy forces like Lebanese Hezbollah, offensive cyber operations, covert intelligence units, and strikes from fixed-wing aircraft, drones, and naval vessels. Among the most important actors on the ground would be Soleimani's Quds Force.

Soleimani's meeting with Russian officials brought together in the same room two of the United States' most significant enemies—Iran and Russia—to counter US activity in the region. The success of this alliance—both long-standing enemies of the United States—would show the true power of irregular warfare.

✳ ✳ ✳ ✳

SOLEIMANI IDENTIFIED as one of the main targets the Syrian city of Aleppo, which had a Shia presence in the southwest that Soleimani wanted to liberate. Aleppo had fallen to Sunni rebel groups in late 2012, led by the Free Syrian Army and Jabhat al-Nusrah.[6] Over the course of 2013 and 2014, Syrian regime forces had encircled Aleppo in an effort to asphyxiate rebels in eastern parts of the city, but they didn't have sufficient firepower to turn the tide. Assad loyalists faced other threats as well: Islamic State forces had stormed into the area and controlled some access routes into the city.

To help retake Aleppo, Soleimani had reached out to an old friend, Hezbollah leader Hassan Nasrallah, for a favor. Would Nasrallah help out Assad, who was fighting for his survival, and send additional Hezbollah fighters to Syria? It was a difficult request.

Nasrallah would be risking the lives of Hezbollah fighters, spending a great deal of money, and opening himself up to domestic criticism for participating in a foreign war. Nasrallah eventually relented, but he cautioned Soleimani about the stakes: "Should Syria fall into the hands of the Americans, the Israelis, the takfiri groups, and America's representatives in the region, which call themselves regional states, the resistance would be besieged and Israel would reenter Lebanon, impose its conditions on Lebanon, and renew its greed and projects in it."[7] Despite the warning, Soleimani was thrilled to have Hezbollah's help. Nasrallah deployed up to 8,000 fighters to participate in combat operations and to train, advise, and assist groups in Syria.[8] But the Quds Force and its Hezbollah partners alone were not enough to tip the balance in Syria. "They couldn't win it unilaterally," said Norm Roule, a thirty-four-year CIA veteran who was serving as the national intelligence manager for Iran. "The Iranians needed airpower; they needed the Russians."[9]

In an effort to break the rebel lock on Aleppo, Soleimani established a headquarters to coordinate the ground campaign. Based out of Aleppo, Soleimani helped bring in roughly 55,000 forces that included Lebanese Hezbollah and foreign fighters from Iraq, Afghanistan, Pakistan, and other areas, trained and equipped by the Quds Force. In 2015, Syrian forces focused their efforts on strategic terrain north of Aleppo, with the help of Russian airpower, Russian *spetsnaz* (special operations forces), Soleimani's Quds Force, and Iranian militias.[10] After several months of Russian strikes on opposition supply lines, two important Shia villages near Aleppo—Nubl and al-Zahraa—fell to the Syrian regime in February 2016.[11] In the spring of 2016, Syrian, Russian, and Iranian forces stepped up their offensive to retake Aleppo, which they called OPERATION DAWN OF VICTORY.[12] In July, Syrian forces and Shia militias cut off the Azaz corridor that linked rebel-controlled Aleppo to Turkey. Soleimani, who had become the overall commander of the Aleppo theater of operations, pushed for a final offensive in the fall.

Proregime forces moved first on the northeastern district of Hanano, pushing west in an attempt to bisect eastern Aleppo.[13] Quds Force–aided groups were essential to the ground operations.[14] Proregime troops next pressed into the central sector, taking the opposition stronghold of al-Sha'ar and then the historic Ancient City by December 7, 2016.[15] Backed by Russian firepower, these forces then made inroads into southeastern Aleppo's Sheikh Saeed district and forced the opposition to withdraw.[16] By December 12, proregime forces held more than three-fourths of eastern Aleppo.[17] Facing slaughter in southern Aleppo's more open terrain, rebels agreed to a cease-fire on December 13. In a political deal negotiated by Soleimani, roughly 35,000 residents left Aleppo for neighboring Idlib province.[18]

By late December 2016, the regime had regained full control of Aleppo. The siege and seizure of Aleppo proved to be a pivotal battle in the Syrian civil war. With the opposition's strategic and symbolic stronghold retaken, proregime forces could now contain the remaining armed opposition in northern Syria to the greater Idlib and eastern Damascus pockets. "Soleimani and the Quds Force were very important in retaking Aleppo," said the CIA's Roule. "The Iranians brought the whole battle space together, which included the Syrians, Russians, Hezbollah, and others."[19]

* * * *

SOLEIMANI WAS ECSTATIC. He visited the ravaged city of Aleppo multiple times in December 2016 to tour the battlefield.[20] In one video released on YouTube, a smiling Soleimani—wearing a black windbreaker, dark baseball cap that hid his weathered face, and tan scarf draped around his neck—stepped out of a pickup truck in Aleppo and was swarmed by local fighters. They treated him like a rock star, snapping selfies and taking videos with their cell phones. Soleimani affectionately hugged and kissed them as if he were at a family reunion.[21]

In Abu Kamal, a city on the Euphrates River in eastern Syria near the Iraqi border, Soleimani left a handwritten note at the house of a Sunni family that he and his staff had used as a military headquarters.

He expressed remorse in broken Arabic, despite the fact that "I am Shia and you are Sunni."

"First, we apologize and hope you will accept our apology, we used your home without your permission," he wrote.

"Second, if there was any damage we are prepared to pay for it."

Soleimani said that he had prayed for the owners and asked God for good "outcomes" for them. "We need your prayers and forgiveness," he concluded the letter, leaving behind a telephone number in case the owners wanted to follow up on any issues.[22]

With Iran's role growing in Syria, Soleimani and his trusted deputy, Ismail Qaani, zigzagged across the Middle East at a dizzying pace over the next several years. Their goal was to enlarge Iran's influence across a massive 1,500-mile expanse from the Mediterranean coasts of Lebanon through Syria, Iraq, the western edges of Afghanistan, and south to the Persian Gulf and the Gulf of Oman. It was part of Iran's "axis of resistance."[23] As the CIA's Mike Morell assessed, "Iran wants to be the hegemonic power in the Middle East. They want to reestablish the Persian Empire."[24] Over at the Pentagon, Mike Vickers, who was the Pentagon's top intelligence official, had a similar take. "Some argue that their goal is Shia dominance. But it's more than that; they back Sunni extremists too," he told me. "My view is that the Iranians want to establish regional hegemony as a Persian power. They believe they are the rightful power in the Middle East."[25]

For Soleimani, the Quds Force was a modern-day foreign legion, and he exerted influence along a contemporary version of the Royal Road—the ancient landbridge built by the Persian king Darius the Great in the fifth century BC.[26] Soleimani took dozens of trips to

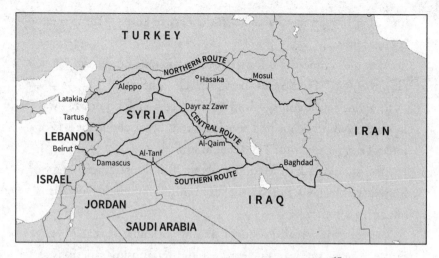

IRAN'S ASPIRATIONAL LANDBRIDGE[27]

Syria, Iraq, and Lebanon to personally oversee Iranian expansion. By the time of his death, he had overseen a transnational Sunni-Shia militancy of over 200,000 fighters. Operating in Iraq, Syria, Lebanon, and Yemen, these forces were capable of simultaneously conducting operations against different foes in disconnected battle spaces. Soleimani and Qaani used these partners to control territory and logistics that enabled the Quds Force to move money, fighters, weapons, and other matériel from battlefield to battlefield.[28]

❋ ❋ ❋ ❋

As the tide of the war turned in Syria, Donald Trump, who was sworn in as US president in January 2017, began to focus his attention on Iran. The following month, on February 6, Trump visited MacDill Air Force Base in Florida to meet with the head of US Central Command, General Joseph Votel, and the head of US Special Operations Command, General Tony Thomas. As Votel briefed the president about US and adversary activity in the region—

including Iranian naval activity in the Persian Gulf—Trump interrupted him.

"Hey, next time those Iranian gunboats come out of the water, blow them up," Trump said. "Seriously, blow them up."

Everyone in the room—from Votel and Thomas on down—was in shock. No president had *ever* been that blunt about the use of force. Trump then paused and caught himself.

"You should talk to Mad Dog about this," he said, referring to Secretary of Defense Jim Mattis. "But I think you should blow them out of the water."[29]

The following year, President Trump announced that he was pulling out of the Iran nuclear deal and reimposing sanctions as part of a "maximum pressure" campaign.[30] As US secretary of state Mike Pompeo explained in more detail, the goal of sanctions was to eliminate—or at least curb—Iran's support to militant organizations, dismantle its ballistic missile program, end its missile support to militant groups, stop its nuclear weapons program, and release all US and allied detainees.[31] Implemented by the US Department of the Treasury's Office of Foreign Assets Control, these sanctions were the most onerous ever placed on Iran by the United States. They targeted Iran's energy, shipping, arms, and financial sectors, including hundreds of individuals, entities, aircraft, and vessels.[32]

The sanctions devastated Iran's economy. They contributed to a GDP growth rate of negative 6 percent, a plummeting of the Iranian currency (the rial), and a dramatic decrease in oil production.[33] The downturn made it difficult for Iranian merchants to import goods or properly price merchandise. Even before the reimposition of US sanctions in 2018, most international banks had left the Iranian market, and they hesitated to return. Many were concerned that the United States might renew sanctions on transactions with Iran, while others worried about corruption and the lack of transparency in Iran's financial sector.

Yet US sanctions did not lead to a significant change in Iranian behavior on the primary issues that the United States cared about. Iran did not end its support to militant organizations, dismantle its ballistic missile program, end its missile support to militant groups, or release most US and allied detainees. In addition, Iran enriched uranium above the 300-kilogram limit negotiated as part of the 2015 nuclear agreement.[34]

The problem, some US officials believed, was that Iran had learned from Muammar al-Qaddafi in Libya. Qaddafi had given up nuclear weapons in 2003, but the United States still overthrew him less than a decade later. "The Iranians took a big lesson out of Libya," said General Tony Thomas. "If you give up nuclear weapons, we will overthrow you." For Iranian leaders—including Soleimani—it made little sense to give up nuclear weapons to a US government they were at war with. Compared with the hardships that Iran had historically faced, sanctions were not *that bad.* "Iran survived the Iran-Iraq War in the 1980s," said Thomas. "They lost an entire generation of people from the war. Do we think that a smaller form of leverage will have more of an effect?"[35]

* * * *

IN THE FACE OF US sanctions, Soleimani turned his attention from Syria back to Iraq. There, the Islamic State had conducted blitz-krieg operations and seized territory in western and northern areas of the country. Now, after helping Assad beat back the Islamic State, Soleimani offered his full support to the besieged Iraqi government.

He made repeated trips to Iraq to provide operational guidance to Shia militia forces assisting the Iraqi military. For decades, Solei-mani and other commanders who lived through the Iran-Iraq War had considered the Iraqi army a potential threat to the Iranian regime. With the collapse of several Iraqi army divisions and the proliferation of the *Hashd al-Shaabi* (Popular Mobilization Forces), Soleimani had an opportunity to promote a parallel security structure to compete with the Iraqi army for legitimacy.[36] One of the most successful operations was in Mosul, where Soleimani's Quds Force worked with Shia militias and Iraqi security forces to retake territory held by the Islamic State. US and other international forces also participated in the campaign, which was known as "OPERATION WE ARE COMING, NINEVEH." By July 2017, these forces had liberated Mosul. Prime Minister Haider al-Abadi praised the Quds Force commander.

"Soleimani is an official of the Iranian military establishment. I'm not denying we are dealing with him," said Abadi. "Everyone knows we are dealing with this man. We very much have respect for him and respect for the Iranian establishment. Iran is a neighbor."[37] In the span of only a few months, Soleimani and his Quds Force had helped turn the tide of the wars in both Syria and Iraq. Aleppo and Mosul were now liberated from the Islamic State, with the United States and its coalition partners also playing a significant role in Iraq.

But Soleimani could not relax. In Yemen, his Quds Force was aiding the Houthi regime in an effort to bloody the nose of Saudi Arabia.

✳ ✳ ✳ ✳

FOR SOLEIMANI AND the Iranian government, support to Houthi forces in Yemen was an inexpensive way to tie down their rival, Saudi Arabia.[38] The Houthi movement, formally called Ansar Allah, included individuals from the Zaidi school of thought, a Shia sect that had emerged in the eighth century in Yemen. Its creed, which it called "the scream," included a series of curses: "Death to America, death to Israel, curse upon the Jews, victory to Islam."[39] Following the Arab Spring and the collapse of the Yemeni city of Sanaa to Houthi rebels in September 2014, the Houthis had seized growing portions of territory in the country.

With the Houthis on the move and willing to accept Iranian aid, Iran crafted a sophisticated irregular warfare campaign. The Quds Force and Lebanese Hezbollah would provide some assistance to the

Houthis—including anti-tank guided missiles, sea mines, drones, 122-millimeter Katyusha rockets, Misagh-2 man-portable air defense systems, RDX high explosives, ballistic and cruise missiles, unmanned explosive boats, radar systems, and mining equipment.[40] The Quds Force and Lebanese Hezbollah also provided training to Houthi fighters in Yemen and Iran, including how to use and maintain the missiles and other weapons provided.[41]

"Iran dramatically improved its strategic reach by equipping and supporting proxies in Yemen with the Houthis and in Iraq with the Shia militias," said Lieutenant General Michael Nagata. "Iran gave the Houthis access to precision-guided anti-ship cruise missiles, sophisticated attack drones, and other advanced capabilities. This kind of high-tech warfare is the future."[42] Mike Vickers, the Pentagon's undersecretary of intelligence, was equally concerned. "The United States lost its primary partner in Yemen when the Saleh government collapsed. Iran took advantage."[43]

The proliferation of advanced ballistic missile technology, armed unmanned aerial vehicles, and explosive remote-controlled boats enabled Iran to significantly improve the Houthis' capabilities in their war with Saudi Arabia. One example was the Borkan-2H mobile, short-range ballistic missiles, which the Houthis used to strike Riyadh and other targets in Saudi Arabia. A United Nations panel of experts concluded that Iran had provided key missile parts to the Houthis.[44]

While Soleimani could not rely on air routes and landbridges for Yemen—which he could for Syria, Lebanon, and Iraq—he could smuggle matériel by maritime routes. Iran frequently broke the weapons systems down, placed them on boats, and moved them through Oman and Yemen ports like Nishtun and al-Ghaydah in al-Mahrah governorate.[45] Lebanese Hezbollah provided training in ground tactics and assisted in the construction and use of missiles and drones.[46] With these capabilities and skills in the hands of the Houthis, Soleimani could target the Saudis indirectly through an irregular approach. Between 2016 and 2021, the Houthis used missiles, drones, and other projectiles to conduct hundreds of attacks against oil infrastructure and other targets in Saudi Arabia. "Iran failed on many of its most important objectives in Yemen, such as controlling the Bab el Mandeb Strait and the Red Sea," said Roule.[47] But Iran nevertheless tied down the Saudis in a quagmire that cost Riyadh over $200 million per day, eroded their international image, embarrassed their military, failed to weaken Iranian influence, killed over 100,000 Yemenis, and displaced more than 4 million people.[48] In 2021, President Joseph Biden announced that he was ending US support to the Saudi-led war in Yemen because the conflict had become a "humanitarian and strategic catastrophe."[49]

Despite some of these setbacks, Iran's irregular campaign in Yemen was remarkably successful. Instead of fighting Saudi Arabia directly in a series of set-piece battles, Iran and Soleimani's Quds Force provided missile technology, drone technology, weapons, and training to the Houthis so that they could bleed Riyadh.

※ ※ ※ ※

IRAN CONTINUED TO wage an irregular campaign against the United States and several of its partners—including Saudi Arabia—across the Middle East. Following the Trump administration's decision to pull out of the nuclear deal, tensions mounted as Iran conducted a series of escalated actions designed to increase the political pressure on Washington and European capitals to restart nuclear negotiations and curb the sanctions.[50] In May 2019, for example, Iran's Islamic Revolutionary Guard Corps sabotaged four commercial ships off the coast of the United Arab Emirates. The next month, Iran used limpet mines to attack Japanese and Norwegian tankers in the Gulf of Oman. Iran then shot down a US Global Hawk, a multimillion-dollar high-altitude, remotely piloted surveillance aircraft, in the Strait of Hormuz. The United States responded by conducting a cyber attack against Iranian computer systems—

including military communications networks—and taking down an Iranian drone in the Strait of Hormuz. Irregular warfare was alive and well.

In the early morning of September 14, 2019, Iran then launched a combination of land-attack cruise missiles and drones from bases in Iran and Iraq against Saudi oil facilities at Abqaiq and Khurais. Abqaiq was the world's largest oil-processing facility and crude oil stabilization plant, with a capacity of more than 7 million barrels per day.[51] Iran likely chose the weapons it used for this attack because of their high maneuverability (which enabled Iran to avoid objects such as power lines), small size, ability to fly close to the ground to evade radar detection, and similarity to weapons systems from other actors (such as the Houthis in Yemen) to mask Iranian involvement.[52] In a further attempt to conceal Iran's actions, Tehran's Houthi partners in Yemen took credit for the attack.

The Iranians were not done. Much like Russia and its use of cyber operations, Iran also perpetrated offensive cyber attacks against Saudi Arabia and other countries—including the United States—as part of its irregular warfare campaign. The Iranian hacking group APT33 (or Elfin) used the destructive malware Shamoon. The attack involved a wiper malware, Trojan.Filerase, that deleted files from infected computers and then wiped the computers' master boot records, making them unusable. The Iranians successfully used Shamoon to target oil and gas infrastructure in Saudi Arabia and the United Arab Emirates.[53] In one attack, Iran erased the hard drives of 30,000 computers from Saudi Arabia's oil company Aramco. Like Russia and China, Iran also leveraged hacktivist organizations to conduct cyber operations. In 2018, for example, the US Department of Justice indicted nine Iranian employees from the Mabna Institute, an Iran-based company that worked closely with the IRGC, for hacking into hundreds of universities and companies to steal sensitive research, proprietary data, and intellectual property.[54]

However, Iran's cyber operations were not always successful. As

US cyber expert Jim Lewis told me: "The Iranians aren't as good at cyber operations as the Russians and Chinese."[55] In May 2020, for example, Iran tried—and failed—to attack the Eshkol water filtration plant in Israel with the intent of causing the water pumps to malfunction so that chlorine levels would increase and poison Israelis.[56]

✳　✳　✳　✳

FOR ALL OF Soleimani's activities in Yemen, Iraq, Lebanon, Syria, and other locations, locals did not always embrace Soleimani or his Quds Force. In Sunni locations, the population often felt disenfranchised by a government in Baghdad that they believed was too closely aligned with Tehran. When Shia militias drove the Islamic State out of Jurf al-Sakhar, a city near Baghdad in central Iraq, it became a ghost town. Thousands of Sunnis became internally displaced, and a local Sunni politician was assassinated with a bullet through his head.[57] An Iranian intelligence report depicted the destruction of Jurf al-Sakhar in nearly biblical terms. "In all the areas where the Popular Mobilization Forces go into action," it concluded, "the Sunnis flee, abandoning their homes and property, and prefer to live in tents as refugees or reside in camps." The assessment described extreme damage to Sunni areas. "In some places, the palm orchards have been uprooted to be burned to prevent the terrorists from taking shelter among the trees. The people's livestock (cows and sheep) have been scattered and are grazing without their owners." Actions by the Quds Force–linked militias alienated Iraq's Sunni population. "Destroying villages and houses, looting the Sunnis' property and livestock turned the sweetness of these successes" against the Islamic State into "bitterness."[58]

Some officers within Iran's Ministry of Intelligence and Security directly blamed Soleimani for an overuse of Shia militias. They also accused him of being a self-promoter and using the campaign against the Islamic State to bolster his political stock in Iran. One Iranian intelligence report, which noted at the top that it should not be shared with the Quds Force, criticized Soleimani for vainly "publishing pictures of himself on different social media sites."[59] Soleimani had an active social media presence, and videos and photographs of him became prevalent as he toured countries like Iraq and Syria. He also taunted foreign leaders like US president Donald Trump on his Instagram account (@sardar_haj_ghasemsoleimani) and Telegram account (T.me/sardar_haj_ghasem). In 2018, for example, Soleimani posted a picture on Instagram of himself giving a speech, with the words: "Mr. Trump, the gambler! Don't threaten our lives! You are well aware of our power and capabilities in the region. *You know how powerful we are at asymmetrical warfare.*"[60]

Soleimani's actions angered Iranian diplomats. In a leaked 2021 audio interview with Iranian journalist Saeed Leylaz, Iranian foreign minister Javad Zarif bitterly complained that Soleimani's actions forced him to "sacrifice diplomacy for the IRGC's operations." Zarif said that Soleimani's influence extended to diplomatic initiatives, such as the 2015 nuclear deal between Iran, the US, and other world powers. "Almost every time I went to negotiate, it was Soleimani who said, 'I want you to make this concession or point.' I was negotiating for the success of the [military field]."[61]

Soleimani's activism created other challenges. Mass demonstrations engulfed Lebanon and Iraq in 2019 and 2020, with some protesters angry about growing Iranian influence in their countries. In Iraq, violent demonstrations erupted as people complained about poor economic conditions. Protesters in the holy Shia city of Karbala torched the Iranian consulate. "Free, free Iraq," some shouted, "Iran get out, get out."[62] In October 2019, Lebanese prime minister Saad Hariri resigned following massive protests that included anger at Iran's excessive influence in the country. The Iranian regime itself faced significant demonstrations in 2020, 2021, and in previous years, including the November 2019 and January 2018 Dey protests. Iran could provide aid to groups like Lebanese Hezbollah, but not good governance.

"Iran's achievements have been incomplete," said General Petraeus. "The economic situation in Lebanon is dire. Syria is incomplete. Iraq is incomplete. And on the home front, Iran is a disaster. Their economy is in shambles."[63] As Admiral Bill McRaven added: "The Iranians have notable limitations. They are a weak conventional power. We know—and they know—there are limits about what they can do."[64]

Yet despite these drawbacks, Soleimani had expanded Iranian influence throughout the region in direct competition with the United States. By the time of his death, militia forces trained, equipped, and funded by Iran extended from Lebanon to Iraq, Syria, Yemen, Afghanistan, and Pakistan.

✳ ✳ ✳ ✳

OVER A DECADE before his death, Soleimani had a premonition. In a speech honoring Iranian soldiers killed during the Iran-Iraq War, he announced to his audience: "In light of the prestige earned by the martyrs, I pray to God for my own end to martyrdom as well, and that He will not deny me this mighty blessing granted to outstanding individuals."[65] On January 3, 2020, Soleimani's prediction came true—courtesy of a US strike.

Between January 4 and January 7, 2020, millions of Iranians flooded into the streets in Baghdad, Beirut, Najaf, Ahvaz, Mashhad, Tehran, Qom, and Soleimani's home province of Kerman to pay tribute to the former Quds Force commander. The January 7 procession in Kerman was so large and unwieldy that a stampede killed at least 56 mourners and wounded over 200 others. In Tehran, the procession of more than 1.3 million people snaked over 4 miles through the center of the city, from west of Azadi Square to several blocks east of Enghelab Square.[66] Mourners chanted "No compromise, no surrender, in the battle against America!" and implored supreme leader Ali Khamenei to avenge Soleimani's death.[67] Many Iranians viewed General Soleimani as a national hero and a "patriot" who guarded the Iranian people from the threats posed by the United States and its partners.

Polling data suggested that Soleimani was not just revered militarily but was also the most popular political figure in Iran, with 82 percent of those polled in Iran viewing him favorably.[68] In addition, Iranians were supportive of Soleimani's activities in the Middle East, with 81 percent responding that the "IRGC's activities in the Middle East have made Iran more secure."[69] Khamenei praised him as a "glorious" martyr, and others, such as Foreign Minister Javad Zarif, referenced his "pure blood."[70] Iran named a surface-to-surface ballistic missile after him—the Martyr Hajj Qassem missile, with a range of 1,400 kilometers, capable of reaching Israel, Saudi Arabia, and US bases in the Middle East.

Still, Soleimani's assassination was a blow to Iran, at least temporarily. "His elimination, I think, has been very detrimental to Iran," former acting US secretary of defense Christopher Miller told me. But he added: "Remarkable figure, wasn't he? I mean, truly charismatic, visionary. Took an organization and really created this whole irregular warfare capability."[71] Even after his death, Soleimani's legacy lived on through his longtime deputy, Ismail Qaani, who carried the irregular warfare flag. Despite a floundering economy—thanks, in part, to US sanctions—Soleimani expanded Iran's influence in such countries as Lebanon, Syria, Iraq, Afghanistan, and Yemen by providing money, arms, training, and technology to nonstate forces. Iran projected power not through conventional capabilities like tanks and fighter jets, but through support to nonstate partners, covert action, espionage, and cyber operations. Soleimani was much more like Sun Tzu than like Carl von Clausewitz.

In approving Qaani as head of the Quds Force, Khamenei promised that the Quds Force's activities would be "exactly the same as that during the period of martyr General Soleimani."[72] As a 2021 US intelligence assessment concluded, "Iran's unconventional warfare operations and network of militant partners and proxies enable

Tehran to advance its interests in the region, maintain strategic depth, and provide asymmetric retaliatory options." The report continued that the Quds Force "and its proxies will remain central to Iran's military power."[73] Soleimani had developed a self-confident "Soleimani strut" over time as the United States helped build up his mythical status. But the CIA's Norm Roule worried that the United States might make the same mistake with Qaani. "We don't want to create what you might call the 'Qaani kick,'" Roule said. "He has everything that Soleimani had except for a fresh conflict."[74] It was not surprising, then, to see Qaani travel to Syria shortly after his appointment to visit Quds Force–backed militias on the ground—just as Soleimani would have done.[75]

Soleimani's lesson for Qaani and other Iranians was clear: Iran *had* to use irregular means to compete with the United States.

PART III
CHINA

ZHANG YOUXIA

8: THE ART OF WAR

On March 10, 2020, Chinese leader Xi Jinping traveled to Wuhan, the epicenter of China's COVID-19 outbreak. It was Xi's first trip to Wuhan since the start of the outbreak in December 2019. He donned a dark, waist-length jacket and sleek protective mask, and waved to jubilant crowds jammed onto balconies and pressed up against windows. The carefully choreographed propaganda event looked more like a celebratory parade than a visit to ground zero of a raging virus. Xi's goal was to demonstrate that China had contained the crisis and that the worst of the national emergency was over—just at the moment that the virus was rampaging through the United States and Europe. Xi praised China's response as a model for the world and volunteered Chinese assistance to countries overseas.[1]

The trip to Wuhan was also a concerted attempt by Xi to salvage China's damaged reputation. The outbreak of COVID-19 was originally linked to the Huanan Seafood Wholesale Market in Wuhan, where live wildlife was sold for food. China's initial response was a blatant cover-up. Li Wenliang, a thirty-four-year-old Chinese doctor from Wuhan, posted in late December on the popular Chinese messaging app WeChat that seven patients from a local seafood market had been diagnosed with a SARS-like illness and quarantined in his hospital. But he was savaged on social media as a traitor. Li, who later died of COVID-19, was hauled into a police station and reprimanded for "spreading rumors online" and "severely disrupting social order."[2] In a statement broadcast throughout the country on China Central Television and posted on China's Twitter-like platform Weibo, the police announced that they had "taken legal measures" against eight people who had recently "published and shared rumors online" about COVID-19. "The internet is not a land beyond the law," the police statement declared. "Any unlawful acts of fabricating, spreading rumors and disturbing the social order will be punished by police according to the law, with zero tolerance."[3]

Over the next month, however, COVID-19 tore through China as the country went into lockdown and the economy ground to a halt. As Xi traveled through Wuhan in March 2020 during his propaganda tour, he was accompanied by several advisers—including Zhang Youxia, vice chairman of China's powerful Central Military Commission. Zhang was little known in the West, but he carried immense weight in China as a onetime "princeling"—the child of an influential senior Communist Party official. Zhang was also a long-standing friend of Xi and one of China's only senior military officers with combat experience. Unlike Valery Gerasimov and Qassem Soleimani, Zhang was neither physically imposing nor charismatic. He was short and pudgy, with a balding head and fleshy chin.

Yet Zhang possessed strategic acumen and political savvy. Along with Xi and other Chinese leaders, he helped oversee Beijing's campaign against the United States that involved information and disinformation operations, espionage to steal some of the United States' most advanced technology, economic warfare, and maritime coercion to expand Chinese influence and territorial control using militias and other paramilitary forces. Zhang also believed that China was engaged in a momentous global competition with the United States. In response to COVID-19, Chinese government operatives forwarded texts to Americans on their cell phones and posted false information on social media platforms, warning that the Trump administration was on the verge of deploying US soldiers to lock down the country. Also on social media, Chinese officials posted lies and conspiracy theories, including that the US Army had brought COVID-19 to Wuhan.

Mirroring KGB forgeries during the Cold War, China fabricated a top secret US government document, which appeared on social media sites in April 2020. The fake document was a memorandum from the US Navy's Pacific Fleet to its sailors. It argued that the actions of Captain Brett Crozier, the commander of the aircraft carrier USS *Theodore Roosevelt* who had been relieved of command after sending a letter to navy leaders asking that most of his crew be taken ashore because of COVID-19 concerns, had "seriously damaged the image of the navy" and "seriously harmed the country."[4] The memorandum, which was translated into Chinese, was designed to highlight US weakness and incompetence. It was also completely fake.

For Zhang and other Chinese leaders, the COVID-19 crisis presented an opportunity to use disinformation to undermine the United States. Four decades earlier, the KGB had conducted a campaign named OPERATION DENVER—or, as East Germany's intelligence agency referred to it, OPERATION INFEKTION. The operation had falsely implicated the US Department of Defense in the emergence of the AIDS virus.[5] In July 1983, the KGB planted an article in a small Indian newspaper, the *Patriot*. The campaign eventually assumed a life of its own, with help from KGB and allied intelligence services abroad. In sub-Saharan Africa, where the KGB focused most of its efforts for OPERATION INFEKTION, media and word of mouth spread the lie that the US military had produced AIDS at a biological research facility at Fort Detrick, Maryland. Both Third World media and Western newspapers like the United Kingdom's *Sunday Express* and *Daily Telegraph* widely reported the AIDS falsehood as true. By late 1987, the story had circulated in the media of 80 countries, appearing in over 200 periodicals in 25 languages.[6]

China's decision to engage in Russian-style operations was a breakout moment for Beijing. "China showed us a lot with COVID-19," Mark Kelton, former head of counterintelligence and counterespionage at the CIA, told me. "Chinese intelligence services are learning institutions. They learned a lot from the Russians in 2016 with the US elections. You can expect to see more of it."[7] The United States may continue to outpace the Chinese in terms of its conventional and nuclear capabilities. But as Zhang and other Chinese leaders believed, America was vulnerable to an irregular campaign. And China was well prepared for one, given its rich history of irregular warfare.

Zhang's life had prepared him for the opportunity.

✻ ✻ ✻ ✻

WHILE QASSEM SOLEIMANI and Valery Gerasimov came from poor, working-class families, Zhang Youxia was born in July 1950 into a privileged household. He had an older brother, Zhang Xinxia, who became director of the Planning Department of the China Aerospace Science and Industry Corporation and the president of the China Great Wall Industry Corporation.[8] Like his siblings, Zhang Youxia was a vaunted princeling. His father was Zhang Zongxun, a prestigious Communist general who served during the Chinese civil war and was one of the first batch of generals after the founding of the People's Republic of China. He came from the Weinan region of Shaanxi province—the same area as Xi Jinping, the future Chinese president and general secretary of the Communist Party. Zhang Youxia's father commanded the Northeast Army Corps in 1947, while Xi Jinping's father, Xi Zhongzun, was a political commissar in the same region. Together, Xi Jinping's and Zhang Youxia's fathers had fought the Kuomintang, which had ruled China from 1927 to 1948.[9]

Zhang Youxia was fortunate. In the upper echelons of the Chinese political system and military, one's status hinges, in part, on who one knows. Because of his father's personal relationship with Xi Zhongzun and his upbringing in Weinan, Zhang Youxia knew Xi Jinping from childhood.[10] "Xi once saw Zhang, who is three years older than him, as his elder brother, and so did Xi's sisters," remarked a retired colonel of the People's Liberation Army (PLA).[11]

Zhang attended the prestigious Beijing Jingshan School and was a competitive athlete. One of Zhang's childhood friends remembers him as being particularly cutthroat on the basketball court, where he was "a man of steel" and played through injuries like a broken wrist. "I still remember him playing basketball and shouting, 'I ask on this boundless land, who rules over man's destiny? We do!'"[12] He joined the PLA in 1968 at the age of eighteen and was assigned to the 14th Group Army, based in Kunming city, Yunnan province. In May 1969, Zhang joined the Communist Party of China—an essential step to promotion in the Chinese military.

One of the unique features of China's Communist political system is that the PLA is not a national army that serves the state, like most Western militaries do. Rather, the PLA serves and falls under the Chinese Communist Party, which controls military strategy. The PLA is, in a very real sense, the Communist Party's army. One of the most important goals of the PLA is to increase power *for the party*. Mao Zedong—founder of the People's Republic of China, chairman of the Communist Party, and erstwhile guerrilla commander— remarked that Chinese are mistaken when they believe that the task of the army is "to merely fight. They do not understand that the Chinese Red Army is an armed body for carrying out the political tasks of the revolution."[13] For Zhang to succeed—and even thrive—in this system, he needed to climb both the military *and* the political ladders to support socialism with Chinese characteristics. In a speech later in life, Zhang hailed the importance of "being bold and loyal, obeying the party's command, and firmly establishing his faith in the party's absolute loyalty." Loyalty to the party was paramount, Zhang explained, and was even a matter of "life and death."[14]

Zhang attended the basic course at the PLA military academy, the precursor to China's National Defense University, and received a junior college education. By all accounts, he was a good soldier and methodically advanced as a squad leader, platoon leader, and deputy commander in the 119th Regiment, 40th Division, 14th Group Army.[15] In 1977, he was promoted to commander of the 8th Company, 3rd Battalion, in the 14th Group Army.[16]

"Like father, like son," remarked one Chinese military analyst. "Zhang was born to be a commander."[17] Part of being a good commander was assiduously studying China's rich history of irregular warfare.

✳   ✳   ✳   ✳

LIKE MOST PLA MEMBERS, Zhang read Sun Tzu's *Art of War*, which had been written over 2,000 years before. In the words of General David Petraeus, *The Art of War* is "one of the world's most influential books on military strategy."[18] For Zhang, Sun Tzu's clear vision, simplicity, and timeless insight made *The Art of War* highly relevant for China—and helped inform the strategy for confronting the United States. Among the most important lessons was how to deal with a more powerful enemy. "Where he is strong," Sun Tzu warned, "avoid him"; strike him where he is weak.[19] Sun Tzu also cautioned that the goal of war should not necessarily be military defeat of the enemy on a battlefield. "For to win one hundred victories in one hundred battles is not the acme of skill," he wrote. But "to subdue the enemy without fighting is the acme of skill."[20] In addition, Sun Tzu emphasized that intelligence and deception were essential skills. "There is no place where espionage is not used," he wrote, and "secret operations are essential in war; upon them the army relies to make its every move."[21]

Zhang also read Mao Zedong.[22] Mao divided warfare into three stages, which had implications for Zhang and competition with a stronger conventional adversary like the United States. During the first stage, when the enemy has a disproportionate advantage in numbers and military power, the goal should be to avoid direct confrontation and focus on defense.[23] During the second stage, which Mao termed "strategic stalemate," the focus should be on asymmetric tactics. During this phase, he advised, forces should "attack; withdraw; deliver a lightning blow, seek a lightning decision . . . withdraw when he advances; harass him when he stops; strike him when he is weary; pursue him when he withdraws."[24] During the third and final stage, the focus should finally be on conducting offensive, conventional operations to vanquish the enemy.[25]

Mao also developed the notion of "people's war," which involves mobilizing and organizing the masses to augment one's capabilities against a stronger enemy.[26] In response to a foreign invasion, "people's war" could also mean luring the invader deep into home territory and utilizing China's massive population to resist the invasion.[27]

Despite a brief period of détente between the United States and China in the 1970s, the United States was an adversary for most of Zhang's life. Beginning in 1949, the Central Military Commission (CMC) of the Chinese Communist Party—which Zhang would eventually serve as vice chairman—adopted a series of military strategies. Known as *zhanlue fangzhen* ("strategic guidelines"), they provided guidance for operational doctrine, force structure, and training of the PLA. As China's leading military body, the CMC directs and commands the national armed forces. It is a party committee that sits under the Central Committee of the Chinese Communist Party.[28]

With the outbreak of the Korean War in 1950, the United States became China's primary adversary. After the United States and China fought to a stalemate on the Korean peninsula, China began preparing for a possible US amphibious assault against the mainland. Because the 1956 strategic guideline identified the United States as China's "strategic opponent," the new strategy focused on how to fight an adversary with technologically superior capabilities.[29] In March 1956, the CMC held a meeting that gathered together senior military officers. Following the meeting, the CMC completed China's first national military strategy. It outlined how to thwart an invasion by US forces using a strategy of "forward defense," which involved attempting to push the front line of a war away from China's borders and coasts.[30] In 1964, Mao reoriented China's military strategy around the concept of "luring the enemy in deep," in which territory would be yielded to an invader to defeat it in a protracted conflict through mobile and guerrilla warfare.[31] As Chinese leader Zhou Enlai noted in February 1962, "The enemy is expanding its force and preparing for war [*kuojun beizhan*]."[32]

When US president Richard Nixon and Chinese premier Zhou Enlai met in 1972 to normalize relations, the threat from the United States temporarily diminished. China was thus able to focus on local enemies, and Zhang was on the front lines.

❊ ❊ ❊ ❊

IN 1979, Zhang had his first taste of combat. He was a green, twenty-six-year-old company commander in the 8th Company of China's 14th Group Army. Following Vietnam's November 1978 defense treaty with the Soviet Union and its December 1978 invasion of Cambodia, China lost patience with its unruly neighbor. As Chinese vice premier Deng Xiaoping remarked to US president Jimmy Carter during a meeting in January 1979, "The little child is getting naughty, it's time he gets spanked."[33]

Zhang and other PLA soldiers invaded Vietnam in February 1979, captured several cities, such as Lang Son, and then began withdrawing in March. China had mobilized as many as 400,000 soldiers against a Vietnamese force that included between 50,000 and 150,000 soldiers.[34] According to Chinese state news sources, Zhang allegedly devised a plan to swing around entrenched Vietnamese forces and surprise them. "Just give me a battalion, and I will raid the enemy formation," he begged his commander.[35] Zhang was given command of a battalion composed of four companies and attacked Vietnamese forces after slicing through thick jungle terrain. He completed the mission and survived several near misses from

Vietnamese bullets. Chinese state-run media claimed that Zhang had performed "well" and with "meritorious service" in Vietnam, though there are few details of his performance except for those from state propaganda.[36] "What matters most is that Zhang was shot at, making him one of the few PLA officers with actual combat experience" by the time Xi Jinping became general secretary of the Chinese Communist Party, said China analyst Dennis Blasko, a former US Army attaché to Beijing and Hong Kong.[37] Most PLA soldiers that fought in the war had long since died or left the army by the era of Xi Jinping.

Several historical accounts of the Sino-Vietnamese conflict concluded that the PLA performed poorly and suffered from weak leadership, lackluster coordination between units at the tactical level, antiquated weapons and logistics equipment, and inadequate training and readiness.[38] Casualties were high. The war lasted less than four weeks, but the costs were staggering. Roughly 60,000 Chinese and Vietnamese soldiers were killed in close fighting, and another 70,000 were wounded.[39]

Zhang was also involved in the 1984 Battle of Laoshan, which yet again pitted China against Vietnam. He commanded the 119th Regiment of the 40th Division of the 14th Group Army. In response to continuing Vietnamese incursions into Cambodia, China had conducted a series of artillery barrages against Vietnamese positions in early 1984. Zhang and others in the PLA's 40th Division crossed into Vietnam, capturing several hamlets and hills just inside Vietnam.[40] According to Chinese state-run news accounts, Zhang held on to "Hill 662.6," known to the Chinese as Songmaoling, despite being outnumbered 7:1 by Vietnamese forces. After receiving intelligence about a surprise Vietnamese attack, Zhang ordered Chinese forces to shell Vietnamese positions. "The Chinese launched a midnight raid, but Zhang Youxia led his troops to persevere, clearly coordinating with artillery to maintain their position," one article summarized. "In the end, he led the regime to successfully repel a three-day counterattack by the Vietnamese, killing over 3,000 enemy troops."[41]

While there is little objective information on Zhang's performance, one thing is certain: Zhang's military career took off after the war. In 1984, he was promoted to deputy commander of the 40th Division in China's 14th Group Army. Much like Gerasimov and Soleimani, Zhang developed a reputation as a soldier's soldier. "He doesn't put on airs and likes getting down in the dirt with ordinary soldiers, to know what their lives are like, how they are living and what they are eating," remarked one Chinese official.[42] He was also politically astute and an active Communist Party member.

In 1990, Zhang was again promoted—this time to commander of the 40th Division in northeastern China's Shenyang Military Region. It was an important post for Zhang. The 40th Division was deployed to a strategically important area, near the potentially explosive Korean peninsula and adjacent to China's border with the Soviet Union. By this time, the world was changing rapidly. The Soviet Union was collapsing, and an emboldened United States invaded Iraq.

* * * *

THE US MILITARY'S rapid defeat of Iraqi forces during the First Gulf War had a profound impact on Chinese military officers like Zhang, much like it did on Valery Gerasimov and Qassem Soleimani.[43] From the perspective of America's enemies, the Gulf War was highly alarming. The United States was now clearly the world's only superpower. No army on earth could match what the Americans had done. The display of logistics, technology, and firepower was overwhelming. Zhang knew that the PLA military was woefully unprepared, should war arise. China lacked sophisticated technology and, as Chinese leader Jiang Zemin warned in March 1991 in a quote borrowed from Soviet leader Joseph Stalin: "Backwards technology means being in a passive position and taking a beating."[44]

In December 1992, PLA leadership began a formal analysis of China's military strategy. Within a month, the PLA established a new strategic guideline that the CMC adopted in early January 1993. As Jiang explained, China's goal must be "winning local wars that may occur under modern technology, especially under high-technology conditions."[45] Unlike previous guidelines in 1956 and 1980, the 1993 version outlined how China could conduct limited wars through, in part, irregular means.[46] Much like Gerasimov, Zhang and other Chinese leaders also studied the US wars in the Balkans later in the decade—including the 1999 Kosovo War. "As an asymmetric conflict," wrote MIT professor Taylor Fravel, "[the Kosovo War] would hold important implications for China, which still viewed itself as relatively weak militarily."[47] Neither the United States nor other NATO countries had used their own ground forces as the main maneuver units. Instead, they leveraged irregular forces from the Kosovo Liberation Army to retake territory.[48]

For Zhang and other Chinese leaders, the United States was revolutionizing warfare by using irregular units—not conventional US forces—to seize and hold territory. As Jiang Zemin remarked, US actions demonstrated that "the new transformation in military affairs is entering into a new stage of qualitative changes and will likely develop into a profound military revolution that spreads around the globe and involves all military fields."[49] China was behind—way behind.[50] The PLA had little or no capability to conduct irregular or even conventional military operations outside of Chinese territory. By the end of the decade, Zhang had become acutely aware of these problems.

✳   ✳   ✳   ✳

IN 1994, the PLA promoted Zhang to become deputy commander of the 13th Group Army. Based in Chongqing, a megacity in southwestern China, the 13th Group Army was one of the most famous in China. Christened the "Tiger in the Mountains," it specialized in mountain and jungle warfare. Its major tasks included ensuring the stability of Tibet and guarding China's borders with India and Vietnam. The 13th Group Army was a Category A force, which meant it was equipped with modern armaments and conducted full-time, high-intensity training. It was distinguished from Category B units with comparatively out-of-date armaments, less training, and lower budgets—similar in some ways to the US National Guard. The 13th Group Army was also one of the few PLA groups with battlefield experience. It had been involved in the 1979 Sino-Vietnamese war— in which Zhang had fought—and had engaged in skirmishes with Indian forces during the 1962 Sino-Indian War.[51]

It was around this time that two little-known PLA colonels— Qiao Liang and Wang Xiangsui—captured the attention of US audiences when they published a controversial book, *Unrestricted Warfare* (or *Chao Xian Zhan*). Qiao and Wang offered an assessment of where warfare was headed, China's distrust of the United States, and where China needed to go—and fast. The authors of *Unrestricted Warfare* were motivated by the advancements and breadth of US power as highlighted during conflicts like the First Gulf War—a war, the authors argued, "that changed the world."[52] The PLA colonels bristled at the United States for its "missionary zeal" and "aspiration of building a new world order with 'USA' stamped on it."[53] The United States' vision looked starkly different from that of Communist China. Despite its conventional superiority, the authors argued, the United States was vulnerable to irregular warfare. They emphasized *fei duicheng* ("asymmetric means") in fighting stronger powers like the United States by using political, economic, information, and psychological warfare.

Just look at the potential of a computer hacker, they pointed out. "This chap, who generally has not received any military training or been engaged in any military profession, can easily impair the security of an army or a nation in a major way by simply relying on his personal technical expertise."[54] Their recommendation was to focus on exploiting US weaknesses:

> This use of asymmetrical measures which create power for oneself and make the situation develop as you want it to, is often hugely effective. It often makes an adversary which uses conventional forces and conventional measures as its main combat strength look like a big elephant charging into a china shop. It is at a loss as to what to do, and unable to make use of the power it has.[55]

Prescient though it may have been, *Unrestricted Warfare* did not represent the official views of the Chinese military establishment. In the end it is unclear—and perhaps unlikely—that it had much influence on Chinese military strategy. "What made the book explosive in the United States was that it was translated into English," Taylor Fravel said to me. "It really wasn't important in China."[56]

A few years later, however, the PLA published a much more authoritative report, *The Science of Military Strategy*. The document represented the views of nearly three dozen influential military strategists at the Academy of Military Science, an organization that reported directly to China's CMC and included some of the most important military thinkers in China.[57] The 2001 *Science of Military Strategy* highlighted the importance of such concepts as "active defense," in which China committed to using offensive actions only if necessary to achieve defensive goals.[58] Echoing Sun Tzu, China's military strategy was to win without fighting—that is, to achieve its national objectives without going to war. The point was that China's military strategy was defensive in nature. China had little interest in a conventional war with a much stronger United States.

But *The Science of Military Strategy* also highlighted the importance of irregular war. One important component was cyber war, which included the possibility of "large information offensives" and the potential for an "electronic Pearl Harbor."[59] *The Science of Military Strategy* noted that China did not need to defeat an adversary on the battlefield by "step-by-step dismembering of the enemy's body," but could do it through irregular means.[60] Where the US Cold War diplomat George Kennan had talked about "the perpetual rhythm of struggle," the PLA report described warfare as a *constant struggle* that involved both the enemy and its population:

> The target of modern psychological warfare is not limited to the enemy forces as it also includes all people of the hostile country ... in order to cause wrong understandings, assessments, and decisions, and shake its thinking and conviction and will of resistance to achieve the objective of defeating the enemy without fighting. It is implemented not only in wartime but also in a massive and continued scale in peacetime.[61]

✳ ✳ ✳ ✳

BY THIS TIME, the PLA had promoted Zhang Youxia to commander of the 13th Group Army, and his influence within the Chinese military continued to grow.[62] In an influential piece around this time, Zhang argued that China needed to "promote a multipolar world" and weaken the United States, which he accused of having hegemonic ambitions.[63] In other words, the United States remained a threat, especially in a conventional war.

But Zhang was not overly concerned about conventional war. The future of warfare was not necessarily in clashes between armies on a battlefield, he concluded, but competition in areas like the information sphere. "The focus point of war is changing from taking cities through conventional operations and seizing land to information operations," Zhang wrote in a perceptive article in 2004.[64] He argued that conventional war was, in many ways, antiquated and that Chinese leaders needed to grasp a new reality. "As human society strides forward from the industrial age to the informatization age, informatization has become the leading melody in our age," Zhang wrote. The term "informatization" (*xinxihua*), as Zhang and other Chinese leaders used it, referred to the transition from the industrial age to the information age caused by the development and use of information technology.[65]

"War has no fixed areas and boundaries," he wrote. "It unfolds in all areas, at any time and space."[66] One of the most important areas for China was increasingly *inside* the United States.

9: THREE WARFARES

ON APRIL 9, 2003, FBI AGENTS ARRESTED KATRINA Leung at her house in San Marino, California, an upscale suburb northeast of Los Angeles in the foothills of the San Gabriel Mountains. She was a shrewd, gregarious forty-nine-year-old businesswoman and well-connected Republican Party member. "Katrina has been a fixture in this city for a long, long time," said Leland Wong, Los Angeles city commissioner.[1] She was born in China in 1954, immigrated to the United States as a teenager, and then attended several prestigious US universities. Leung earned her undergraduate degree from Cornell University and her MBA from the University of Chicago. In early 1980, she moved to Los Angeles with her husband, where she initially resided in an apartment building that the FBI characterized as a "nest of spies."[2] She lived a lavish lifestyle in California and became the general manager of an import-export company suspected by the FBI of engaging in the illegal transfer of technology from the United States to China.

In February 1981, the FBI opened a counterintelligence investigation of Leung, one that would become one of the most dramatic—and bizarre—in the bureau's history. Instead of prosecuting her, however, the FBI had other ideas. FBI agent James J. Smith—or "J.J." to those who knew him—recruited Leung as an FBI asset, with the code name PARLOR MAID. She was one of the bureau's highest-paid assets, raking in nearly $2 million over eighteen years for providing information on Chinese intelligence agents and the activity of high-ranking Chinese officials.[3]

But there were two problems for the FBI.[4] The first was that Leung was a double agent. She was actively spying for China and had passed substantial amounts of classified information on US counterintelligence efforts and sensitive technologies to China's main foreign intelligence service, the Ministry of State Security.[5] The second problem was that Leung had engaged in sexual relationships with not one—but two—FBI counterintelligence agents. The first was with J. J. Smith, her primary handler, in an affair that persisted for two decades.[6] The second was with supervisor William Cleveland from the FBI's San Francisco field office. It was an extraordinary lapse in judgment by two seasoned FBI counterintelligence agents. Over a twenty-year period, until her arrest in 2003, Leung did grave damage to US national security. "The PARLOR MAID case was a tremendous blow to FBI counterintelligence," the CIA's Mark Kelton explained to me. "Leung was able to gather a lot of information from them. The damage was twofold," he said. "First, she was being tasked by FBI agents, so she passed information on to China about what FBI counterintelligence was interested in. Second, she passed along information to her Chinese handlers from general conversations with FBI agents—what you might call 'loose talk.'"[7]

Yet PARLOR MAID was only the beginning. By 2003, China was engaging in a massive espionage effort to narrow the military and economic gap that Zhang Youxia had long identified between the United States and China. To catch up, China needed to steal US information and technology. "An army without secret agents," Sun Tzu warned, "is exactly like a man without eyes or ears."[8] China had long had spies, of course, such as Larry Wu-Tai Chin, a translator for the CIA's Foreign Broadcast Information Service who provided classified documents to China. But now China was improving its tradecraft. As former CIA chief of counterintelligence James Olson noted: "There are spies, and then there are Chinese spies. China is in a class by itself in terms of its espionage, covert action and cyber capabilities. It is also in a class by itself because of its absolute obsession with stealing America's secrets."[9]

Over the previous decade, China had stolen information on some of the United States' most sensitive weapons systems and technologies, such as the W62 Minuteman III intercontinental ballistic missile, W76 Trident C4 submarine-launched ballistic missile, and W88 Trident D5 submarine-launched ballistic missile.[10] These thefts were just the beginning. China's espionage campaign in the United States grew exponentially over the next decade to include sensitive information about cruise missile systems, US Navy warship technologies, stealth technology, F-16 jet engine design, trade secrets from US corporations such as General Motors and Ford Motor Company, computer chip design and development, and the development and design of the F-35—the United States' cutting-edge stealth aircraft.

And there were many others besides PARLOR MAID. There was Peter Lee, a physicist at Los Alamos National Laboratory; Edward Lin, a US Navy signals intelligence specialist; Szuhsiung Ho, a nuclear engineer at the Tennessee Valley Authority; and Greg Chung, an engineer at Boeing, to note just a few spies. Several Chinese intelligence agencies—including the Ministry of State Security and multiple departments within the PLA—used these individuals and many others to steal sensitive information and bring it back to China. The scale, scope, and impact were significant. China's use of espionage was not new or surprising. All countries, including the United States, spied. What was different, however, was how China integrated intelligence into a broader irregular campaign that involved economic, military, and political competition with the United States. While US intelligence agencies did not steal secrets and give them to US companies to maximize their competitiveness, China regularly provided the fruits of espionage to its state-run companies. Paul Moore, a China analyst at the FBI, summed up China's strategy in comparison to the United States and Russia:

If a beach was an espionage target, the Russians would send in a sub, frogmen would steal ashore in the dark of night and with great secrecy collect several buckets of sand and take them back to Moscow. The Americans would target the beach with satellites and produce reams of data. The Chinese would send in a thousand tourists, each assigned to collect a single grain of sand. When they returned, they would be asked to shake out their towels. And they would end up knowing more about the sand than anyone else.[11]

* * * *

AS CHINESE SOURCES collected grains of intelligence, PLA officials like Zhang evolved their thinking about warfare, in part as a result of the US invasions of Afghanistan and Iraq.[12] In 2003, the Central Committee of the Communist Party and the Central Military Commission—the body for which Zhang would eventually become vice chairman—approved a pivotal concept for the PLA called *san zhong zhanfa*, or "three warfares."[13] It included three components: *yulun zhan* (public opinion or media warfare), *xinli zhan* (psychological warfare), and *falu zhanzheng* (legal warfare).[14] Building on Mao's contention that the military's goal was to carry out "the political tasks of the revolution," three warfares offered a way for the PLA to establish and expand Chinese political power at home and abroad.[15] In this sense, the PLA was a major instrument for conducting inherently *political* work.[16] The components of three warfares were not intended to be mutually exclusive, but rather reinforcing. Together, they were intended to help China wage information warfare against the United States and other competitors across the globe.

The first component, public opinion warfare, involved the use of broadcast, print, and online efforts to influence domestic and international public opinion in ways that supported Chinese interests and undermined its competitors. China recognized that newspapers, television, radio, social media, and even organizations like civilian institutes were all legitimate media for waging information warfare.[17] Overseas, China waged public opinion warfare through global broadcasts of the state-run China Central Television (CCTV), Chinese government–paid inserts in newspapers like the *Washington Post* and *New York Times*, and educational institutes established around the world.[18]

The second component, psychological warfare, was designed to sow dissent, disaffection, and discord among soldiers and the civilian population of competitors like the United States.[19] Psychological warfare also leveraged television, radio broadcasts, leaflets, and other media—much like public opinion warfare—but it was designed to achieve military purposes. As one analysis in the PLA journal *China Military Science* concluded, the goal of psychological warfare should be to "sap the enemy's morale, disintegrate their will to fight, ignite the anti-war sentiment among citizens at home, heighten international and domestic conflict, weaken and sway the will to fight among its high level decision makers, and in turn lessen their superiority in military strength."[20]

The third component of three warfares, legal warfare, involved the exploitation of international and domestic law to assert the legitimacy of Chinese claims. The 2001 *Science of Military Strategy* had argued that for the PLA, "international law is a powerful weapon to expose the enemy, to win over sympathy and support of the international community [for China], and to strive to gain the position of strategic initiative." It went on to explain that China needed to publicize its "own humanitarianism and reveal a lot of the war crimes committed by the opponent in violation of law . . . to compel [the] opponent to bog down in isolation and passivity."[21] Influential Chinese military texts emphasized that the PLA should justify its military actions through legal means before beginning any conflict.[22]

None of these components—media, psychological, or legal

warfare—were new for China. "All warfare," Sun Tzu wrote, "is based on deception."[23] What was new, however, was China's attempt to use the three warfares to expand its power overseas. After receiving assessments of US operations in Iraq, Chinese leader Jiang Zemin remarked that "the conduct of public opinion warfare, psychological warfare, and legal warfare by the use of modern mass media is an important measure for warring countries that attempt to grasp the political initiative and military victory."[24]

The battlefield was now global, and China was shifting to the offense. As Zhang wrote in an influential article, conventional war with the United States was a low probability.[25] One of China's most significant targets in waging public opinion warfare was elite US universities—the heartbeat of the United States' education system.

✳ ✳ ✳ ✳

IN 2009, the University of Chicago—where I went to graduate school—quietly approved the establishment of a Confucius Institute on its main campus on Chicago's south side.[26] The institute, which included sparingly furnished offices and a seminar room, was tucked away on the fourth floor of Judd Hall, a stately Victorian Gothic building. The Chinese government had established the Confucius Institute program several years earlier, in 2004, after publication of the "three warfares" doctrine. Hanban, a Chinese government agency chaired by a member of the politburo and the vice premier of the People's Republic of China, oversaw the program. Its stated goals were to promote Chinese language and culture, support local Chinese teaching overseas, and facilitate cultural exchanges.[27] Over the next several years, Confucius Institutes began to pop up across the United States. By 2009, there were 90 Confucius Institutes housed at US universities—including prestigious institutions like Columbia, Stanford, and Chicago—and a total of 440 across the globe.[28]

But the Confucius Institutes quickly became a lightning rod for controversy. At the University of Chicago, more than 100 professors signed a petition calling on the university to terminate its contract with Hanban.[29] Bruce Lincoln, the Caroline E. Haskell Distinguished Service Professor of the History of Religions at the University of Chicago, helped lead the charge, arguing that the institute was a potentially dangerous "sort of arrangement where an entity outside the university . . . is in effect seriously influencing who's teaching and what's taught under our name and inside our curriculum."[30]

The core problem was that the Confucius Institutes stifled open and free debate. Hanban hired and trained teachers to oversee academic courses within US universities, and research proposals had to be approved by Hanban.[31] Numerous examples of censorship began to emerge at Confucius Institutes across the globe—such as in Sweden, Portugal, Australia, and Canada—suffocating discussion in classrooms and at conferences.[32] Hanban instructed teachers in Confucius Institutes to discourage the discussion of issues that were politically taboo in China, such as the status of Taiwan, the 1989 Tiananmen Square massacre orchestrated by PLA forces, human rights, China's prodemocracy movement, and the status of China's beleaguered Uyghur population.[33] Marshall Sahlins, an anthropology professor at the University of Chicago, argued that "by hosting a Confucius Institute, [universities] have become engaged in the political and propaganda efforts of a foreign government in a way that contradicts the values of free inquiry and human welfare to which they are otherwise committed."[34]

Some US intelligence and law enforcement officials also expressed alarm that the Chinese Ministry of State Security was using organizations like the Confucius Institutes to recruit spies and collect intelligence on Chinese in the United States. "The Chinese have multiple goals with Confucius Institutes, including to monitor Chinese communities in the United States and other Western countries," the CIA's Mark Kelton said to me. "The Chinese have also been interested in influencing the tone of debate on campuses and traditional espionage—including spotting and recruiting individuals."[35] The CIA's James Olson explained that China's Ministry of State Security "has an elaborate spotting program to identify those students who show political or cultural sympathy for China."[36]

But the Chinese government hit back hard, excoriating its detractors as xenophobic. "The great Chinese sage Confucius might have pardoned . . . their criticism of Confucius Institutes, as it probably stemmed from either fear or ignorance of other cultures, perhaps both," an article in the *China Daily* argued.[37] Another article accused critics of "McCarthyism"—a nod to the 1950s anticommunist campaign led by US senator Joseph McCarthy—and of being mired in "cultural racism."[38] These were strong words, particularly within university communities. Yet the charge of racism was fallacious, since the critiques focused on China's efforts to stifle debate about issues that the Communist Party considered sensitive. Several articles in the Chinese press also erroneously argued that the Confucius Institutes were no different from the United Kingdom's British Institutes, France's Alliance Française, and Germany's

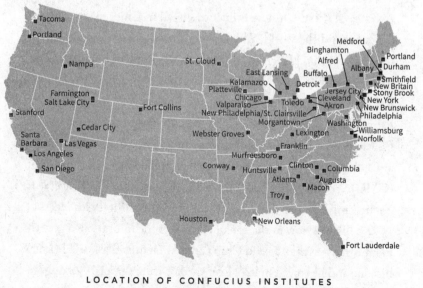

**LOCATION OF CONFUCIUS INSTITUTES
IN THE UNITED STATES, 2021**[39]

Goethe-Instituts—which were all funded by their respective governments.[40] But unlike the Confucius Institutes, these organizations were not housed at universities and didn't attempt to directly influence foreign education systems from within.[41] Over the next decade, a growing number of US colleges and universities closed down institutes on their campuses. By 2021, the number of Confucius Institutes had decreased to sixty-three in cities across the United States.[42]

The Confucius Institutes were part of a broader effort by China to wage three warfares overseas. Many of these efforts were tied to the activity of China's overseas United Front Work Department, or UFWD. Overseen by the Central Committee of the Communist Party of China, the UFWD attempted to protect and bolster the image of the Communist Party by monitoring and countering criticism overseas—often by recruiting or pressuring Chinese diaspora. The Chinese government considered diaspora *huaqiao tongbaomen* ("overseas compatriots"), who owed a measure of loyalty to the Chinese motherland.[43]

* * * *

AS FEARS OF Chinese influence spread in Chicago and on campuses around the world, Zhang's fortunes changed dramatically in the fall of 2012. His childhood friend, Xi Jinping, became general secretary of the Communist Party and then president of the People's Republic of China, taking over from Hu Jintao.[44] With Xi at the helm, Zhang's career took off. He was promoted to director of the PLA General Armaments Department in 2012 and, most important, selected to China's prestigious Central Military Commission (CMC).[45] Zhang's position on the CMC gave him direct access to Xi, making him one of China's most powerful military leaders.

"Zhang was now at the top of the top of the military in a government run by civilians," said China analyst Dennis Blasko. "He knew his lane and he stayed in it."[46] Ever the faithful politician, Zhang frequently reminded his soldiers that loyalty to the Communist Party came first.[47] In a speech a few years earlier, Zhang had urged young PLA soldiers to "listen to the party's command." The good soldier, he said, "has the courage to make sacrifices, always put the interests of the people first, and always maintain the political nature of the people's army."[48] Zhang had become one of China's leading military figures through political adroitness and unrelenting party loyalty. "What Xi now needs is not talent, but people who absolutely obey his orders, and Zhang is one of the people in his camp he can rely on," said a senior PLA colonel.[49]

Zhang's promotion to the top of China's military leadership occurred just as China began to expand its power in Asia. While nominally adhering to a "defensive defense," China's foreign policy under Xi, Zhang, and other Chinese leaders shifted to "peaceful expansion."[50] As China's most recent defense white paper had argued in a nod toward the United States: "International military competition remains fierce. Major powers [such as the United States] are stepping up the realignment of their security and military strategies, accelerating military reform, and vigorously developing new and more sophisticated military technologies," such as space and cyber capabilities.[51]

With Xi at the helm, Chinese foreign policy also became increasingly assertive.

* * * *

ZHANG VISITED the United States in 2012 for a firsthand look at his main adversary.[52] While at the US Marine Corps base at Camp Lejeune, North Carolina, Zhang inspected a US M4 assault rifle, the US military's premier infantry weapon. He was deeply impressed. "It is much better than the 95," he marveled, referring to the Type 95 automatic rifle used by the PLA.[53] As Zhang recognized in a more hands-on way than he had before, China lacked the high-end capabilities of the US military. PLA soldiers also lacked combat experience.[54] "Today, it has been many years since our army has engaged in actual combat, though the world is constantly at war," Zhang remarked. "In this regard, the gap between our army and foreign troops is widening day by day. That is a reality."[55] Some in China called the PLA's lack of combat experience *hépíng bing* ("peace disease").[56]

Yet China was interested in multiple facets of power. The 2013 *Science of Military Strategy* had cited Sun Tzu's emphasis on *fei duicheng* ("asymmetric means") against adversaries, emphasizing that China needed to "develop its special asymmetric, contactless, and nonlinear warfare style."[57] China became increasingly involved in irregular operations: seizing and militarizing contested territory, waging economic warfare, conducting offensive cyber operations to steal sensitive technology and data, and orchestrating information and disinformation campaigns against the United States and its partners under the rubric of China's "three warfares."

The goal of Zhang and other Chinese leaders was to maintain uncontested Communist Party rule at home, restore China as the preponderant land and maritime power in Asia, become equal— if not superior—to the United States, and export China's model of political control and a managed economy.[58] China's 2013 *Science of Military Strategy* painted a zero-sum picture of competition with the United States. It argued that "Western nations led by the United States [are] carrying out strategic encirclement against our country."[59] It continued that the United States was aggressively trying to integrate China into a US-led international order, engage in balance-of-power politics against China in the Pacific, and control the world's major strategic channels and natural resources. Zhang was increasingly focused on competition with the United States. He openly talked about "marching toward the Chinese dream of the great rejuvenation of the Chinese nation" so that China could "build a world-class army" and "win modern wars."[60] In a speech in May 2014, Xi called for an end to "external blocs" and an end—or at least a downgrading—of US alliances in Asia.[61]

"China was now unmasked and revisionist," said Asia expert Mike Green. "This was not the China of Deng Xiaoping anymore. The Chinese were coming directly at the United States."[62]

10: THE GREAT WALL OF SAND

MISCHIEF REEF, LOCATED ROUGHLY 450 MILES west of Vietnam in the warm waters of the South China Sea, is an atoll—a coral reef that surrounds a lagoon. It boasts rich marine life, including schools of whitemargin unicornfish, hammerhead sharks, and green and hawksbill sea turtles. China, the Philippines, Vietnam, Brunei, Malaysia, Indonesia, and Taiwan had all claimed ownership of various reefs and islands in the South China Sea. These weren't simply piles of rock and coral. They represented nodes of power in a lucrative waterway. In 2020, roughly $4 trillion in global trade passed through the South China Sea.[1] Oil tanker traffic through the Strait of Malacca, which leads into the South China Sea, was nearly five times greater than in the Suez Canal in Egypt and eighteen times more than in the Panama Canal.[2] The Spratly Islands also boasted significant untapped oil and gas reserves.

As Xi and Zhang recognized, anyone who controlled the Spratly Islands was master of a strategically important part of the South China Sea. For Zhang, maritime security was essential for China.[3] The 2015 Chinese defense white paper argued that China was increasingly engaged in a "maritime military struggle." It highlighted the "continuous expansion of China's national interests," in which access to foreign markets and unencumbered sea lines of communication "have become prominent." The white paper also noted that the focus of China's navy would "shift from 'near-seas defense' [*jinhai fangyu*] to the combination of 'near-seas defense' and 'far-seas protection' [*yuanhai huwei*]."[4] The inclusion of far-seas operations indicated that China was attempting to project power outside of East Asia.

"Under Xi, China has several strategic objectives," said the CIA's Mike Morell. "First, they want to have significant influence, particularly in East Asia. Second, they want to expand their economic activity; they have a mercantilist view of the world. Third, they want to compete with the United States on who gets to set the rules of the global road."[5]

Zhang had been thinking about maritime competition for years. He had supported a position of "non-direct engagement," rather than all-out war, to achieve Chinese objectives. It would be counterproductive to seize territory through an amphibious invasion, he believed.[6] Instead, China used irregular means—covertly building islands, spreading disinformation, harassing local maritime forces and fishermen, and using the China Coast Guard, the People's Armed Forces Maritime Militia, and fishing boats to patrol the areas. Over the next several years, China's leaders—led by Xi, Zhang, and others—waged an aggressive irregular warfare campaign against the United States and other Western countries. China seized territory in the South China Sea, conducted sophisticated cyber operations, developed an extensive Belt and Road Initiative to expand Chinese economic and political power, and attempted to influence individuals and companies inside the United States—from Hollywood notables to college students and professors. These types of actions were critical to compete with a United States that, in Zhang's words, was committed to global "hegemony" and "containment" of China.[7]

In the South China Sea, China achieved a result almost as dramatic as Gerasimov and Putin's annexation of Crimea: China seized the islands without firing a shot.

* * * *

OVER A MATTER of weeks in early 2015, US intelligence analysts from the National Geospatial-Intelligence Agency examined disturbing satellite images. Clusters of Chinese vessels at Mischief Reef were busily dredging white sand by sucking it up from the seabed and pumping it onto the formerly undeveloped reef. It looked like they were building a military base. China replaced the few dilapidated fishing shacks on stilts with an airfield, control tower, hangars to store aircraft, and radar installations. Chinese amphibious warships, capable of holding 500–800 troops, began to patrol the reef's southern flank.[8] In case anyone had questions about the true nature of Mischief Reef, China then added HQ-9B surface-to-air missiles and YJ-12B anti-ship cruise missiles.

"Chinese actions were deeply concerning," said Mike Vickers, the top US intelligence official in the Pentagon. "This was part of Beijing's effort to restore China's dominance in Asia."[9] Mischief Reef was only the beginning. China used hundreds of dredgers and barges to transform other atolls and reefs into military bases: Subi Reef, Hughes Reef, Gaven Reefs, Fiery Cross Reef, Cuarteron Reef, and Johnson South Reef. One of the most impressive dredgers was the *Tian Jing Hao*, a 2,400-ton ship that could excavate 4,500 cubic meters of sand per hour. It was eventually replaced by the *Tian Kun Hao*—dubbed the "magic island maker"—an even larger Chinese-built dredging vessel that was 460 feet long and could excavate 6,000 cubic meters of sand per hour.[10]

The story was similar across the South China Sea. On Fiery Cross Reef, roughly 200 miles west of Mischief Reef, China created an island 9,850 feet long and 985 feet wide with a harbor capable of docking warships and a runway that could support military aircraft. Other islands across the Spratlys now had military barracks, fuel depots, antiaircraft and antimissile systems, and high-frequency radar installations. They served as important logistics hubs for the PLA across the South China Sea. Over time, China placed anti-ship cruise missiles, long-range surface-to-air missiles, sensors, elec-

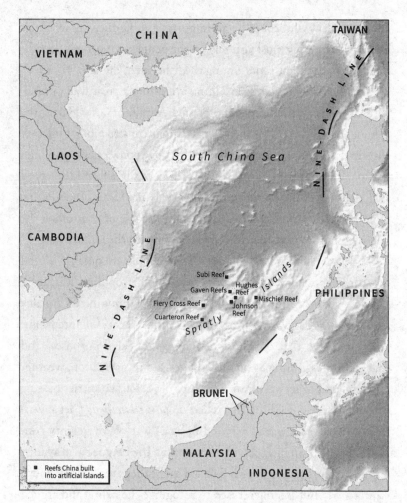

**CHINESE TERRITORIAL CLAIMS
IN THE SPRATLY ISLANDS**[11]

tronic warfare systems, space-based systems, and signals intelligence (SIGINT) platforms on these outposts.[12]

China claimed sovereignty over *all* these islands, ignoring the long-standing claims of its neighbors. To protect its interests, China employed a suite of irregular capabilities: coast guard cutters, vessels from the People's Armed Forces Maritime Militia, and even fishing boats. Mao Zedong had long argued that the PLA needed to leverage fishermen, who could be an important component of irregular warfare. "The navy must also rely on the people; it must rely on fishermen. It must plant roots among the fishermen," he said.[13]

US officials were alarmed. "China is creating a great wall of sand, with dredgers and bulldozers," protested Admiral Harry Harris, the commander of the US Pacific Fleet.[14] China's construction of military bases in the South China Sea gave the PLA power projection capabilities to expand its influence in the region. China was in a formidable position. Admiral Philip Davidson, head of the United States Indo-Pacific Command, remarked that "China is now capable of controlling the South China Sea in all scenarios short of war with the United States."[15]

With the support of Zhang, Chinese officials quickly played down the threat by using *yulun zhan* ("public opinion warfare"). Chinese state-run media—from CCTV to Xinhua News Agency and the *People's Daily*—proclaimed China's peaceful intentions. They suggested that the construction was for "civil purposes" and that "China is aiming to provide shelter, aid in navigation, weather forecasts and fishery assistance to ships of various countries passing through the sea."[16] China also relied on *falu zhanzheng* ("legal warfare")—what Zhang had referred to as a "war of sovereignty control."[17] In 2016, an international tribunal at The Hague ruled against China's claims to the Spratly Islands and other areas in the South China Sea.[18] But Beijing refused to recognize the ruling and argued that the international tribunal itself lacked legal jurisdiction.[19]

In the face of these actions, however, the Obama administration was inconsistent in responding to China. In 2016, Xi Jinping backed down after President Obama warned the Chinese leader there would be serious consequences if China claimed Scarborough Shoal. But the United States did not attempt to block Chinese ships from dredging the reefs. "We talked a big game," I was told by a US Navy commander who had deployed multiple times to the Pacific—including the Spratly Islands. "But we did little in the end."[20]

After seizing islands in the South China Sea, where would

China go next? Zhang and others saw plenty of good targets in the United States.

✳ ✳ ✳ ✳

ON MARCH 7, 2017, the Apache Software Foundation, an open-source nonprofit corporation, announced a bug in certain versions of its Apache Struts software that companies use to develop customer-facing web applications. Apache urged users to fix the patch imme-diately.[21] At the US Department of Homeland Security, the United States Computer Emergency Readiness Team (US-CERT)—which was responsible for analyzing cyber threats, disseminating alerts, and coordinating responses to incidents—issued a warning about a vulnerability in certain versions of the Apache Struts software.[22] If companies failed to fix the bug, hackers could exploit the vulner-ability and access the computer networks of organizations using the software.

Equifax, one of the United States' largest consumer credit report-ing agencies, failed to patch the vulnerability. Equifax compiles and stores massive amounts of consumer information, which it sells to other businesses and organizations that seek to assess the credit of individuals. Its servers had the full names, addresses, Social Secu-rity numbers, birth dates, and driver's license numbers of millions of Americans. Equifax used Apache Struts on its online dispute portal, the location on Equifax's website where users went to correct errors on their credit reports. The bug opened an unguarded back door into a gold mine of data.

Operatives from the PLA's 54th Research Institute—including Wu Zhiyong, Wang Qian, Xu Ke, and Liu Lei—took notice. The secretive 54th Research Institute was situated within the PLA's recently created Strategic Support Force, which centralized China's space, cyber, electronic, and psychological warfare missions.[23] This was a first for China. The Strategic Support Force combined tech-nology and information systems together in an organization that was crucial for offensive operations.[24] For Zhang and other Chinese military leaders, the US homeland was a legitimate target. After all, as Zhang had argued, the United States and other "external forces" had violated Chinese sovereignty by conducting covert operations in Hong Kong.[25]

Wu Zhiyong and his PLA colleagues hacked into Equifax's computer system through the dispute portal. The PLA team then obtained log-in credentials to navigate Equifax's network. Wu and his collaborators spent several weeks running queries to better understand Equifax's database structure and hunting for sensitive information. Once they had accessed files of interest, they stored the information in temporary output files, compressed and divided the files, and ultimately downloaded and exfiltrated the data. Wu and his team took careful steps to evade detection. They routed traffic through approximately thirty-four servers located in nearly twenty countries, used encrypted communication channels within Equifax's network to blend in with normal network activity, deleted compressed files, and wiped log files on a daily basis to eliminate records of their activity.[26]

The size and scope of this cyber robbery was virtually unparalleled. Wu and his PLA colleagues obtained the full names, birth dates, and Social Security numbers of a whopping 145 million Americans, as well as the driver's license numbers for at least 10 million Americans. The PLA hackers also collected credit card numbers and other information belonging to 200,000 American consumers. It was one of China's most significant cyber attacks ever. As US attorney general William Barr remarked in February 2020: "This was an organized and remarkably brazen criminal heist of sensitive information *of nearly half of all Americans.*"[27]

As large as the Equifax cyber operation was, it was still only one among many perpetrated by the PLA under Zhang and other Chinese military leaders. In 2015, the PLA had stolen a massive trove of information from the Office of Personnel Management

(OPM), including the security clearance records of over 20 million Americans—7 percent of the US population.[28] China seized Social Security numbers, passport numbers, birth dates, birthplaces, and multiple modes of contact information. PLA hackers also stole other valuable information about those with security clearances: their residential, employment, travel, educational, criminal, financial, addiction, and mental health history, as well as detailed information on spouses, cohabitants, other family members, and foreign contacts. I was one of the many victims whose information was compromised, and I received a cryptic letter from OPM alerting me that my personal information had been stolen.

In 2015, the FBI assessed that there was a shocking 53 percent increase in economic espionage against US companies from the previous year—and China was the main culprit. "The enormity of the Chinese espionage effort is staggering," lamented the CIA's James Olson. "And it is getting worse."[29] These attacks had now become the norm.

✳   ✳   ✳   ✳

By 2017, Zhang had become one of Xi's most valuable allies not just because of his military advice, political acumen, and childhood relationship—though all of these were important. Zhang had also established a reputation for integrity and aggressiveness in rooting out the pervasive corruption in China, including in the PLA.[30] Two of the PLA's most important generals—Xu Caihou and Guo Boxing—had been detained and prosecuted for corruption. Xu was vice chairman of the CMC, where Zhang now sat, and he had accumulated substantial wealth by demanding bribes for the promotion of officers. Guo also served as vice chairman of the CMC and was expelled from the Communist Party and sentenced to life imprisonment for similarly taking bribes in exchange for PLA promotions. Hundreds of other PLA officers were removed for corruption. "Zhang is well known for his good character and sociability, which will help unify opinion to help Xi carry out his reforms," said one Hong Kong–based military analyst.[31]

In October 2017, Xi promoted Zhang to vice chairman of the CMC, making Zhang one of China's top two most powerful military figures. Zhang had repeatedly warned PLA officers that they needed to work their way up the PLA hierarchy through honesty, hard work, and commitment to the Communist Party—not through personal gain.[32] "Be an upright and clean Communist," Zhang implored.[33]

Under Zhang, the PLA targeted US firms and government agencies at a torrid pace.[34] Chinese government spies obtained confidential information about some of the US Department of Defense's most advanced weapons systems and platforms, including the F-35 Lightning II—the United States' next-generation stealth fighter. Through its involvement with a hacking group known as Advanced Persistent Threat 10 (APT10), China stole hundreds of gigabytes of sensitive data and targeted companies in such fields as aviation, space, satellites, manufacturing, pharmaceuticals, oil and gas exploration and production, communications, computer processing, and maritime systems.[35] A cyber group with links to PLA Unit 78020— called Naikon—used a cyber attack tool termed "Aria-body" to target foreign governments.

Chinese espionage activities were well known, as highlighted by the FBI's arrest of Americans spying for China, such as Alexander Yuk Ching Ma, Kevin Patrick Mallory, and Jerry Chun Shing Lee. But it was not always easy for the US government to attribute cyber attacks to the Chinese government, since the PLA attempted to mask its involvement. Even in cases where the United States had high confidence of PLA activity, US intelligence agencies sometimes worried about publicly acknowledging the attack if it meant revealing their sources and methods. Many US corporations were also leery about acknowledging PLA hacks, because it was bad publicity.

Yet China hardly limited its activity to cyber and covert action.

Its largest and most expensive campaign to expand its economic, political, and military power—the Belt and Road Initiative—was conducted entirely in the open, covered widely by the global media, and undeniable in its initial impact.

✻ ✻ ✻ ✻

IN SEPTEMBER 2018, Zhang met with Amir Hatami, Iran's defense minister, in Beijing. As he stood with Iranian leaders, Zhang discussed one of China's boldest and most important endeavors: the Belt and Road Initiative.[36] Announced by Xi five years earlier, the Belt and Road Initiative was an ambitious global development strategy that used infrastructure investments to expand China's political, economic, and military power.[37] Chinese leaders did not advertise it as irregular warfare. But it was—especially China's use of economic assistance to pressure foreign governments to adopt favorable policies on such issues as Taiwan, Hong Kong, control of islands in the South China Sea, and the plight of Uyghurs in western China. The Belt and Road Initiative was extraordinary in its scope and vision. Xi's goal was to create a vast network of railways, highways, energy pipelines, maritime trade routes, and ports to connect China with the rest of Asia, Europe, the Middle East, and Africa. "Belts" referred to the network of land routes that connected China to Central Asia, the Middle East, Russia, and Europe. "Roads" referred—somewhat confusingly—to the maritime routes, including ports, that connected Chinese seaports to countries in the South China Sea, Indian Ocean, South Pacific, and Mediterranean Sea.

In one sense, China's strategy was not new. The Romans built more than 250,000 miles of road to expand their empire.[38] The Incas constructed a 25,000-mile road system, which ran nearly the length of South America's west coast.[39] China's original Silk Road, established during the Han dynasty 2,000 years ago, was an ancient series of maritime and overland trade routes that connected Asia to Europe. These routes played a key role in China's economic develop-

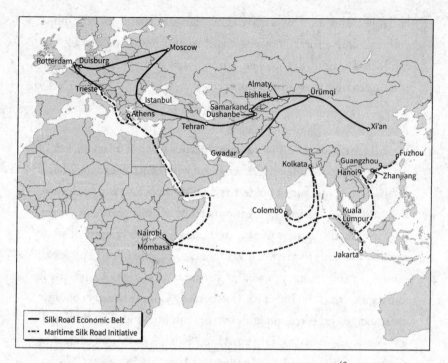

CHINA'S BELT AND ROAD INITIATIVE [40]

ment and helped the country establish political and cultural connections with the rest of the world. But the Belt and Road Initiative was even more ambitious.[41]

More than sixty countries—over two-thirds of the world's population—eventually signed on to projects or expressed a willingness to do so. The countries accounted for 40 percent of global gross domestic product growth and 44 percent of the world's population. According to the US investment bank Morgan Stanley, China's overall expenses over the life of the Belt and Road Initiative could reach $1.3 trillion by 2027.[42] Participating countries found the economic benefits alluring. China agreed to invest in sectors such as transport, construction, manufacturing, and energy—as well as "soft" sectors like banking, culture, and tourism. Beijing promised that such investments would help generate local jobs, secure tax revenues, boost trade, and promote economic growth. In addition to physical infrastructure, China vowed to build fifty special economic zones.

But the flip side was that Beijing used its investments—and the possibility of future investment—as a cudgel against governments to enact policies favorable to China. The issues in play included human rights, the status of Taiwan, crackdowns in Hong Kong, the status of Tibet, Chinese sovereignty in the South China Sea, and China's oppression of Uyghurs. After meeting with Zhang, Serbian president Alexander Vučić—whose country had received nearly $6 billion in investment financing and loans as part of the Belt and Road Initiative—issued a statement that could have been written by the Chinese government itself.[43] "The Serbian government, people and armed forces follow the One-China policy," Vučić remarked, referring to the diplomatic acknowledgment that there is one China, not two: the People's Republic of China and Taiwan. Vučić continued by noting that Serbs "firmly support China's position and propositions on issues concerning China's core interests."[44]

Countries that could not pay back their loans were often indebted to China. Perhaps the quintessential example was Sri Lanka. After the Sri Lankan government failed to pay back loans for an ambitious port project in Hambantota—a project initially proposed by former Sri Lanka president Mahinda Rajapaksa—China took control of the port under a ninety-nine-year lease, along with 150,000 acres of land around the port. In addition, Djibouti racked up a debt to China worth more than 70 percent of its gross domestic product because of Chinese infrastructure projects.[45]

Yet the Belt and Road Initiative was not profitable, and China incurred significant financial costs for some troubled projects.[46] Growth in Chinese overseas construction contracts actually flattened by the end of 2017 and then fell.[47] Local governments and populations were frequently irate at Beijing's preference for Chinese labor and its heavy-handedness, which extended beyond the

Belt and Road Initiative to other projects, like 5G networks. In late 2019, German politicians chastised the Chinese ambassador in Germany—Wu Ken—after he threatened that "there [would] be consequences" if Germany excluded Huawei from its 5G network. Wu issued a thinly veiled threat that Germany's automotive industry could be punished. "Can we also say that German cars are not safe because we're in a position to manufacture our own cars?" Wu asked.[48] Since China was the largest foreign market for German car companies like Volkswagen, many German officials interpreted Wu's comment as a threat to place tariffs on German cars if Germany refused to work with Huawei.[49]

The Belt and Road Initiative was not all politics and economics. Major Belt and Road infrastructure projects also enabled China to expand its military power projection capabilities. One US military assessment concluded that the initiative would likely "drive [China's] military overseas basing" requirements by creating a need for the Chinese military to secure the country's economic investments.[50] China constructed deep-water ports that could be used by PLA blue-water naval vessels, as well as airfields for the PLA Air Force, in such locations as Djibouti; Hambantota, Sri Lanka; and Gwadar, Pakistan. As one US Defense Intelligence Agency assessment concluded:

> China's efforts to enhance its presence abroad, such as establishing its first foreign military base in Djibouti and boosting economic connectivity by reinvigorating the New Silk Road Economic Belt and 21st Century Maritime Road under the "Belt and Road Initiative" (BRI), could enable the PLA to project power at even greater distances from the Chinese mainland.[51]

Pakistan was a prime example. After 9/11, the United States provided massive assistance to Pakistan to capture and kill al-Qaeda leaders and fight the Taliban in neighboring Afghanistan. But with US involvement in the Afghan war winding down and Washington's relationship with Islamabad fraying, Chinese leaders like Zhang dangled the prospect of Chinese investments at an opportune time.[52] China used its economic zone under the China-Pakistan Economic Corridor, a portion of the Belt and Road Initiative, to provide Islamabad with a new generation of fighter jets like the JF-17, navigation systems, radar systems, and onboard weapons. Many Pakistan politicians took the bait, though not all of them. Some Pakistan officials, such as General Qamar Javed Bajwa, who served as chief of army staff, repeatedly complained that it was maddeningly difficult to develop a close rapport with China. On one trip to China, Bajwa brought his wife, Ayesha. She returned exasperated after a half day of shopping and lamented: "We have nothing in common with these people!"[53] Pakistan also became mired in debt and received a multibillion-dollar bailout from the International Monetary Fund. And Chinese officials worried about Pakistan's corruption, persistent project delays, and failure to make payments on time.[54]

Senior US officials became increasingly concerned about Chinese activity outside of Asia. "It became regular to see a Chinese presence in the Middle East," said General Joseph Votel, head of US Central Command. "We saw Chinese construction companies, businesses, and military vessels throughout the region."[55] The same was true in Africa and Latin America, said General Tony Thomas, head of US Special Operations Command. "I ran into the Chinese in Panama and other Latin American countries," he said. "They were in our backyard."[56]

General Thomas was correct, of course. But the Chinese were also in America's front yard.

✳   ✳   ✳   ✳

CHINESE INFLUENCE WAS pervasive inside the United States. In Hollywood, China dangled access to its market of 1.4 billion people in return for positive public relations coverage. The China Film Administration, which is governed by the Chinese

Communist Party, reviews all films and dictates whether, when, and how a movie is released. For unflattering depictions of China and other reasons, it banned numerous US films, including *Seven Years in Tibet* with Brad Pitt and *Lara Croft Tomb Raider: The Cradle of Life* with Angelina Jolie. In the remake of the movie *Red Dawn*, MGM changed the invading army from China to North Korea during the postproduction phase because of fears about the Chinese response.[57]

"Hollywood now regularly censors its own movies to appease the Chinese Communist Party," noted US attorney general William Barr in a stinging rebuke. "This censorship infects not only versions of movies that are released in China, but also many that are shown in American theaters to American audiences."[58] In the Marvel Studios blockbuster *Doctor Strange*, filmmakers altered the nationality of a major character from Tibetan to Celtic out of concern that the China Film Administration would refuse release of the movie in China. Screenwriter C. Robert Cargill explained that "if you acknowledge that Tibet is a place and that he's Tibetan, you risk alienating one billion people." He added that there was a serious risk of "the Chinese government going, 'Hey, you know one of the biggest film-watching countries in the world? We're not going to show your movie because you decided to get political.'"[59]

US sports leagues also faced significant pressure from China. In 2019, the Chinese government reacted angrily when Daryl Morey, the general manager of the Houston Rockets basketball team, supported protesters in Hong Kong. He tweeted: "Fight for Freedom. Stand with Hong Kong."[60] In response, the Chinese consulate in Houston released a statement expressing its "strong dissatisfaction" with Morey's tweet, noting that "anybody with conscience would support the efforts made by the Hong Kong Special Administrative Region to safeguard Hong Kong's social stability."[61] The Chinese government then punished the NBA by canceling television deals and pulling merchandise off the shelves of Chinese stores—which amounted to as much as $400 million in losses for the NBA.[62] As NBA commissioner Adam Silver remarked: "The financial consequences have been and may continue to be fairly dramatic."[63] In 2020, the US government retaliated by ordering China to close its consulate in Houston.[64]

The NBA case was yet another example of Chinese efforts to pressure US companies to comply with China's political positions—in this instance to muzzle criticism of Beijing's authoritarian crackdown in Hong Kong. When companies refused to comply, China was willing to punish them by cutting off market access. The entertainment industry was only one of many sectors. China used access to its huge market to threaten US companies in such sectors as information technology, retail, aerospace, and automobiles. It also strong-armed US and other foreign companies to provide sensitive information to the Chinese government. Former FBI deputy director Sean Joyce resigned from a senior position at Airbnb, Inc., following concerns that the company was sharing customer data—including the phone numbers, email addresses, and messages between users and the company—with the Chinese Communist Party.[65] As Airbnb explained in a filing with the US Securities and Exchange Commission, the company risked losing the ability to operate in China if it didn't comply with the country's data-sharing requirements.[66]

In addition, US universities, which had pushed back against Confucius Institutes and closed many of them, continued to be targeted by an evolving Chinese influence campaign.[67]

✻ ✻ ✻ ✻

IN JANUARY 2020, FBI agents arrived at the office of Charles Lieber, chair of Harvard University's Department of Chemistry and Chemical Biology. Neatly dressed in a Brooks Brothers polo shirt, hiking boots, and cargo pants, Lieber politely greeted the FBI agents. He was a star researcher who had become one of the world's leading experts on nanoscale materials, which involved research on tiny structures—like medical sensors and computer chip components—measured in atoms rather than bulky inches or millimeters. Ironically, Lieber's hobby was growing colossal, award-winning pumpkins—some the size of Volkswagen Beetles—at his gabled house in Lexington, Massachusetts. Several years before, he had won the Giant Pumpkin Grower's weigh-off at Frerichs Farm in Warren, Rhode Island, with a whopping 1,870-pound pumpkin.[68]

FBI agents arrested the flabbergasted professor and charged him with making false statements to federal authorities about his financial relationship with the Chinese government, particularly his participation in China's "Thousand Talents Plan." China established the program to recruit leading experts to bring their knowledge and experience to China and to reward those experts for providing proprietary information.[69] As Zhang argued, scientific and technological advancement and innovation were essential to create a powerful Chinese military.[70] It was not illegal for Americans to participate in the program. "The Thousand Talents Plan is not traditional espionage," the CIA's Mark Kelton said to me. "But the Chinese are essentially trying to recruit people as agents of influence, as well as building their knowledge base on key technologies."[71]

In its bid to acquire—and steal, if necessary—sensitive technology from the United States, the Chinese government saw Lieber as an attractive target. He was a world-renowned expert in nanoscience, a technology with the potential to reshape the world and lead to revolutionary breakthroughs in fields from manufacturing to health care. His Lieber Research Group had received more than $15 million in funding from the National Institutes of Health and the US Department of Defense, which required recipients to disclose significant foreign financial conflicts of interest—including financial support from foreign governments. Lieber had lied both to Harvard and to federal investigators that had interviewed him in 2018 and 2019. Unbeknownst to Harvard, Lieber became a "strategic scientist" in 2011 at the Wuhan University of Technology in

China—which was ground zero of COVID-19 when Lieber was arrested. The university paid Lieber $50,000 per month, provided reimbursement for living expenses of up to $158,000, and awarded him more than $1.5 million to establish a research lab in China.[72]

China's interest in Lieber was part of a much broader campaign to penetrate US universities, research institutions, and companies. "Anything the Chinese can get their hands on, they will try," said Kari Bingen, who served as the number two intelligence official in the US Department of Defense until January 2020. "Artificial intelligence, quantum computing, semiconductors."[73] In January 2021, for example, the FBI indicted MIT mechanical engineering professor Gang Chen for allegedly failing to disclose extensive Chinese government funds in grant applications to the US Department of Energy.[74] In 2021, the FBI opened a new counterintelligence case involving China *every ten hours*, and approximately half of the FBI's counterintelligence investigations involved China.[75]

China was dedicated to becoming a world leader in the development of advanced technology. It pursued researchers working on robotics, nanotechnology, 5G wireless technology, and cloud computing. Xi Jinping outlined his goal of transforming the PLA into a "world-class military" that could compete with the United States.[76] To do so, he would need advances in military technology such as hypersonic and directed-energy weapons. But China also sought other advantages. As Zhang remarked, China's space-based capabilities included the BeiDou positioning system, which established nearly worldwide coverage, on par with American GPS.[77] Its "Made in China 2025" program was a ten-year plan to "transform China into a leading manufacturing power by the year 2049," the 100th anniversary of the founding of the People's Republic of China.[78]

* * * *

IN LIGHT OF these developments, a recent Chinese national defense white paper was frank about security competition. "International strategic competition is on the rise," it said, blaming the United States as the aggressor. "The U.S. has adjusted its national security and defense strategies, and adopted unilateral policies," it concluded. "It has provoked and intensified competition among major countries, significantly increased its defense expenditure, pushed for additional capacity in nuclear, outer space, cyber and missile defense, and undermined global strategic stability."[79] Zhang made similar remarks during a meeting with Russian officials. "The United States and other Western countries are compulsively implementing the politics of hegemony and resorting to harassment, pursuing a containment policy against Russia, China and other countries," said Zhang.[80] China and the United States were fated to be global competitors.

Several months before the FBI arrested Lieber, Xi Jinping gave a speech on a "great national rejuvenation." He heralded a rising China to as-yet-unseen greatness by 2049. In the speech he used the word *douzheng* ("struggle") nearly sixty times.[81] For Xi, Zhang, and other officials, that struggle will inevitably involve competition with China's chief rival, the United States. Since coming to power, Xi—with the support of Zhang and other leaders—attempted to expand Chinese power and weaken the United States and its international partners through a range of irregular activities: building islands through clandestine means, waging cyber espionage that targeted most Americans, coercing countries using transnational projects like the Belt and Road Initiative, expanding information and intelligence collection through China's Digital Silk Road and Huawei, and co-opting US scholars and students through programs like the Thousand Talents Plan.

Although Zhang was one of the few Chinese military officers with any combat experience, his views on warfare had dramatically evolved since the late 1970s and 1980s when he fought Vietnam. Back then, warfare had been largely conventional. Now it was predominantly irregular and occurred daily, if not hourly. In the future, much of China's competition with the United States will likely occur not on a conventional battlefield but in the information and disinformation sphere, on atolls in the Pacific, in the cyber arena, through global investment projects, and in US and other Western universities and companies. As Zhang explained to Chinese military leaders in December 2020, China's ability to compete in the future hinges, in part, on the PLA's effectiveness in the "ideological and political" spheres.[82]

Yet the United States remains ill equipped to compete with China in most of these areas. The US military continues to focus primarily on low-probability conventional war with China, while China's military strategy is to *avoid* a major war. In the economic arena, the United States has neglected to create an attractive alternative to China's Belt and Road Initiative, struggled to push back against Chinese political influence around the globe, and failed to develop an information campaign to counter China's three warfares and the activities of China's United Front Work Department.

PART IV

THE
WAY
FORWARD

11: COUNTERING THE WOLF WARRIORS

THE MOVIE CHARACTER LENG FENG IS THE EPIT-ome of a Chinese superhero. He is a suave former Chinese special operations soldier with jet-black hair, lean physique, skin-tight shirt that highlights his rippling muscles, and supremely confident smile. He is part Rambo, part Bruce Lee. He can handle his AK-47 assault rifle and P226 9-mm pistol just as deftly as his alloy claw knife and bare knuckles. He is a martial arts expert that can jump, kick, and dodge bullets. Most important, he is the main character in China's wildly popular movie franchise, *Wolf Warrior*, whose tagline is, "Anyone who offends China, no matter how remote, must be exterminated." In *Wolf Warrior II*, the franchise's second film and the highest-grossing film in Chinese history, Leng travels to Africa. With help from the Chinese Navy, he rescues helpless African and Chinese civilians from "Big Daddy"—you guessed it, a ruthless American who heads a mercenary company.

The *Wolf Warrior* movies depict China as the only power-ful, trustworthy, and generous world power, which helps foreign countries build their economies, protects them from marauding Americans, and cures deadly pandemics. In the climactic scene of *Wolf Warrior II*, Big Daddy sneers at Leng as they exchange skull-crushing blows. "People like you will always be inferior to people like me," Big Daddy drawls in a perfect American accent as he pre-pares to kill Leng. "Get used to it. Get f*****g used to it!" Leng has been knocked down and stabbed in the gut. Blood pours from his mouth and a gruesome gash above his left eye. But he summons his remaining strength, kills Big Daddy, and—in the movie's most salient line—responds, "That's f*****g history." China is the future; America is the past.

"They think our days are over," said the CIA's Mike Morell. "They think the future is China."[1] Even during the Biden administration, Chinese newspapers trumpeted the end of Pax Americana.[2] The rise of China is a recognizable motif in *Wolf Warrior*. The movie franchise highlights China's global ambitions, the nature of competition with the United States, and—importantly—irregular methods. Leng Feng isn't a knuckle-dragging infantry officer fighting the Americans on conventional battlefields in Asia or Africa. He is a Spiderman-like special operations warrior that uses irregular tactics to out-think, outmuscle, and outperform his American nemesis and win the hearts and minds of populations across the globe.

✳   ✳   ✳   ✳

WOLF WARRIOR II was notable for its international success. It grossed over $800 million worldwide and was seen by millions—though mostly outside of the United States.[3] While American and Western culture continue to dominate the global landscape, Chinese cultural products are catching up. But China's ascendance—at least as portrayed in *Wolf Warrior II*—is not inevitable.

During the United States' last major global struggle, with the Soviet Union, America eventually outmaneuvered its authoritarian competitor, which crumbled in December 1991. Throughout the Cold War, NATO planners prepared for nuclear and conventional war with the Red Army and other Warsaw Pact militaries. But the fear of large-scale destruction—including of cities like New York, Washington, Moscow, and Saint Petersburg—deterred conventional and nuclear war despite several close calls, including the 1962 Cuban Missile Crisis. Instead, the United States and Soviet Union engaged in intense security competition at the irregular level across Latin America, Africa, Asia, and Europe. Both countries backed substate groups and states in an effort to expand their own power and influence. Under the Reagan Doctrine, for example, the United States provided overt and covert assistance to anticommunist governments and resistance movements to roll back communist gains across the globe. The Soviets did the same for the other side. This type of irregular war was anything but "cold."

In the past few years, a growing body of Russian literature—very little of it translated into English—has examined why the United States won the Cold War. As many Russians now understand, they did not lose on a conventional battlefield. They lost in the hearts and minds of Russians, Eastern Europeans, and others across the globe who became disillusioned with the disastrous performance of communism. As the Russian military theorist Igor Panarin wrote, Russia lost the information war. George Kennan was right, Panarin said: "It was Kennan, a person who lived in Russia for many years, who accurately defined the direction of the main attack in the information war against the USSR."[4] Panarin contended that by the 1980s, Soviet political leaders and intelligence professionals had failed to adequately respond to an increasingly successful US information war: "The Central Committee of the Communist Party and the KGB were acting formulaically," he wrote. "Although the true intentions of the adversary in the informational-ideological struggle were revealed, adequate counter-measurements were not implemented. . . . the Soviet special agencies failed to prevent the dissolution of the USSR."[5]

Similarly, Russian colonel Sergey Chekinov and lieutenant general Sergey Bogdanov concluded that US irregular activities were more effective than conventional operations.[6] Some of these arguments doubtless exaggerated what the United States did—including its impact. They also underplayed the weaknesses of the Soviet Union's communist system. But the broader point is unmistakable: a growing body of Russian history now argues that the United States won the Cold War through irregular means.

✳ ✳ ✳ ✳

TODAY, the United States is in a period somewhat akin to the early years of the Cold War—"a 1947 redux," as Undersecretary of Defense Mike Vickers told me—where the United States has an opportunity to refashion what it stands for, what it does, and what it represents in the world.[7] US foreign policy is in the process of a cataclysmic shift from two decades of countering terrorist groups to competing with illiberal powers. The good news is that the United States has the capabilities to fight disinformation, economic coercion, espionage, and authoritarianism—as it showed during the Cold War. But Americans need to reconceptualize what competition is and how to compete more effectively. China, Russia, and Iran are vastly different countries from the Soviet Union, and the world has changed dramatically since the Cold War—from globalization to technology, and from the internet and social media to robotics, artificial intelligence, and nanotechnology.

Americans and future administrations need to ask: What are America's principles as a nation? What are the US objectives at home and abroad? What instruments should the United States use (and not use) to achieve its main objectives? This final chapter argues that the principles and objectives that guide US foreign policy should be linked to the country's democratic values, and US policy should leverage *all* the instruments of power, such as military, diplomatic, financial, development, intelligence, and ideological.

There are several components of an effective US strategy against the likes of Valery Gerasimov, Qassem Soleimani (and his replacement Ismail Qaani), Zhang Youxia, and their successors. These components include building on America's core principles as a nation; understanding US adversaries through a better appreciation of what is occurring "on the other side of the hill," as the 1st Duke of Wellington put it; focusing on the irregular aspects of competition, not just the conventional; improving and expanding influence operations; conducting an offensive, not just defensive, irregular campaign; and rebuilding relationships with allies and partners.

CORE US PRINCIPLES

Perhaps the single most important step in competition is to refashion US foreign policy on the United States' core principles, which have been in place since America's founding. Competition today is, to a great extent, a struggle between rival political, economic, and military *systems*. China is a good example, as former secretary of defense Robert Gates told me: "The Chinese are saying 'Hey, if you want an example of a country that works, just look at us.'" While Gates argued that Maoism is "as dead as a doornail," he nevertheless acknowledged that the Chinese "build great infrastructure. They've brought hundreds of millions of people out of poverty." But that is not all that the Chinese bring, Gates continued with a wry grin: "You have to give up your political rights, and if you're a Uyghur you will end up in a concentration camp. And there is political repression that gets worse every day."[8]

China, Russia, and Iran are all undemocratic and eschew free markets and a free press. They have violently cracked down on democratic movements, developed largely state-run economic systems, and tried to suppress information by creating, respectively, a "Great Firewall," a Russian-language "Runet," and a Persian "halal net." China's digital firewall, for example, banned over 18,000 websites that the government assessed had content unfavorable to China, as well as such platforms and services as Gmail, Google, YouTube, Facebook, Instagram, and numerous virtual private network (VPN) providers.[9] In April 2021, Beijing blocked access in China to the website of the Center for Strategic and International Studies (CSIS), the Washington-based research institution where I work, in response to articles critical of the Chinese government. Overseas, China attempted to stifle critics by jailing dozens of Chinese citizens that used foreign social media platforms like Twitter to criticize Xi Jinping and his government.[10] These three countries are challenging a US-led international system that has been committed since World War II to free market international economic institutions, bilateral and regional security organizations, and democratic political norms.

A failure to revolutionize US strategic thinking and planning will have enormous implications for the United States. "The United States is backing into a Cold War, but without a strategy. It is like the proverbial bus to Abilene," General David Petraeus said to me—a reference to the paradox in which a group of individuals decide on a course of action that is counter to the preferences of most of them. "How did we get on this bus? Where is it going?"[11]

Countries like China and Russia aim to undermine US democratic institutions at home, weaken US power and influence overseas, and spread authoritarian principles across the globe. US president Ronald Reagan described competition with Moscow in black-and-white terms, as a "struggle between right and wrong and good and evil."[12] Similarly, America's competitors today do not have a desirable ideology to sell to foreign countries. "The Chinese don't have political values that others want to model themselves after. But they do have money," said Mike Morell.[13] The same is true of Russia. "No one wants Russian television. No one wants to be like Russia," said former JSOC commander General Stanley McChrystal.[14]

During the Reagan administration, National Security Decision Directive 75, "U.S. Relations with the USSR," bluntly stated that US policy toward the Soviet Union would consist of three interrelated objectives: to reverse Soviet expansionism by competing on a sustained basis in all international arenas, to promote change in the Soviet Union toward a more pluralistic political and economic system, and to engage in negotiations with the Soviet Union (when feasible) that protected and enhanced US interests.[15] To accomplish these objectives, the directive argued that the United States needed to use military, economic, political, and other instruments—

including ideological ones: "U.S. policy must have an ideological thrust which clearly affirms the superiority of U.S. and Western values of individual dignity and freedom, a free press, free trade unions, free enterprise, and political democracy over the repressive features of Soviet Communism." The document noted that Eastern Europe—situated in Moscow's backyard—was an essential battleground: "The primary U.S. objective in Eastern Europe is to loosen Moscow's hold on the region while promoting the cause of human rights in individual East European countries."[16]

Today, the core principles of the United States are succinctly explained in the preamble to the US Constitution: "to form a more perfect Union, establish justice, insure domestic Tranquility, provide for the common defense, promote the general Welfare, and secure the Blessings of Liberty to ourselves and our Posterity."[17] Freedom—of the ballot box, the press, and even religion—is what the United States is about. It is a nation, as Abraham Lincoln reminded us, "conceived in Liberty, and dedicated to the proposition that all men are created equal."[18] These principles were tested when far too many Americans—including President Trump himself—attempted to undermine the outcome of the November 2020 elections. As one Chinese newspaper columnist argued: "There are so many American double standards . . . how hypocritical are the 'freedom' and 'equality' they advertise."[19] Moving forward, US foreign policy must be grounded, first and foremost, in protecting the freedom of Americans from external enemies, advancing US prosperity, and setting an example for governments and populations overseas.

But there are limits to what the United States can and should do overseas, particularly with military force. "One of the errors in Iraq and Afghanistan," Gates reminded me in our discussion, "was trying to impose democracy at the point of a gun."[20] The goal of US foreign policy should not be what some have called "liberal hegemony": to spread liberal democracy by toppling regimes and attempting to force liberal values on foreign populations through military intervention.[21] The United States has a responsibility to encourage free trade, democracy, human rights, and other core values—but not by military force. The Cold War ended not because NATO countries invaded Poland, East Germany, and other Warsaw Pact countries, but because their populations rose up against tyranny.

THE OTHER SIDE OF THE HILL

The next step is to better understand how China, Russia, and Iran—including future Gerasimovs, Soleimanis, and Zhangs—view competition with the United States. This step is about comprehending what is happening on the "other side of the hill." What are their objectives? What are the main instruments they use? What are their exploitable vulnerabilities and weaknesses? In his "Long Telegram," George Kennan encouraged the United States to study the Soviet Union "with [the] same courage, detachment, objectivity, and...determination...with which [a] doctor studies [an] unruly and unreasonable individual."[22] The same is true today with China, Russia, and Iran. As this book highlights, a close analysis of Russian, Iranian, and Chinese activity indicates that all three countries have established irregular campaigns against the United States. In many cases, their leaders, exemplified by Gerasimov, Soleimani, and Zhang, were influenced by US activity over the past several decades in countries like Kosovo, Afghanistan, Iraq, and Libya.

Unfortunately, the United States has not learned from its own past. Beijing invests substantial resources in translating and exploring the contours of American culture and politics. Unlike during the Cold War, the US government and private sector have failed to invest in the language skills and expertise to effectively compete with the Chinese Communist Party. US national security documents argue that the United States and China are engaged in a long-term strategic competition. But you wouldn't know it by looking at the US media and the general lack of funding for Chinese language programs—a role that was filled by Beijing's Confucius Institutes at US college campuses.[23]

COVID-19 highlighted the problem. There were dueling narratives from the highest levels of the US and Chinese governments about the origins of—and responses to—the pandemic, including those peddled by Xi Jinping and Zhang Youxia. Yet when Americans talked about Beijing's side of the story, they generally referred to a small selection of commentary in English that consisted largely of statements by the Chinese foreign ministry's spokesperson, Twitter accounts of prominent Chinese commentators, and the Communist Party's newspapers. Americans might be forgiven for not even realizing there was a debate inside China about the government's slow response, cover-ups, and doctored numbers. The problem is that these discussions are happening in Chinese, not English. "The lack of translated material from Chinese into English is a real travesty," MIT professor Taylor Fravel told me. "There is no understanding of context, no understanding of what the Chinese are saying to themselves, and no understanding of how Chinese views have changed over time."[24]

Beijing has not made the same mistake. *Cankao Xiaoxi*, the Chinese newspaper with the largest domestic circulation, is a compilation of foreign news articles—including English-language reports—translated into Chinese.[25] There is sadly no equivalent in the United States. China has also invested significant resources into English-language training to better understand its main competitor. China's Foreign Languages Publishing Administration, which is part of the Communist Party's Central Propaganda Department, distributes the party line on myriad issues to overseas audiences, conducts research on foreign media, and implements language training programs. Its operating budget doubled from $48 million in 2009 to $97 million in 2019.[26] The market for English-language training in China ballooned to $18 billion, with 70 percent of that revenue coming from the instruction of children. In contrast, the market size for all language instruction in the United States was a paltry $1.6 billion.[27] Even though China's population outstrips America's, Beijing still spends more than twice as much per capita.

American leaders during the Cold War would have been appalled at this discrepancy. The "Long Telegram," one of the most influential US government documents of the Cold War, was written by George Kennan, a Russian speaker par excellence and an expert on the Soviet Union. Many of the influential US Cold War thinkers, such as Kennan, Charles Bohlen, and Richard Pipes, were true experts with a deep knowledge of Soviet politics, culture, history, and language. The American government also invested significant resources in conducting information campaigns and translating Soviet documents into English. Among the most important US organizations was the Foreign Broadcast Information Service, which monitored, translated, and disseminated massive amounts of news from the Soviet Union, Cuba, and other countries. Researchers, activists, journalists, and policy makers—including this author—relied on its invaluable translations. When the Cold War ended, however, the US slashed the budgets for these types of organizations. In 2019, with little fanfare, the United States shut down all outside access to the Open Source Enterprise, the successor of the Foreign Broadcast Information Service.

There is still time to fix these mistakes. One step is to build a twenty-first-century open-source information service with congressional aid. The United States should start by translating materials from its main competitors—such as China, Russia, and Iran—and making them publicly available. Every Xi Jinping speech, for example, should be available in English within twenty-four to forty-eight hours. Machine learning and translation technology from programs like Google Translate have been helpful stopgaps. But they cannot replace translation by humans with a nuanced understanding of local culture, politics, and history.

In addition, the US government needs to increase the resources devoted to educating its diplomats, soldiers, and spies in Chinese, Russian, and Persian language, history, politics, and culture. China should be the main focus. In the "Long Telegram," Kennan urged Americans to study the Soviet Union and truly understand "the nature of the movement with which we are dealing."[28] He would certainly say the same today. "We are way behind," said General McChrystal. "We need to make sure our soldiers and diplomats learn languages—Russian, Chinese, Persian."[29] Even elite US soldiers and spies are way behind. "How many of our special operations forces speak Farsi, Russian, or Mandarin?" asked Stu Bradin, a career US special operations soldier. "Not many," he responded. "We are not prepared."[30] The same is true of spies. "We need language and cultural expertise on countries like China," Mark Kelton, former head of counterintelligence at the CIA, told me.[31]

But the United States is not there—and is not even close yet.

IRREGULAR WARFARE: REBALANCING PRIORITIES

The United States also needs to get over its obsession with conventional war. The issue is not whether to focus on conventional *or* irregular aspects of competition. Both are important, as Secretary of Defense Gates reminded me.[32] The challenge, then, is to find an equilibrium. "It is important to get a balance between conventional and irregular activities," said Admiral Bill McRaven. "You have to plan for conventional war. But you also need irregular capabilities."[33] As the lives and experiences of Gerasimov, Soleimani, and Zhang attest, they and their countries established irregular strategies and capabilities based, in part, on closely watching the successes and failures of US warfare over the past several decades. As Deputy Secretary of Defense Kathleen Hicks explained, these countries have turned to irregular activities "because US supremacy at the conventional and strategic levels of military conflict remains unsurpassed."[34]

Yet the United States today is far too heavily weighted toward conventional war.[35] The unclassified portion of the Trump administration's *National Defense Strategy* was virtually silent on irregular competition.[36] Not until the end of the administration—one month before the 2020 presidential election—did the Department of Defense finally release an unclassified irregular warfare annex to the *National Defense Strategy*.[37] "Many of you spent most of your career fighting irregular warfare or engaging in it," said Secretary of Defense Mark Esper to a gathering at the US Naval War College in Newport, Rhode Island. "But times have changed," he continued, suggesting that the United States needed to focus on conventional war.[38] It was an erroneous statement from a sitting secretary of defense. In separate remarks, Esper emphasized what he considered the most serious threat to the United States. "Our strategic competitors are China and Russia and we must be prepared for *a high-end fight* with them in the future," he remarked, again repeating the mantra of needing "to conduct *regular warfare*."[39] As has been repeatedly highlighted in this book, US adversaries are not focused mainly on conventional warfare.

When senior US special operations officials, led by Assistant Secretary of Defense Owen West, briefed US undersecretary of defense John Rood in the spring of 2018 about developing an irregular warfare annex to the *National Defense Strategy*, Rood was skeptical. "Why are we bothering to do this?" he asked in one meeting. "We aren't doing irregular warfare anymore." Those in the room were incredulous, since Rood was conflating irregular warfare and counterterrorism. "He just didn't get it," said one official present at the meeting. "John had an ossified view of competition; all he cared about was conventional warfare."[40] To get anything done, West had to go straight to the then deputy secretary of defense Patrick Shanahan. "Rood just didn't care about irregular competition."[41]

But the problem is not just at the Pentagon. Members of Congress, such as Senator Tom Cotton of Arkansas, advocated spending billions of dollars on US submarines, jet fighters, and missile defense systems in the Asia-Pacific for a conventional war with China, showing little interest in irregular warfare.[42] Most of the war games funded by the US Department of Defense over the past several years—including those I participated in—focused on conventional wars. Long-term US Department of Defense research and development, budget planning, training, and force structure are fixated on conventional war. Professional military education at such locations as the US Army War College, US Army Command and General Staff College, and National Defense University is heavily biased toward conventional war.

"This is a strategically bankrupt approach to competition," said Lieutenant General Michael Nagata. "We are building a military for the struggle we *want* to have. We are not building a military for the struggle we are *going* to have—and we are having right now."[43] In their professional education curriculum, military schools need to include more about Chinese, Russian, and Iranian irregular activity, as well as such issues as irregular warfare, influence operations, denial and deception, and economic coercion. Just as important, the military needs to establish defense planning scenarios, operational plans (or OPLANs—detailed plans that combatant commanders develop for conducting joint military operations), and war games for irregular competition.

One example is Taiwan, where the vast majority of classified planning scenarios, OPLANs, and war games focus on a conventional war with China. But how well is the United States prepared for a Chinese attempt to overthrow the government in Taiwan through subversion and sabotage? The answer is bleak: not well prepared. "The Taiwan Strait is the new Fulda Gap," said Mark Mitchell, who served as acting assistant secretary of defense for special operations.[44] He was referring to a lowland corridor near the border between East and West Germany, which Western military strategists identified as a possible route for a Soviet invasion of Western Europe during the Cold War. "There are some senior navy officers who long to be the next winner of the Battle of Midway," added Nagata. "Some may have grown up hoping for it. Yet that type of war is not likely to happen in a Taiwan scenario. It is the wrong model, especially since Taiwan could be lost today without a shot being fired."[45]

Nevertheless, some US officials understood the importance of irregular warfare. As acting secretary of defense Christopher Miller told me: "We're not going to go force on force [with countries like China and Russia]. That's ridiculous. Why would anybody fight us force on force? They're going to use these irregular tools and these irregular techniques to try to, you know, gain advantage on us."[46]

INFLUENCE OPERATIONS: OFFENSE AND DEFENSE

In a letter to US painter and Revolutionary War veteran John Trumbull, George Washington wrote that "offensive operations, often times" are "the surest, if not the only ... means of defence."[47] The United States needs to devote substantial resources and expertise in influence campaigns to compete directly with China's three warfares (*san zhong zhanfa*), Russia's active measures (*aktivnyye meropriyatiya*) and asymmetrical actions (*asimmetrichnym*), and Iran's soft war (*jang-e narm*). As Gerasimov remarked, Russia clearly understood that "the information sphere, having no pronounced national borders, provides opportunities for remote, covert influence ... on the population of countries" like the United States.[48]

Unfortunately, organizations like the US Department of State are woefully underfunded. The State Department's budget is roughly thirteen times smaller than the Department of Defense budget.[49] To the degree that US policy makers are thinking about—and planning for—information campaigns at all, they are an afterthought, stovepiped among multiple government agencies and poorly resourced. The US government lacks an integrated information campaign or organization to combat Russian, Iranian, and Chinese propaganda and disinformation. During the Reagan administration, the US government broadcast radio programs into Eastern Europe and the Soviet Union. The administration took information campaigns seriously, more than doubling the budget for Radio Free Europe and Radio Liberty, and nearly doubling the budget for the US Information Agency.[50] But in 1999, the US State Department shut down the US Information Agency, which had been responsible for some of the United States' most effective efforts against the Soviet Union. And despite the creation of organizations like the Global Engagement Center at the State Department—which focuses on countering foreign propaganda and disinformation—these types of organizations are starved of resources and undervalued.

Conducting an effective irregular campaign requires both defensive *and offensive* operations. The United States needs to wage offensive information operations against China, Russia, and Iran to advance US interests and deter its adversaries from aggressive actions. "Putin and Xi share a similar fear," said Mike Morell. "They are nervous about instability in their own countries."[51] US support for democratic reforms and a free press threaten the authoritarian control in these countries.

There are at least three components of an effective offensive campaign. First, US efforts should be based, in part, on leveraging US democratic strengths and encouraging reforms in Beijing, Moscow, and Tehran. Their authoritarian political systems and attempt to control access to information—including through state-run media—make them vulnerable to a US and Western information campaign.

Second, the United States and its partners should proactively highlight examples of malign activity, human rights abuses, and corruption by its adversaries. Zhang Youxia's obsessive focus on corruption demonstrated that it is a serious problem in China—

including in the People's Liberation Army.[52] Some of the best work may come from investigative journalists at Western newspapers and magazines, not just US or other Western governments. Examples of vulnerabilities include:

* Chinese, Russian, and Iranian involvement in human rights abuses, such as their participation in the arrest, torture, or assassination of defectors, political opponents, and those investigating or prosecuting corruption and human rights abuses (such as journalists and lawyers). China already has its hands full, from protesters in Hong Kong and Taiwan to Uyghurs in the Xinjiang autonomous region of China. So does Russia with the poisoning of former Russian intelligence officer Sergei Skripal in the United Kingdom, as well as the attempted assassination and then arrest of Russian opposition leader Aleksei Navalny.

* Problems with regional and international economic campaigns like China's Belt and Road Initiative, which sometimes placed exorbitant debt on countries and for which Beijing often relied on Chinese labor overseas rather than local workers.

* Corruption and cheating scandals, which are pervasive in China, Russia, and Iran. In China, for example, PLA officers have frequently paid bribes to get promoted. Both Russia and China also have been embroiled in massive doping scandals with their athletes, including for the Olympics.

* Economic problems, including high unemployment, local growth rates, and massive income disparity that Beijing, Moscow, and Tehran may—and already do—try to hide from their populations.

✳ Economic coercion against foreign countries, companies, and educational institutions. Chinese pressure in the United States has ranged from Hollywood to the NBA to virtually any US company that wants to do business in China. But it is not just the United States. After Australia called for an investigation into the origins of COVID-19, for example, China slapped restrictions on imports of Australian coal, wine, barley, cotton, and other goods.

✳ Attempts to control information through China's "Great Firewall," Iran's "halal net," and Russia's "Runet." Most populations want access to other sources of news—not just state-run media.

✳ Instances of malign intelligence collection overseas, including leveraging Chinese corporations such as Huawei and access to its 5G network. In 2018, French newspapers leaked a story—which turned out to be true—that Chinese intelligence agencies had siphoned off data from the African Union headquarters in Ethiopia, which the Chinese had built.[53]

✳ Espionage and clandestine influence in the United States, including at US universities, corporations, and government agencies. China's Confucius Institutes and Thousand Talents Plan have been controversial because of their connection to the Communist Party of China. Russia has conducted numerous aggressive cyber operations inside the United States—including the massive attack orchestrated by Russia's Foreign Intelligence Service, or SVR, against US companies and government agencies that involved compromising the US software company SolarWinds.

✳ Antiregime riots, protests, and demonstrations that highlight the weakness of the regimes in China, Russia, and Iran.

All three of these countries have faced—and will likely face again—protests from their local populations because of economic, political, and other grievances.

* Political and health failures, such as the outbreak of COVID-19 in Wuhan, China.

As CIA director Michael Hayden said to me: "Russia, China, and Iran are all vulnerable to information campaigns. The United States should be supporting protest movements calling for democracy."[54] During the Cold War, irregular warfare involved taking risks. In some cases, as with the CIA's covert support of Poland's Solidarity during the 1980s, those risks paid off by weakening the Soviet Union and its partners. But in other cases, as in Nicaragua, the Reagan administration made significant mistakes—including during the Iran-Contra affair. Because of these risks, some US officials will strongly resist engaging in irregular activities. While it is important to weigh the pros and cons of specific actions, the United States would *never* have succeeded in undermining Soviet power and influence without taking prudent risks that exploited its adversary's vulnerabilities.

Third, offensive operations require leveraging defectors, émigrés, and dissidents from China, Russia, and Iran—including intellectuals and scientists—for information campaigns. Soviet and Eastern European defectors and dissidents were an important tool in the irregular warfare battles of the Cold War and a critical source of information. Their testimonies were helpful in constructing powerful, emotional, and truthful narratives that undermined the Soviet Union and its ideology. Defectors like Stanislav Levchenko and Ladislav Bittman also provided critical insights into how active measures worked and how to fight back.[55] The United States needs to find opportunities to effectively identify and exploit defectors and dissidents from all of its competitors—including China, Russia, and Iran.

ALLIES AND PARTNERS

Finally, effective competition will not be possible without the active support of US allies and partners. During the Cold War, allies and partners played a critical role in irregular warfare against the Soviet Union. As highlighted in a memo from US secretary of state George Shultz to President Reagan, "maintaining the vitality of our alliances" was essential to competition.[56] A Reagan National Security Council paper emphasized the importance of "our ability to build and maintain domestic and allied support for the competitive aspects of our Soviet policy."[57] US partners were helpful in publicly undermining the falsities of Soviet disinformation campaigns and forgeries, providing aid to state and nonstate partners against Soviet-backed groups and regimes, imposing economic sanctions, and aiding covert action programs. They were also a target of Soviet active measures.

Effective irregular warfare today requires the assistance of US allies and partners. Australia blocked the purchase of Huawei 5G telecommunications gear for its national network and was an outspoken critic of China's human rights abuses and anti-democratic practices. France, Germany, and the United Kingdom condemned Vladimir Putin's assassination of dissidents and offensive cyber operations in the West, including their respective countries. In many cases, the United States will need to train, advise, and assist state and nonstate actors across the globe to balance against China, Russia, and Iran—and to work by, with, and through its partners. This is classic irregular warfare.[58]

But rallying that support will be a difficult task. The relationship between the United States and virtually all of its friends suffered under the Trump administration. Every single former US official I interviewed—from Secretary of Defense Gates to CIA director Hayden—bemoaned the damage done to US partners. All were frustrated by President Trump's condescending tone toward far too many foreign leaders, the transactional nature of US foreign policy, the disregard for institutions like NATO, and the absence of an appealing message to foreign countries. "'Make America Great Again' was not an attractive narrative for the rest of the world," said General McChrystal. "What is our message to the world?"[59] It did not help that organizations like the US State Department became backwaters of US foreign policy. "Of the eighteen countries we have diplomatic relations with in the US Central Command area, we had confirmed ambassadors in only seven at one point," said General Joseph Votel, the head of US Central Command. "Think of the terrible message we have sent to countries like Jordan—critical to our regional security strategy. We have given them a series of short-term chargés d'affaires—great public servants, but without the weight that comes with presidential appointment and Senate confirmation."[60]

* * * *

THANKFULLY, there is hope. But hope needs to begin with a recognition that competition with China, Russia, and Iran is inevitable. The authoritarianism and illiberalism at the root of Chinese, Russian, and Iranian political and economic systems are antithetical to Western values. All of these countries view the United States as their main adversary. Competition is, to a great extent, a struggle over ideologies and systems. Much is at stake, including the shape and makeup of political norms, the international trading system, multilateral security organizations, and international institutions like the United Nations.[61] The penalty for a US and broader Western failure will not likely be a conventional or nuclear war between major powers, but rather a devolution of the international system into spheres of influence and a deterioration in the number of democratic countries.

This is not to say that cooperation is impossible or even unpalatable. Competition and cooperation are not zero-sum. Reagan and Gorbachev reached a historic arms control agreement during the height of the Cold War. China will remain an important trading partner in the future and a critical market for US companies. China's economy is growing, its manufacturing sector is the largest in the world by a wide margin, its population of 1.4 billion is an attractive market for US companies, and the country boasts 400 million millennials—five times the number in the United States.[62] Russia and the United States also share common interests in nonproliferation, global energy markets, counterterrorism, trade, and other areas. In addition, not all competition is bad. Athletes, spelling-bee contestants, corporations, and universities all compete with each other.

The United States should ultimately take solace in the fact that China, Russia, and Iran are vulnerable to a campaign that exploits their weaknesses at home and abroad by encouraging democratic reforms, opening up financial markets, and undermining the state's control of information. Many of their citizens likely want greater transparency, more access to objective sources of news and information, and more influence in choosing their leaders.

In the Chinese movie *Wolf Warrior II*, the only virtuous American in the movie, Rachel Smith, attempts to contact the US embassy when marauders attack African and Chinese civilians inside a factory. "Why are you calling the Americans?" asks the movie's hero, Leng Feng. "Where are they? It is a waste of time." A "Fortress America" that pulls back from the world may not answer. But is that the kind of country most Americans want? Or is it closer to the one described by the American poet Langston Hughes?

> *Let America be America again.*
> *Let it be the dream it used to be.*
> *Let it be the pioneer on the plain*
> *Seeking a home where he himself is free.*[63]

ACKNOWLEDGMENTS

Sweet are the uses of adversity,
Which, like the toad, ugly and venomous,
Wears yet a precious jewel in his head;
And this our life, exempt from public haunt,
Finds tongues in trees, books in the running brooks,
Sermons in stones, and good in every thing.

—William Shakespeare, *As You Like It*, act 2, scene 1

THIS BOOK IS THE PRODUCT OF OVER TWO DECADES of "adversity" as described by the immortal William Shakespeare— of thinking about, and struggling with, the concept of competition. Thankfully, I had lots of help along the way. The book would not have been possible without early discussions with Eric Lupfer, my agent, and Tom Mayer, my editor at W. W. Norton. Eric helped shape the concept of the book in the early stages, when I needed his assistance the most. Tom was a true inspiration to work with—a gifted editor, a thoughtful colleague, and a wonderful team player. The entire Norton team was an extraordinary pleasure to work with—yet again. William Warder Norton launched the firm in 1923 with a commitment to publish "books that live," and it has been more like a family to me than a publishing house. Many others were extraordinarily helpful during the copyediting and publication phases, including Lauren Abbate, Nneoma Amadiobi, Rebecca Homiski, Rachel Salzman, and Dassi Zeidel. Stephanie Hiebert did an outstanding job in copyediting the manuscript, clarifying numerous passages, and catching several errors.

As with any book, there is a long list of individuals that contributed to the research, writing, rewriting, and editing over the course of its evolution. Thanks to James Suber, Alex Friedland, Jacob Ware, and Grace Hwang for their superb research assistance along the way—especially tracking down articles and information on Valery Gerasimov, Qassem Soleimani, and Zhang Youxia. We went down numerous rabbit holes together and occasionally struck gold. The Mason Library at Johns Hopkins University's School of Advanced International Studies, where I teach, was helpful in tracking down obscure books through interlibrary loan on everything from the Islamic Revolutionary Guard Corps's history of the Iran-Iraq War to biographies of Qassem Soleimani.

I also owe a special debt of gratitude to several individuals who read and commented on the manuscript: Jude Blanchette, Hal Brands, Samuel Charap, Christopher Chivvis, James Dobbins, Michael Mazarr, Eric Robinson, Norman Roule, and Fred Suria. Their critiques were invaluable and saved me from faulty logic and countless empirical mistakes. Thanks also to several individuals involved in translating documents into English from Russian, Mandarin, and Persian—including Joaquim Ferreira and his team at Etcetera Language Group, Inc., Ashley Lane, and Ivan Khokhotva. I took two years of Russian in graduate school at the University of Chicago but had forgotten most of it by the time I started this book.

In addition, thanks to those who agreed to discuss their thoughts on warfare and competition. One of the most gracious was Charles Cleveland. I spent countless mornings sitting on his front porch, sipping coffee, munching on pastries, and talking about the finer points of irregular warfare. Others included Jeff Benson, Kari Bingen, Jude Blanchette, Dennis Blasko, Ryan Crocker, James Dobbins, Michael Donofrio, Taylor Fravel, Mike Green, John Hamre, Timothy Heath, Robert Gates, Michael Hayden, Mark Kelton, James Lewis, Carter Malkasian, Michael Mazarr, Stanley McChrystal, William McRaven, Christopher Miller, Mark Mitchell, Michael Morell, Michael

Nagata, David Petraeus, Norman Roule, Tony Thomas, Michael Vickers, Joseph Votel, and Juan Zarate. Stuart Bradin, Meaghan Keeler-Pettigrew, Keenan Yoho, Chelsea Hamashin, Rick Lamb, and others involved with the Global SOF Foundation provided a particularly useful environment for discussing thoughts and concepts on irregular warfare.

At CSIS, a special thanks to John Hamre, Craig Cohen, and Josie Gabel for their stewardship and friendship. I had numerous conversations with John Hamre about competition, cooperation, and American values. He is a gold mine of wisdom. Also thanks to Deputy Secretary of Defense and former CSIS colleague Kathleen Hicks. My numerous conversations with her over the years, along with her extensive work on "gray zone" activities, significantly influenced my views. Numerous CSIS experts also helped shape my views on Russia, Iran, China, and competition—including Jon Alterman, Samuel Brannen, Mark Cancian, James Cartwright, Seth Center, Victor Cha, Heather Conley, Anthony Cordesman, Shannon Culbertson, Melissa Dalton, Rachel Ellehuus, Alice Friend, Bonnie Glaser, Timothy Goyer, Jason Gresh, Todd Harrison, Jonathan Hillman, Andrew Hunter, Tom Karako, Brian Katz, Clare Linkins, Edmund Loughran, Eric McQueen, Joe Moye, Gregory Poling, John Schaus, Lindsey Sheppard, Suzanne Spaulding, and Tobias Switzer. Those that I worked with at the CSIS Transnational Threats Project were instrumental along the way, including Catrina Doxsee, Nicholas Harrington, Grace Hwang, Max Markusen, Danika Newlee, and Charles Vallee.

Thanks to my parents (Alec and Sethaly) and brothers (Alex, Josh, and Clark) for their support and humor during the research and writing phases. They helped me see the good in everything, to paraphrase Shakespeare. My father breezed through the entire manuscript over a weekend in the summer of 2020—and offered helpful comments. Finally, thanks to my wife (Suzanne) and daughters (Elizabeth and Alexandra) for making me smile and creating a happy and loving home. I dedicate this book to you.

NOTES

Note: Where interviewees are not identified by name, the interviews were conducted in confidentiality, and the names are withheld by mutual agreement.

CHAPTER 1: THE WRONG WAR

1. Edward Wong, Matthew Rosenberg, and Julian E. Barnes, "Chinese Agents Helped Spread Messages That Sowed Virus Panic in U.S., Officials Say," *New York Times*, April 23, 2020.

2. Mihir Zaveri, "Be Wary of Those Texts from a Friend of a Friend's Aunt," *New York Times*, March 16, 2020.

3. National Security Council (@WHNSC), Twitter, March 15, 2020, 11:48 p.m.

4. Interview with former US intelligence agency leader, 2020.

5. Lijian Zhan (@zlj517), Twitter, March 12, 2020, 10:37 a.m.

6. The interview was published by CGTN Arabic TV on March 17, 2020, with Chinese vlogger "Ms. V." To watch the video, see "On China's Official Arabic-Language TV: COVID-19 Does Not Appear to Have Originated in China," *MEMRI*, Special Dispatch no. 8704, April 17, 2020.

7. Юлия Папшева [Julia Papsheva], "Коронавирус: биологическая война США против России и Китая" [Coronavirus: American biological warfare against Russia and China], Звезда, [Star], January 29, 2020.

8. "Coronavirus May Be a Product of U.S. 'Biological Attack' Aimed at Iran and China, IRGC Chief Claims," RT, March 5, 2020.

9. "Coronavirus May Be U.S. 'Biological Attack': IRGC Head Hossein Salami," Al Arabiya, March 5, 2020.

10. See, for example, Mark F. Cancian, *U.S. Military Forces in FY 2021: Navy* (Washington, DC: Center for Strategic and International Studies, November 9, 2020); Mark F. Cancian, *U.S. Military Forces in FY 2021:*

Army (Washington, DC: Center for Strategic and International Studies, October 28, 2020); Michael R. Gordon, "Biden to Review Nuclear-Arms Programs," *Wall Street Journal*, December 26, 2020.

11. Robert Gates, interview by the author, June 17, 2020.

12. See, for example, "美方对待暴力示威的荒谬逻辑" [The absurd logic of the United States' treatment of violent demonstrations], 人民日报 [People's daily], January 14, 2021; "人民锐评：世界见证美式"双标"大型翻车现场" [People's daily editorial commentary: The world watches as the American "double standard" collides in real-time], 人民日报 [People's daily], January 8, 2021.

13. See Richard Wike, Jacob Poushter, Janell Fetterolf, and Mary Mordecai, *U.S. Image Plummets Internationally as Most Say Country Has Handled Coronavirus Badly* (Washington, DC: Pew Research Center, September 15, 2020); Jacob Poushter and Christine Huang, *Climate Change Still Seen as the Top Global Threat, but Cyberattacks a Rising Concern* (Washington, DC: Pew Research Center, February 10, 2019); John Gramlich and Kat Devlin, *More People around the World See U.S. Power and Influence as a 'Major Threat' to Their Country* (Washington, DC: Pew Research Center, February 14, 2019).

14. Michael Morell, interview by the author, May 21, 2020.

15. Charles Cleveland, interview by the author, May 15, 2020.

16. Michael Hayden, interview by the author, May 18, 2020.

17. William McRaven, interview by the author, May 21, 2020.

18. Kathleen H. Hicks and Melissa Dalton, *By Other Means Part II: US Priorities in the Gray Zone* (Lanham, MD: Rowman and Littlefield, 2019), 2.

19. Joseph Votel, interview by the author, May 21, 2020.

20. B. H. Liddell Hart, *The Other Side of the Hill: Germany's Generals, Their Rise and Fall, with Their Own Account of Military Events, 1939–1945* (London: Pan Books, 1999).

21. Louis J. Jennings, ed., *The Croker Papers: The Correspondence and Diaries of the Late Right Honourable John Wilson Croker*, vol. 3 (London: John Murray, 1884), 275.

22. Tony Thomas, interview by the author, May 22, 2020.

23. John Pomfret, "What America Didn't Anticipate about China," *Atlantic*, October 16, 2019.

24. Валерий Герасимов [Valery Gerasimov], "Влияние современного характера вооруженной борьбы на направленность строительства и развития Вооруженных Сил Российской Федерации. Приоритетные задачи военной науки в обеспечении обороны страны" [The influence of the contemporary nature of armed struggle on the focus of the con-

struction and development of the armed forces of the Russian Federation. Priority tasks of military science in safeguarding the country's defense], Вестник Академии военных наук [Journal of the Academy of Military Sciences] 62, no. 2 (2018): 16–22.

25. 张又侠, 王西欣 [Zhang Youxia and Wang Xixin], "在一体化训练实践中推进中国特色军事变革" [Promoting military transformation with Chinese characteristics through integrated training practices], 解放军报 [PLA daily], May 25, 2004.

26. George F. Kennan, "Organizing Political Warfare," April 30, 1948, History and Public Policy Program Digital Archive, Wilson Center, Washington, DC.

27. General Sir Nick Carter, interview by the author, April 28, 2021. Emphasis added.

28. The US government's formal definition of "irregular warfare" can be found in US Department of Defense, *Summary of the Irregular Warfare Annex to the National Defense Strategy* (Washington, DC: Department of Defense, 2020). Also see, for example, Charles T. Cleveland, *The American Way of Irregular Warfare: An Analytical Memoir* (Santa Monica, CA: RAND, 2020); David H. Ucko and Thomas A. Marks, *Crafting Strategy for Irregular Warfare: A Framework for Analysis and Action* (Washington, DC: National Defense University Press, July 2020).

29. See, for example, the "toolkit" highlighted in Kathleen H. Hicks and Alice Hunt Friend, *By Other Means, Part I: Campaigning in the Gray Zone* (Lanham, MD: Rowman and Littlefield, 2019). Also see Linda Robinson, Todd C. Helmus, Raphael S. Cohen, Alireza Nader, Andrew Radin, Madeline Magnuson, and Katya Migacheva, *Modern Political Warfare: Current Practices and Possible Responses* (Santa Monica, CA: RAND, 2018).

30. See, for example, Hal Brands, *How to Wage a Twilight Struggle: Lessons from America's Cold War* (unpublished manuscript, 2020); Tim Weiner, *The Folly and the Glory: America, Russia, and Political Warfare 1945–2020* (New York: Henry Holt, 2020); Thomas Rid, *Active Measures: The Secret History of Disinformation and Political Warfare* (New York: Farrar, Straus and Giroux, 2020); Mark Galeotti, *Russian Political War: Moving Beyond the Hybrid* (New York: Routledge, 2019). Robinson et al., *Modern Political Warfare*; Frank G. Hoffman, "Examining Complex Forms of Conflict: Gray Zone and Hybrid Challenges," *Prism* 7, no. 4 (2018): 31–47; Kennan, "Organizing Political Warfare"; Hal Brands and Toshi Yoshihara, "How to Wage Political Warfare," *National Interest*, December 16, 2018; B. H. Liddell Hart, *Strategy: The Indirect Approach* (London: Faber, 1967); Hicks and Friend, *By Other Means, Part I*.

31. On the distinctions between irregular and conventional warfare, see US Special Operations Command, US Marine Corps Combat Development Command, and US Joint Chiefs of Staff, *Irregular Warfare (IW): Joint Operating Concept (JOC)* (Washington, DC: US Department of Defense, September 2007), 7–9.

32. Merriam-Webster.com, s.v. "warfare," accessed October 17, 2020.

33. See, for example, 姜玉坤, 阎永峰 [Mei Yushen and Yan Yongfeng], "沈阳军区某集团军拉开'三战'序幕" [A certain group army of the Shenyang military region pulls back the curtain on the "three warfares"], 中国青年报 [China youth daily], July 17, 2004; 侯宝成 [Hou Baocheng], "政治工作为什么要加强对'三战'的研究" [Why political work should step up the study of the "three warfares"], 解放军报 [PLA daily], July 29, 2004.

34. Sun Tzu, *The Art of War*, trans. Samuel B. Griffith (New York: Oxford University Press, 1971), 77; emphasis added.

35. Валерий Герасимов [Valery Gerasimov], "По опыту Сирии" [On the Syrian experience], Военно-промышленный курьер [Military-industrial courier], no. 44 (March 9, 2016).

36. Charles K. Bartles, "Getting Gerasimov Right," *Military Review* 96, no. 1 (January–February 2016): 30.

37. Carl von Clausewitz, *On War*, trans. J. J. Graham (Harmondsworth, England: Penguin, 1968), 101. On Sun Tzu versus Clausewitz, also see Sean McFate, *The New Rules of War: Victory in the Age of Durable Disorder* (New York: HarperCollins, 2019).

38. "Inside the KGB: An Interview with Retired KGB Maj. Gen. Oleg Kalugin," CNN, 1998.

39. Sun, *Art of War*, 64.

40. Condoleezza Rice, *Democracy: Stories from the Long Road to Freedom* (New York: Twelve, 2017), 140.

41. Morell, interview.

42. On the activities of Military Unit 74455 within the GRU, see United States of America v. Yuriy Sergeyevich Andrienko et al., United States District Court, Western District of Pennsylvania, Indictment, Criminal no. 20-316, October 15, 2020.

43. National Intelligence Council, *Foreign Threats to the 2020 Federal Elections*, ICA 2020–00078D (McLean, VA: Office of the Director of National Intelligence, March 10, 2021), i.

44. See, for example, US Department of Homeland Security, "DHS Statement on the Issuance of Binding Operational Directive 17-01," September 13, 2017; US Department of the Treasury, "Treasury Targets Assets of Russian Financier Who Attempted to Influence 2018 US Elections,"

September 13, 2019; Robert S. Mueller III, *Report on the Investigation into Russian Interference in the 2016 Presidential Election*, vol. 1 (Washington, DC: US Department of Justice, March 2019).

45. See, for example, Mueller, *Report on the Investigation into Russian Interference*; US Department of the Treasury, "Treasury Targets Assets of Russian Financier"; US Department of the Treasury, "Treasury Increases Pressure on Russian Financier," September 23, 2020.

46. Interviews with FBI officials, 2019 and 2020.

47. Interview with senior Middle East leader, 2019.

48. Morell, interview.

49. The data come from an Iranian proxy database at the Transnational Threats Project at the Center for Strategic and International Studies. See, for example, Seth G. Jones, *Containing Tehran: Understanding Iran's Power and Exploiting Its Vulnerabilities* (Washington, DC: Center for Strategic and International Studies, 2020), 11. I updated the data through early 2021.

50. United Nations Security Council, "Identical Letters Dated 7 April 2021 from Permanent Representative of Israel to the United Nations Addressed to the Secretary-General and the President of the Security Council," S/2021/338, April 8, 2021; Jeremy Binnie, "Israel Says Iranian Missile Could Have 5,000 Kilometer Range," *Jane's Defence Weekly*, April 21, 2021.

51. Daniel R. Coats, *Worldwide Threat Assessment of the U.S. Intelligence Community* (Washington, DC: Office of the Director of National Intelligence, January 29, 2019), 6.

52. Norman Roule, interview by the author, July 13, 2020.

53. David Petraeus, interview by the author, May 22, 2020.

54. Stanley McChrystal, interview by the author, June 8, 2020.

55. National Counterintelligence and Security Center, "How China Operates on University Campuses," 2019.

56. Aynne Kokas, *Hollywood Made in China* (Oakland: University of California Press, 2017).

57. The data come from *The Military Balance 2020* (London: International Institute for Strategic Studies, 2020), 21. According to *Military Balance* data, US defense spending is roughly equivalent to defense spending of the next eleven countries combined: China, Saudi Arabia, Russia, India, United Kingdom, France, Japan, Germany, South Korea, Brazil, and Italy.

58. The United States has almost certainly lost "overmatch"—an overwhelming advantage in all aspects of warfare against countries like Russia and China—especially in areas such as the Baltics, the Taiwan Strait, and the South China Sea. Nevertheless, a conventional or nuclear war would be

extremely costly. On the US loss of overmatch, see, for example, David Ochmanek, "Restoring the Power Projection Capabilities of the U.S. Armed Forces," Testimony Presented before the Senate Armed Services Committee, February 16, 2017.

59. David C. Gompert, Astrid Stuth Cevallos, and Cristina L. Garafola, *War with China: Thinking through the Unthinkable* (Santa Monica, CA: RAND, 2016), xiv.

60. Gompert et al., *War with China*, xiv.

61. Michèle A. Flournoy, "How to Prevent a War in Asia," *Foreign Affairs*, June 18, 2020.

62. Gates, interview.

63. Ronald Reagan, "Farewell Address to the Nation," January 11, 1989.

64. See Wike et al., *U.S. Image Plummets Internationally*.

65. Сергей Чекинов и Сергей Богданов [Sergey Chekinov and Sergey Bogdanov], "Влияние непрямых действий на характер современной войны" [The influence of indirect actions on the character of contemporary war], Военная мысль [Military thought] 6 (2011): 7, 10.

66. Gates, interview.

67. The quote is from Thomas Jefferson's first inaugural address on March 4, 1801. See Barbara E. Oberg, ed., *The Papers of Thomas Jefferson*, vol. 33, *17 February to 30 April 1801* (Princeton, NJ: Princeton University Press, 2006), 152.

CHAPTER 2: ACTIVE MEASURES

1. Interviews with US, European, and Afghan government officials, 2020. Some of this information was first publicly reported in Charlie Savage, Eric Schmitt, and Michael Schwirtz, "Russia Secretly Offered Afghan Militants Bounties to Kill U.S. Troops, Intelligence Says," *New York Times*, June 26, 2020.

2. Interviews with US, European, and Afghan government officials, 2020. See also, for example, Charlie Savage, Eric Schmitt, Rukmini Callimachi, and Adam Goldman, "New Administration Memo Seeks to Foster Doubts about Suspected Russian Bounties," *New York Times*, July 3, 2020; Mujib Mashal, Eric Schmitt, Najim Rahim, and Rukmini Callimachi, "Afghan Contractor Handed Out Russian Cash to Kill Americans, Officials Say," *New York Times*, July 13, 2020; Charlie Savage, Mujib Mashal, Rukmini Callimachi, Eric Schmitt, and Adam Goldman, "Suspicions of Russian Bounties Were Bolstered by Data on Financial

Transfers," *New York Times*, July 30, 2020; Seth G. Jones, "Afghanistan's Future Emirate? The Taliban and the Struggle for Afghanistan," *CTC Sentinel* 13, no. 11 (November/December 2020): 1–10.

3. See, for example, А. В. Хомутов [A. V. Khomutov], "О решении проблем применения общевойсковых формирований тактического звена в современных военных конфликтах" [On solving the problems of the use of combined arms tactical units in modern military conflicts], Военная мысль [Military thought], no. 6 (June 2020); А. А. Михлин, В. В. Молочный, С. Н. Охремчук, В. А. Баландин, Т. М. Коэметс [A. A. Mikhlin, V. V. Molochny, S. N. Okhremchuk, V. A. Balandin, and T. M. Koemets], Новые вызовы и угрозы национальным интересам России в Средиземноморском регионе [New challenges and threats to Russia's national interests in the Mediterranean region], Военная мысль [Military thought], no. 6 (June 2020); А. С. Брычков, В. Л. Дорохов, Г. А. Никоно́ров [A. S. Brychkov, V. L. Dorokhov, and G. A. Nikonorov], "О гибридном характере войн и вооруженных конфликтов будущего" [On the hybrid nature of future wars and armed conflicts], Военная мысль [Military thought], no. 2 (February 2019).

4. See, for example, Maria Tsvetkova and Anton Zverev, "After Deadly Syrian Battle, Evidence of Russian Losses Was Obscured," Reuters, February 5, 2019; Seth G. Jones, ed., *Moscow's War in Syria* (Washington, DC: Center for Strategic and International Studies, 2020), 37–38.

5. Tony Thomas, interview by the author, May 22, 2020.

6. Robert O. Crummey, *The Formation of Muscovy, 1304–1613* (New York: Routledge, 1987), 145.

7. Валерий Герасимов [Valery Gerasimov], "Сила Великой Победы" [The power of the great victory], Военно-промышленный курьер [Military-industrial courier], no. 45 (May 11, 2015). The comments were from a conference on April 25, 2015, on lessons from World War II, the "Great Patriotic War."

8. Герасимов [Gerasimov], "Сила Великой Победы" [The power of the great victory].

9. See the interview with Gerasimov in Наби Набиев [Nabi Nabiyev], "Горячие будни генерала Герасимова" [Gen. Gerasimov's busy routine], Красная звезда [Red star], March 12, 2001.

10. Catherine Merridale, *Ivan's War: Life and Death in the Red Army, 1939–1945* (London: Faber and Faber, 2005), 168.

11. Константин Симонов [Konstantin Simonov], Жди меня... (стихотворение) [Wait for me... (poem)] (Moscow: Detskaya Literatura, 2010).

12. Набиев [Nabiyev], "Горячие будни генерала Герасимова" [Gen. Gerasimov's busy routine].

13. "Герасимов Валерий Васильевич" [Gerasimov Valery Vasilyevich], Министерство обороны Российской Федерации [Ministry of Defense of the Russian Federation], 2019; Набиев [Nabiyev], "Горячие будни генерала Герасимова" [Gen. Gerasimov's busy routine].

14. Zvezda TV Video Transcript. Телеканал «Звезда» [Zvezda TV], Видеорепортаж, "Замминистра обороны Валерий Герасимов отмечает 60-летний юбилей" [Deputy Defense Minister Valery Gerasimov celebrates his 60th birthday], YouTube, September 8, 2015.

15. Телеканал «Звезда» [Zvezda TV], Видеорепортаж "Замминистра обороны Валерий Герасимов отмечает 60-летний юбилей" [Deputy Defense Minister Valery Gerasimov celebrates his 60th birthday].

16. Телеканал «Звезда» [Zvezda TV], Видеорепортаж "Замминистра обороны Валерий Герасимов отмечает 60-летний юбилей" [Deputy Defense Minister Valery Gerasimov celebrates his 60th birthday].

17. "Герасимов Валерий Васильевич" [Gerasimov Valery Vasilyevich], Министерство обороны Российской Федерации [Ministry of Defense of the Russian Federation], 2019.

18. Александр Андреевич Свечин [Alexander Andreyevich Svechin], Стратегия [Strategy] (Moscow: Gosvoenizdat, 1926).

19. Валерий Герасимов [Valery Gerasimov], "Современные войны и актуальные вопросы организации обороны страны" [Contemporary warfare and current issues for the defense of the country], Вестник Академии военных наук [Journal of the Academy of Military Sciences] 2, no. 59 (2017).

20. Валерий Герасимов [Valery Gerasimov], "Влияние современного характера вооруженной борьбы на направленность строительства и развития Вооруженных Сил Российской Федерации. Приоритетные задачи военной науки в обеспечении обороны страны" [The influence of the contemporary nature of armed struggle on the focus of the construction and development of the armed forces of the Russian Federation. Priority tasks of military science in safeguarding the country's defense], Вестник Академии военных наук [Journal of the Academy of Military Sciences] 62, no. 2 (2018): 16–22.

21. On Soviet use of the term "active measures," see, for example, "Report by the Chairman of the Delegation of the Committee for State Security (KGB) of the USSR, General-Colonel V. M. Chebrikov during Soviet Bloc Meeting on Western Radio," April 23, 1980, Cold War International History Project, History and Public Policy Program Dig-

ital Archive, Wilson Center, Washington, DC; *Soviet Active Measures: Hearings before the Permanent Select Committee on Intelligence, House of Representatives, Ninety-Seventh Congress, Second Session, July 13, 14, 1982* (Washington, DC: US Government Printing Office, 1982), 231.

22. Vasili Mitrokhin, "KGB Active Measures in Southwest Asia in 1980–82," n.d., Cold War International History Project, History and Public Policy Program Digital Archive, Wilson Center, Washington, DC.

23. John McMahon, statement, in *Soviet Covert Action (the Forgery Offensive): Hearings before the Subcommittee on Oversight of the Permanent Select Committee on Intelligence, House of Representatives, Ninety-Sixth Congress, Second Session, February 6, 19, 1980* (Washington, DC: US Government Printing Office, 1980), 6.

24. *Soviet Active Measures: Hearings*, 5.

25. Interagency Intelligence Study, "Soviet Active Measures," in *Soviet Active Measures: Hearings*, 31; emphasis added.

26. See, for example, the testimony of former KGB operative Stanislav Levchenko in *Soviet Active Measures: Hearings*, 138–45.

27. Ladislav Bittman (former deputy chief of the Disinformation Department of the Czechoslovak Intelligence Service), statement, in *Soviet Covert Action (the Forgery Offensive)*, 43–44.

28. The photo was available at http://www.sgvavia.ru as of January 2021.

29. Thomas M. Troy Jr., "A Secret Life," *Studies in Intelligence* 48, no. 2 (2004).

30. Benjamin Weiser, *A Secret Life: The Polish Officer, His Covert Mission, and the Price He Paid to Save His Country* (New York: Public Affairs, 2004).

31. Central Intelligence Agency, "A Look Back . . . a Cold War Hero: Colonel Ryszard Kuklinski," January 14, 2010.

32. Quoted in Mark Kramer, *The Kuklinski Files and the Polish Crisis of 1980–1981: An Analysis of the Newly Released CIA Documents on Ryszard Kuklinski*, Working Paper (Cold War International History Project), no. 59 (Washington, DC: Woodrow Wilson International Center of Scholars, 2009), 17.

33. See, for example, "Telegram to Directors of Voivode Police," circa December 12, 1981, in *From Solidarity to Martial Law: The Polish Crisis of 1980–1981*, ed. Andrzej Paczkowski and Malcolm Byrne (New York: Central European University Press, 2007), 459.

34. Gregory F. Domber, *Empowering Revolution: America, Poland, and the End of the Cold War* (Chapel Hill: University of North Carolina Press, 2014), 41.

35. Wojciech Jaruzelski, "Commentary," *Cold War International History Project Bulletin*, no. 11 (Winter 1998): 33.

36. Seth G. Jones, *A Covert Action: Reagan, the CIA, and the Cold War Struggle in Poland* (New York: W. W. Norton, 2018).

37. Benjamin B. Fischer, "Solidarity, the CIA, and Western Technology," *International Journal of Intelligence and Counterintelligence* 25, no. 3 (2012): 443.

38. Валерий Герасимов [Valery Gerasimov], "Ценность науки в предвидении: Новые вызовы требуют переосмыслить формы и способы ведения боевых действий" [The value of science is in the foresight: New challenges demand rethinking the forms and methods of carrying out combat operations], Военно-промышленный курьер [Military-industrial courier], no. 8 (February 26, 2013).

39. Michael R. Beschloss and Strobe Talbot, *At the Highest Levels: The Inside Story of the End of the Cold War* (Boston: Little, Brown, 1993), 302.

40. See, for example, Jaanus Piirsalu and Madis Jürgen, "Vene relvajõude juhib kindral, kes viis punaväed Eestist välja" [The Russian armed forces are led by a general who took the Red Army out of Estonia], Eesti Ekspress [Estonian express], November 16, 2012. Also see "Russia/Estonia—Yeltsin Border Inspection" (video), Story no. w074340, AP Archive, November 23, 1994.

41. Набиев [Nabiyev], "Горячие будни генерала Герасимова" [Gen. Gerasimov's busy routine].

42. The data came from the CIA *World Factbook*, various issues; Central Intelligence Agency, *USSR: Demographic Trends and Ethnic Balance in the Non-Russian Republics*, GI 90-10013U (Langley, VA: Directorate of Intelligence, Central Intelligence Agency, April 1990); Saul Bernard Cohen, *Geopolitics of the World System* (New York: Rowman and Littlefield, 2003), 198.

43. Владимир Серебрянников и Александр Капто [Vladimir Serebryanikov and Alexander Kapko], "Невоенные средства оборонной безопасности России" [The non-military means of the defense security of Russia], Диалог [Dialog] 2 (2000): 23.

44. On Gerasimov's reference to US support to the mujahideen in Afghanistan, see Валерий Герасимов [Valery Gerasimov], "По опыту Сирии" [On the Syrian experience], Военно-промышленный курьер [Military-industrial courier], no. 44 (March 9, 2016).

45. "Герасимов Валерий Васильевич" [Gerasimov Valery Vasilyevich], Министерство обороны Российской Федерации [Ministry of Defense of the Russian Federation], 2019.

46. Mark Kramer, "The Perils of Counterinsurgency: Russia's War in Chechnya," *International Security* 29, no. 3 (Winter 2004/2005): 17.

47. Olga Oliker, *Russia's Chechen Wars 1994–2000: Lessons from Urban Combat* (Santa Monica, CA: RAND, 2001).

48. Валерий Герасимов [Valery Gerasimov], interview by Владимир Тихонов [Vladimir Tikhonov], Военно-промышленный курьер [Military-industrial courier], May 25, 2005.

49. Maura Reynolds, "Russia's 'Cruel' Soldier Comes Home," *Los Angeles Times*, January 19, 2001.

50. Anna Politkovskaya, *A Dirty War: A Russian Reporter in Chechnya*, trans. John Crowfoot (London: Harvill, 2001), 180. Also see, for example, "A Military 'Super-hawk' Speaks Out on Chechnya," *Chechnya Weekly* 1, no. 4 (November 20, 2000).

51. Isayeva, Yusupova and Bazayeva v. Russia, European Court of Human Rights, Application no. 57947-49/00, Judgment of February 24, 2005.

52. Human Rights Watch, " 'No Happiness Remains': Civilian Killings, Pillage, and Rape in Alkhan-Yurt, Chechnya," April 1, 2000.

53. See "Chechnya: Russia Takes Control of Border" (video), Story no. 160695, AP Archive, October 23, 1999.

54. Набиев [Nabiyev], "Горячие будни генерала Герасимова" [Gen. Gerasimov's busy routine].

55. The video of Gerasimov was available on YouTube: Настоящая война (Дагестан-Чечня) [Real war (Dagestan-Chechnya)], posted February 11, 2018, by Faye Walker. In addition, see the footage of Gerasimov in Ingushetia in "Russia Fighting 2" (video), Story no. 351110, AP Archive, September 26, 2002.

56. Набиев [Nabiyev], "Горячие будни генерала Герасимова" [Gen. Gerasimov's busy routine].

57. Набиев [Nabiyev], "Горячие будни генерала Герасимова" [Gen. Gerasimov's busy routine].

58. Anna Politkovskaya, *Putin's Russia: Life in a Failing Democracy*, trans. Arch Tait (New York: Henry Holt, 2004), 52.

59. Oliker, *Russia's Chechen Wars 1994–2000*, 77–79. Also see, for example, Politkovskaya, *Dirty War*, 163–70.

60. Ray Finch, "Snapshot of a War Crime: The Case of Russian Colonel, Yuri Budanov," *Journal of Power Institutions in Post-Soviet Societies*, no. 12 (August 2011), 1–15.

61. Politkovskaya, *Putin's Russia*, 47.

62. Usam Baysayev, "The Yuri Budanov Case," *Prague Watchdog*, January 8, 2009.

63. Politkovskaya, *Putin's Russia*, 53.

64. Politkovskaya, *Putin's Russia*, 52–53.

65. Douglas Birch, "Chechens Fear to Leave Russia Camps for Home," *Baltimore Sun*, December 16, 2002.

66. "Military 'Super-Hawk' Speaks Out," *Chechnya Weekly*.

67. Politkovskaya, *Putin's Russia*, 42.

68. Birch, "Chechens Fear to Leave Russia Camps for Home."

69. Набиев [Nabiyev], "Горячие будни генерала Герасимова" [Gen. Gerasimov's busy routine].

70. See, for example, Mark Galeotti, *Russia's Wars in Chechnya 1994–2009* (New York: Osprey, 2014); Anatol Lieven, *Chechnya: Tombstone of Russian Power* (New Haven, CT: Yale University Press, 1998).

71. Hannah Levintova, "The U.S. Military Is Set to Meet with the Russian General Who Called for Cyberattacks against the West," *Mother Jones*, January 11, 2018.

CHAPTER 3: THE MAIN ENEMY

1. Gary Schroen, *First In: An Insider's Account of How the CIA Spearheaded the War on Terror in Afghanistan* (New York: Ballantine, 2005), 28.

2. Gary Berntsen and Ralph Pezzullo, *Jawbreaker: The Attack on Bin Laden and Al Qaeda: A Personal Account by the CIA's Key Field Commander* (New York: Crown, 2005), 312.

3. On the overthrow of the Taliban regime, see Schroen, *First In*; Henry A. Crumpton, *The Art of Intelligence: Lessons from a Life in the CIA's Clandestine Service* (New York: Penguin, 2013); Stephen Biddle, *Afghanistan and the Future of Warfare: Implications for Army and Defense Policy* (Carlisle, PA: Strategic Studies Institute, US Army War College, November 2002); Berntsen and Pezzullo, *Jawbreaker*; Bob Woodward, *Bush at War* (New York: Simon and Schuster, 2002).

4. Валерий Герасимов [Valery Gerasimov], "Влияние современного характера вооруженной борьбы на направленность строительства и развития Вооруженных Сил Российской Федерации. Приоритетные задачи военной науки в обеспечении обороны страны" [The influence of the contemporary nature of armed struggle on the focus of the construction and development of the armed forces of the Russian Federation. Priority tasks of military science in safeguarding the country's defense],

Вестник Академии военных наук [Journal of the Academy of Military Sciences] 62, no. 2 (2018): 16–22.

5. See, for example, Ariel Cohen, *The "Primakov Doctrine": Russia's Zero-Sum Game with the United States* (Washington, DC: Heritage Foundation, December 15, 1997); Eugene Rumer, *The Primakov (Not Gerasimov) Doctrine in Action* (Washington, DC: Carnegie Endowment for International Peace, June 5, 2019).

6. Валерий Герасимов [Valery Gerasimov], "Ценность науки в предвидении: Новые вызовы требуют переосмыслить формы и способы ведения боевых действий" [The value of science is in the foresight: New challenges demand rethinking the forms and methods of carrying out combat operations], Военно-промышленный курьер [Military-industrial courier], no. 8 (February 26, 2013).

7. Валерий Герасимов [Valery Gerasimov], Доклад на тему: "Влияние современного характера вооруженной борьбы на направленность строительства и развития Вооруженных Сил Российской Федерации" [The influence of the contemporary nature of armed struggle on the Trends in Construction and Development of the Armed Forces of the Russian Federation].

8. Valery Gerasimov, PowerPoint slides, Moscow Conference on International Security, May 23, 2014, published in Anthony H. Cordesman, *Russia and the 'Color Revolution': A Russian Military View of a World Destabilized by the U.S. and the West* (Washington, DC: Center for Strategic and International Studies, May 28, 2014).

9. Валерий Герасимов [Valery Gerasimov], "Военные опасности и военные угрозы Российской Федерации в современных условиях" [Military dangers and military threats of the Russian Federation in modern conditions], Армейский сборник [Army journal], no. 5 (April 16, 2015).

10. В. Герасимов [V. Gerasimov], Выступление на тему: "Военные опасности и военные угрозы Российской Федерации в современных условиях" [Military dangers and military threats to the Russian Federation in Today's World].

11. Treaty on the Limitation of Anti-Ballistic Missile Systems (ABM Treaty), signed by the United States and the Union of Soviet Socialist Republics in Moscow on May 26, 1972.

12. В. Герасимов [V. Gerasimov], "Развитие военной стратегии в современных условиях" [The development of military strategy under contemporary conditions], Вестник Академии военных наук [Journal of the Academy of Military Sciences] 67, no. 2 (2019): 6–11.

13. Walter L. Perry, Richard E. Darilek, Laurinda L. Rohn, and Jerry M. Sollinger, eds., *Operation Iraqi Freedom: Decisive War, Elusive Peace* (Santa Monica, CA: RAND, 2015), xxii.

14. US Department of Defense, "President Bush Proclaims End to Major Combat Ops in Iraq," May 1, 2003.

15. Gerasimov, PowerPoint slides, May 23, 2014.

16. Герасимов [Gerasimov], "Ценность науки в предвидении" [The value of science is in the foresight].

17. Валерий Герасимов [Valery Gerasimov], "О роли военной силы в современных конфликтах" [On the role of military force in modern conflicts] (III Московской конференции по международной безопасности [III Moscow Conference on International Security], May 23, 2014).

18. Gerasimov, PowerPoint slides, May 23, 2014; Герасимов [Gerasimov], "Ценность науки в предвидении" [The value of science is in the foresight].

19. Joel D. Rayburn and Frank K. Sobchak, eds., *The U.S. Army in the Iraq War*, vol. 1, *Invasion, Insurgency, Civil War, 2003–2006* (Carlisle, PA: Strategic Studies Institute, US Army War College Press, 2019), 82.

20. Perry et al., *Operation Iraqi Freedom*, 153–55.

21. Rayburn and Sobchak, *U.S. Army in the Iraq War*, 1:104.

22. Герасимов [Gerasimov], "Развитие военной стратегии в современных условиях" [The development of military strategy under contemporary conditions].

23. Gerasimov, PowerPoint slides, May 23, 2014.

24. Владимир Путин [Vladimir Putin], "Выступление и дискуссия на Мюнхенской конференции по вопросам политики безопасности" [Speech and discussion at the Munich Conference on Security Policy] (Munich, Germany, February 10, 2007).

25. Валерий Герасимов [Valery Gerasimov], "Вооруженные Силы Российской Федерации и борьба с международным терроризмом" [The armed forces of the Russian Federation and the fight against international terrorism] (V Московской конференции по международной безопасности [V Moscow Conference on International Security], April 27, 2016).

26. Герасимов [Gerasimov], "О роли военной силы в современных конфликтах" [On the role of military force in modern conflicts].

27. Герасимов [Gerasimov], "О роли военной силы в современных конфликтах" [On the role of military force in modern conflicts].

28. Валерий Герасимов [Valery Gerasimov], "ИГИЛ начался с

'Талибана'" [ISIS began with the "Taliban"], Военно-промышленный курьер [Military-industrial courier], October 12, 2015.

29. The Afghan data come from World Bank, "World Development Indicators" dataset, 2020.

30. Gerasimov, PowerPoint slides, May 23, 2014.

31. Charles K. Bartles, "Getting Gerasimov Right," *Military Review* 96, no. 1 (January–February 2016): 32.

32. Gerasimov, PowerPoint slides, May 23, 2014.

33. Gerasimov, PowerPoint slides, May 23, 2014.

34. Герасимов [Gerasimov], "Ценность науки в предвидении" [The value of science is in the foresight].

35. Peter Graff, "Libyan Rebels Overrun Gaddafi HQ, Say He's 'Finished,'" Reuters, August 23, 2011.

36. Karl Mueller, ed., *Precision and Purpose: Airpower in the Libyan Civil War* (Santa Monica, CA: RAND, 2015), 123.

37. Mueller, *Precision and Purpose*, 4, 124.

38. On the US and broader NATO campaign, see Christopher S. Chivvis, *Toppling Qaddafi: Libya and the Limits of Liberal Intervention* (New York: Cambridge University Press, 2013).

39. Герасимов [Gerasimov], "Ценность науки в предвидении" [The value of science is in the foresight].

40. Валерий Герасимов [Valery Gerasimov], "Современные войны и актуальные вопросы организации обороны страны" [Contemporary warfare and current issues for the defense of the country], Вестник Академии военных наук [Journal of the Academy of Military Sciences] 2, no. 59 (2017).

41. Герасимов [Gerasimov], "Ценность науки в предвидении" [The value of science is in the foresight].

42. В. Герасимов [V. Gerasimov], "Вооруженные Силы Российской Федерации" [The armed forces of the Russian Federation].

43. Gerasimov, PowerPoint slides, May 23, 2014.

44. See the comments by senior Russian leaders on Libya and the color revolutions in Александр Тихонов [Alexander Tikhonov], "'Цветные революции'—угроза миру" ["Color revolutions"—A threat to peace], Красная звезда [Red star], May 23, 2014.

45. Quoted in Alexander D. Chekov, Anna V. Makarycheva, Anastasia M. Solomensteva, Maxim A. Suchkov, and Andrey A. Sushentsov, "War of the Future: A View from Russia," *Survival* 61, no. 6 (December 2019–January 2020): 35. The remarks come from Andrey Ilnytsky (an adviser

to Russian defense minister Sergey Shoigu), Valdai International Discussion Club, Moscow, October 10, 2018.

46. Валерий Герасимов [Valery Gerasimov], "По опыту Сирии" [On the Syrian experience], Военно-промышленный курьер [Military-industrial courier], no. 44 (March 9, 2016).

47. "Mikhail Gorbachev Calls for Vladimir Putin to Resign," *Telegraph* (London), December 24, 2011.

48. Евгений Никитенко [Evgeniy Nikitenko], "Конфликты будущего: сценарно-аналитический прогноз" [Conflict of the future—Scenario-analytical forecast], Ситуационные анализы [Case studies] 3 (2013).

49. Chekov et al., "War of the Future," 29.

50. Gerasimov, PowerPoint slides, May 23, 2014; emphasis added.

51. Герасимов [Gerasimov], "Ценность науки в предвидении" [The value of science is in the foresight].

52. See the interview with Gerasimov in Наби Набиев [Nabi Nabiyev], "Горячие будни генерала Герасимова" [Gen. Gerasimov's busy routine], Красная звезда [Red star], March 12, 2001.

53. Interview with senior US Department of Defense official, 2020.

54. В. Герасимов [V. Gerasimov], Выступление на тему: "Военные опасности и военные угрозы Российской Федерации в современных условиях" [Military dangers and military threats to the Russian Federation under contemporary conditions].

55. Even in Ukraine, the role of the United States was minimal. Some of the US diplomats (such as Assistant Secretary of State Victoria Nuland) and politicians (such as Senator John McCain) met with protesters in the streets. But the motivation and legwork came from Ukrainians themselves.

56. Valery Gerasimov, PowerPoint slides, Moscow Conference on International Security, May 23, 2014, published in Anthony H. Cordesman, *Russia and the 'Color Revolution': A Russian Military View of a World Destabilized by the U.S. and the West* (Washington, DC: Center for Strategic and International Studies, May 28, 2014).

57. Michael Morell, *The Great War of Our Time: The CIA's Fight against Terrorism—from al Qa'ida to ISIS*, with Bill Harlow (New York: Twelve, 2015), 179.

58. Алексей Николаевич Бельский, Ольга Витальевна Клименко [Alexey Nikolaevich Belsky and Olga Vitalievna Klimenko], "Политические технологии 'цветных революций': пути и средства

противодействия" [The political engineering of "color revolutions": The ways and means of counteraction], Военная мысль [Military thought], no. 9 (2014): 20–29.

59. В. Герасимов [V. Gerasimov], "Вооруженные Силы Российской Федерации" [The armed forces of the Russian Federation]; Герасимов [Gerasimov], "О роли военной силы в современных конфликтах" [On the role of military force in modern conflicts].

60. Сергей Шойгу [Sergey Shoigu], "Глобальная безопасность и региональная стабильность" [Global security and regional stability], Красная звезда [Red star], May 23, 2014.

61. Российской Федерации [Russian Federation], "Стратегия национальной безопасности России" [Russian national security strategy], December 31, 2015.

62. В. Герасимов [V. Gerasimov], Выступление на тему: "Военные опасности и военные угрозы Российской Федерации в современных условиях" [Military dangers and military threats to the Russian Federation under contemporary conditions].

63. See the account in Michael McFaul, *From Cold War to Hot Peace: An American Ambassador in Putin's Russia* (Boston: Houghton Mifflin Harcourt, 2018), 401.

CHAPTER 4: RUSSIAN CHESS

1. "Путин рассказал анекдот про кортик и часы" [Putin told a joke about a dagger and a watch], Газета.Ru [Gazeta.ru], December 14, 2017.

2. Виктор Баранец [Victor Baranets], "Начальник Генштаба Вооруженных сил России генерал армии Валерий Герасимов: 'Мы переломили хребет ударным силам терроризма'" [Chief of the General Staff of the Armed Forces of Russia, army general Valery Gerasimov: "We have broken the ridge of the shock forces of terrorism"], Комсомольская правда [Komsomolskaya pravda], December 26, 2017.

3. Валерий Герасимов [Valery Gerasimov], "Ценность науки в предвидении: Новые вызовы требуют переосмыслить формы и способы ведения боевых действий" [The value of science is in the foresight: New challenges demand rethinking the forms and methods of carrying out combat operations], Военно-промышленный курьер [Military-industrial courier], no. 8 (February 26, 2013).

4. Quoted in Герасимов [Gerasimov], "Ценность науки в предвидении"

[The value of science is in the foresight]. I left the quote in Gerasimov's words because his interpretation of Isserson is important to understand. It is from Георгий Самойлович Иссерсон [Georgii Samoilovich Isserson], Новые формы борьбы [New forms of combat] (Moscow: Voenizdat, 1940). Also see, for example, Георгий Самойлович Иссерсон [Georgii Samoilovich Isserson], Эволюция оперативного искусства [The evolution of operational art] (Fort Leavenworth, KS: Combat Studies Institute Press, US Army Combined Arms Center, 2013).

5. Герасимов [Gerasimov], "Ценность науки в предвидении" [The value of science is in the foresight].

6. Крым. Путь на Родину [Crimea: The way home], directed by Sergey Kraus broadcast on России-1 [Russian-1], March 15, 2015. For excerpts, see Андрей Кондрашов [Andrey Kondrashov], "Путин рассказал 'России 1', как вернул Крым и спас Януковича" [Putin told Russia-1 how he returned Crimea and saved Yanukovych], Vesti.ru, March 9, 2015; emphasis added.

7. On the Russian campaign in Ukraine, see Samuel Charap and Timothy J. Colton, *Everyone Loses: The Ukraine Crisis and the Ruinous Contest for Post-Soviet Eurasia* (New York: Routledge, 2017).

8. Международный дискуссионный клуб Валдай [Valdai International Discussion Club], Современная российская идентичность: измерения, вызовы, ответы [Contemporary Russian identity: Dimensions, challenges, answers], September 2013.

9. On the development of Russian special operations forces, see, for example, Владимир Квачков [Vladimir Kvachkov], Спецназ России [Russian special forces] (Moscow: Algoritm, 2015). Kvachkov was a former *spetsnaz* colonel.

10. Quoted in Илья Крамник [Ilya Kramnik], "Иностранные корни нового российского спецназа" [Foreign roots of new Russian *spetsnaz*], *Lenta.ru*, December 20, 2016.

11. Christopher Marsh, *Developments in Russian Special Operations: Russia's Spetsnaz, SOF and Special Operations Forces Command* (Ottawa: Canadian Special Operations Forces Command, 2017), 21.

12. Marsh, *Developments in Russian Special Operations*, 21.

13. Michael Kofman, Katya Migacheva, Brian Nichiporuk, Andrew Radin, Olesya Tkacheva, and Jenny Oberholtzer, *Lessons from Russia's Operations in Crimea and Eastern Ukraine* (Santa Monica, CA: RAND, 2017), 7–8.

14. Interview with senior US government official, 2020.

15. Kofman, *Lessons from Russia's Operations*, 8–9.

16. Sun Tzu, *The Art of War*, trans. Samuel B. Griffith (New York: Oxford University Press, 1971), 77.

17. See McCain's comments in Jay Newton-Small, "Senator John McCain: 'We Are All Ukrainians,'" *Time*, February 28, 2014.

18. Tony Thomas, interview by the author, May 22, 2020.

19. William McRaven, interview by the author, May 21, 2020.

20. See, for example, Евгений Месснер [Evgeny Messner], "Горе и побежденным и победителям" [Grief to the defeated and the victors], Сегодня [Segodnya], no. 71 (1931); Евгений Месснер [Evgeny Messner], Всемирная мятежевойна [The worldwide subversion war] (Buenos Aires: South American Division of the Institute for the Study of the Problems of War and Peace, 1971); Александр Дугин [Alexander Dugin], Русская вещь [The Russian thing] (Moscow: Arktogeya, 2001); Александр Дугин [Alexander Dugin], Философия войны [The philosophy of war] (Moscow: Yauza, Eksmo, 2004); Игорь Панарин, Любовь Панарина [Igor Panarin and Lyubov Panarina], Информационная война и мир [Information war and the world] (Moscow: OLMA-PRESS, 2003); Сергей Чекинов, Сергей Богданов [Sergey Chekinov and Sergey Bogdanov], "Эволюция сущности и содержания понятия 'война' в XXI столетии" [The evolution of the nature and the content of the concept of 'war' in the twenty-first century], Военная мысль [Military thought], no. 1 (2017); Сергей Чекинов, Сергей Богданов [Sergey Chekinov and Sergey Bogdanov], "Военное искусство на начальном этапе XXI столетия: проблемы и суждения" [Military art at the beginning of the twenty-first century: Problems and opinions], Военная мысль [Military thought], no. 1 (2015); Сергей Чекинов, Сергей Богданов [Sergey Chekinov and Sergey Bogdanov], "О характере и содержании войны нового поколения" [The nature and content of a new-generation war], Военная мысль [Military thought], no. 10 (2013).

21. Герасимов [Gerasimov], "Ценность науки в предвидении" [The value of science is in the foresight].

22. Alexander D. Chekov, Anna V. Makarycheva, Anastasia M. Solomensteva, Maxim A. Suchkov, and Andrey A. Sushentsov, "War of the Future: A View from Russia," *Survival* 61, no. 6 (December 2019–January 2020): 36.

23. Ben Smith, *Russian Intelligence Services and Special Forces* (London: House of Commons, October 20, 2018), 10.

24. On April 17, 2014, during a call-in show on Russian television, Putin used the term *Novorossiya* and recalled that eastern and southern Ukraine were historically part of the Russian empire. See the English translation

in "Direct Line with Vladimir Putin," The Kremlin, April 17, 2014. The event was broadcast live by Channel One, Rossiya-1, and Rossiya-24 TV channels; and Radio Mayak, Vesti FM, and Radio Rossii radio stations.

25. Kofman, *Lessons from Russia's Operations*, 33–71.

26. Marsh, *Developments in Russian Special Operations*, 23.

27. *"Little Green Men": A Primer on Modern Russian Unconventional Warfare, Ukraine 2013–2014* (Fort Bragg, NC: US Army Special Operations Command, 2014), 44.

28. Interviews with law enforcement and intelligence officials from the United Kingdom, France, Germany, Netherlands, and Belgium, 2019 and 2020. Also see, for example, Soufan Center, *White Supremacy Extremism: The Transnational Rise of the Violent White Supremacist Movement* (New York: Soufan Center, September 2019).

29. United States of America v. Yuriy Sergeyevich Andrienko et al., United States District Court, Western District of Pennsylvania, Indictment, Criminal no. 20-316, October 15, 2020; US Department of Justice, "U.S. Charges Russian GRU Officers with International Hacking and Related Influence and Disinformation Operations," October 4, 2018. One of the best accounts of Russian operations in Ukraine can be found in Andy Greenberg, *Sandworm: A New Era of Cyberwar and the Hunt for the Kremlin's Most Dangerous Hackers* (New York: Doubleday, 2019).

30. David E. Sanger, *The Perfect Weapon: War, Sabotage, and Fear in the Cyber Age* (New York: Crown, 2018), 1–5, 152–56; Greenberg, *Sandworm*.

31. United States of America v. Yuriy Sergeyevich Andrienko et al.

32. *"Little Green Men,"* 3.

33. Michael Hayden, interview by the author, May 18, 2020.

34. Comments by John Brennan in Ken Dilanian, "Former CIA Director: We Worried Arming Ukraine Would Hand Technology to Russian Spies," NBC News, November 22, 2019.

35. See, for example, Петр Матковский, Александр Нещадимов [Peter Matkovsky and Alexander Neshchadimov], "Донбасс – наше дело!" [Donbass is our business!], Военно-промышленный курьер [Military-industrial courier], no. 14, April 14, 2020.

36. С. А. Караганов, Д. В. Суслов [S. A. Karaganov and D. V. Suslov], Новое понимание и пути укрепления многосторонней стратегической стабильности [New understanding and ways to strengthen multilateral strategic stability] (Moscow: National Research University Higher School of Economics, 2019).

37. Валерий Герасимов [Valery Gerasimov], "Вооруженные Силы Российской Федерации и борьба с международным терроризмом"

[The armed forces of the Russian Federation and the fight against international terrorism] (V Московской конференции по международной безопасности [V Moscow Conference on International Security], April 27, 2016).

38. В. Баранец [V. Baranets], "Начальник Генштаба Вооруженных сил" [Chief of the General Staff of the Armed Forces].

39. See, for example, the US government map titled "Areas of Influence, August 2014–2015," published in Lead Inspector General for Overseas Contingency Operations, *Operation Inherent Resolve* (Washington, DC: US Department of Defense, US Department of State, and US Agency for International Development, September 30, 2015), 26.

40. В. Баранец [V. Baranets], "Начальник Генштаба Вооруженных сил" [Chief of the General Staff of the Armed Forces].

41. В. Баранец [V. Baranets], "Начальник Генштаба Вооруженных сил" [Chief of the General Staff of the Armed Forces].

42. Central Intelligence Agency, "Relations between Syria and the USSR," June 1, 1976; Central Intelligence Agency, "Soviet General Purpose Naval Deployments outside Home Waters: Characteristics and Trends," June 1973; Roy Allison, "Russia and Syria: Explaining Alignment with a Regime in Crisis," *International Affairs* 89, no. 4 (July 2013); Gordon H. McCormick, *The Soviet Presence in the Mediterranean* (Santa Monica, CA: RAND, October 1987).

43. See, for example, Герасимов [Gerasimov], "Ценность науки в предвидении" [The value of science is in the foresight]. Also see later statements, such as Valery Gerasimov, "Speech at the Annual Meeting of the Academy of Military Sciences," March 2, 2019. The speech was published in English in "Russian First Deputy Defense Minister Gerasimov: 'Our Response' Is Based on the 'Active Defense Strategy,'" MEMRI, Special Dispatch no. 7943, March 14, 2019.

44. В. Герасимов [V. Gerasimov], "Вооруженные Силы Российской Федерации" [The armed forces of the Russian Federation].

45. Byron Tau, "Obama Renews Call for Assad to Step Down," *Wall Street Journal*, February 24, 2015.

46. "John McCain Leads U.S. Delegation of Senators on Tour to Train Syrian Rebels," *Guardian*, January 18, 2015.

47. See, for example, John McCain (@SenJohnMcCain), "Important visit with brave fighters in #Syria who are risking their lives for freedom and need our help," Twitter, May 28, 2013, 2:58 p.m.

48. Kristina Wong, "McCain Meets Syrian Rebels, Presses for Military Aid to Fight ISIS," *Hill*, July 2, 2014.

49. "John McCain and Lindsey Graham Call for 20,000 Troops in Syria and Iraq," *Guardian*, November 29, 2015.

50. Валерий Герасимов [Valery Gerasimov], "По опыту Сирии" [On the Syrian experience], Военно-промышленный курьер [Military-industrial courier], no. 44 (March 9, 2016).

51. Владимир Путин [Vladimir Putin], "70-я сессия Генеральной Ассамблеи ООН" [70th Session of the UN General Assembly] (speech, September 28, 2015).

52. Соглашение между Российской Федерацией и Сирийской Арабской Республикой о размещении авиационной группы Вооруженных Сил Российской Федерации на территории Сирийской Арабской Республики от 26 августа 2015 года [Agreement between the Russian Federation and the Syrian Arab Republic on the deployment of an aviation group of the armed forces of the Russian Federation on the territory of the Syrian Arab Republic, August 26, 2015].

53. On Russian military preparations in Syria, see Валерий Половинкин [Valery Polovinkin, ed.], Российское оружие в сирийском конфликте [Russian weapons in Syrian conflict] (Moscow: STATUS, 2016).

54. Stephen Tanner, *Afghanistan: A Military History from Alexander the Great to the Fall of the Taliban* (New York: Da Capo Press, 2002), 266.

55. On Russian support to organizations like the Wagner Group, see James Bingham and Konrad Muzyka, "Private Companies Engage in Russia's Non-linear Warfare," *Jane's Intelligence Review*, January 29, 2018. On activity by Lebanese Hezbollah and the Islamic Revolutionary Guard Corps-Quds Force, see Nader Uskowi, *Temperature Rising: Iran's Revolutionary Guards and Wars in the Middle East* (Lanham, MD: Rowman and Littlefield, 2019), 77–96.

56. On Russian special operations in Syria, see Michael Kofman, "Russian Spetsnaz: Learning from Experience," *Cipher Brief*, March 15, 2017; Marsh, *Developments in Russian Special Operations*.

57. Michael Kofman and Matthew Rojansky, "What Kind of Victory for Russia in Syria?" *Military Review* 98, no. 2 (2018): 6–23.

58. Anton Lavrov, *The Russian Air Campaign in Syria: A Preliminary Analysis* (Arlington, VA: Center for Naval Analysis, June 2018), 3.

59. See, for example, Ralph Shield, "Russian Airpower's Success in Syria: Assessing Evolution in Kinetic Counterinsurgency," *Journal of Slavic Military Studies* 31, no. 2 (2018): 214–39; Kofman and Rojansky, "What Kind of Victory for Russia in Syria?"; Lavrov, *Russian Air Campaign in Syria*.

60. On Russian weapons and platforms used in Syria, see, for exam-

ple, Половинкин [Polovinkin], Российское оружие в сирийском конфликте [Russian weapons in Syrian conflict].

61. Michael Nagata, interview by the author, May 19, 2020.

62. Герасимов [Gerasimov], "По опыту Сирии" [On the Syrian experience].

63. Interview with senior US Department of Defense official, 2019.

64. Interview with senior US Department of Defense official, 2019.

65. Interview with senior US Department of Defense official, 2019.

66. Interview with senior US Department of Defense official, 2019.

67. Office of the Director of National Intelligence (ODNI), "Assessing Russian Activities and Intentions in Recent U.S. Elections," ICA 2017-01D, January 6, 2017, ii.

68. United States of America v. Viktor Borisovich Netyksho et al., United States District Court for the District of Columbia, Criminal Indictment, filed July 13, 2018.

69. Sanger, *Perfect Weapon*, 19–20.

70. Robert S. Mueller III, *Report on the Investigation into Russian Interference in the 2016 Presidential Election*, vol. 1 (Washington, DC: US Department of Justice, March 2019).

71. Mueller, *Report on the Investigation into Russian Interference*, 1:36–37.

72. United States of America v. Viktor Borisovich Netyksho et al.

73. Mueller, *Report on the Investigation into Russian Interference*, 1:38, 40.

74. Mueller, *Report on the Investigation into Russian Interference*, 1:37, 50.

75. ODNI, "Assessing Russian Activities and Intentions," 4.

76. Mueller, *Report on the Investigation into Russian Interference*, 1:25.

77. "Пресс-конференция по итогам переговоров президентов России и США" [Press conference following talks between the presidents of Russia and the United States], Президент России [President of Russia], July 16, 2018.

78. Mark Kelton, interview by the author, June 2, 2020.

79. Баранец [Baranets], "Начальник Генштаба Вооруженных сил" [Chief of the General Staff of the Armed Forces]. Also see, for example, Руслан Пухов [Ruslan Pukhov], "Война, которую Россия выиграла" [The war that Russia won], Известия [Izvestia], October 13, 2017.

80. Stephen Biddle, *Afghanistan and the Future of Warfare: Implications for Army and Defense Policy* (Carlisle, PA: Strategic Studies Institute, US Army War College, November 2002).

81. On punishment campaigns, see Seth G. Jones, *Waging Insurgent Warfare: Lessons from the Vietcong to the Islamic State* (New York: Oxford University Press, 2017), 47–52; Ivan Arreguín-Toft, *How the Weak Win Wars: A Theory of Asymmetric Conflict* (New York: Cambridge Univer-

sity Press, 2005), 31–32; Robert B. Asprey, *War in the Shadows: The Classic History of Guerrilla Warfare from Ancient Persia to the Present* (New York: Little, Brown, 1994), 108; Nathan Leites and Charles Wolf Jr., *Rebellion and Authority: An Analytic Essay on Insurgent Conflicts* (Santa Monica, CA: RAND, February 1970), 90–131.

82. Human Rights Watch, *World Report 2019: Events of 2018* (New York: Human Rights Watch, 2019); "Indiscriminate Bombing of Syria's Idlib Could Be War Crime, Says France," Reuters, September 12, 2018; Sanu Kainikara, *In the Bear's Shadow: Russian Intervention in Syria* (Canberra, Australia: Air Power Development Centre, Department of Defence, 2018), 90; Brian Glyn Williams and Robert Souza, "Operation 'Retribution': Putin's Military Campaign in Syria, 2015–2016," *Middle East Policy* 23, no. 4 (Winter 2016): 42–60.

83. Jason Lyall, "Does Indiscriminate Violence Incite Insurgent Attacks? Evidence from Chechnya," *Journal of Conflict Resolution* 53, no. 3 (2009): 331–62.

84. Human Rights Watch, *World Report 2019*, 487.

85. "Government Assessment of the Syrian Government's Use of Chemical Weapons on August 21, 2013," US Intelligence Community, released by the White House, Office of the Press Secretary, August 30, 2013; Human Rights Watch, *Attacks on Ghouta: Analysis of Alleged Use of Chemical Weapons in Syria* (New York: Human Rights Watch, 2013); Joby Warrick, "More Than 1,400 Killed in Syrian Chemical Weapons Attack, U.S. Says," *Washington Post*, August 30, 2013.

86. "Seventh Report of the Organisation for the Prohibition of Chemical Weapons-United Nations Joint Investigative Mechanism," United Nations Security Council, October 26, 2017; "Both ISIL and Syrian Government Responsible for Use of Chemical Weapons, UN Security Council Told," *UN News*, November 7, 2017; Rodrigo Campos, "Syrian Government to Blame for April Sarin Attack: UN Report," Reuters, October 26, 2017; Stephanie Nebehay, "Syrian Government Was behind April Sarin Gas Attack, UN Says," *Independent*, September 6, 2017.

87. "French Declassified Intelligence Report on Syria Gas Attacks," Reuters, April 14, 2018.

88. On Russia's diplomatic and disinformation campaign, see Seth G. Jones, ed., *Moscow's War in Syria* (Washington, DC: Center for Strategic and International Studies, 2020), 41–51.

89. Thomas Gibbons-Neff, Jeremy White, and David Botti, "The U.S. Has Troops in Syria. So Do the Russians and Iranians. Here's Where," *New York Times*, April 11, 2018.

90. *Iran's Priorities in a Turbulent Middle East* (Brussels: International Crisis Group, April 13, 2018).

91. On the number of Islamic Revolutionary Guard Corps-Quds Force (IRGC-QF) troops in Syria, see, for example, the data from Gadi Eisenkot, former chief of staff of the Israel Defense Forces, in Bret Stephens, "The Man Who Humbled Qassim Suleimani," *New York Times*, January 12, 2019. On IRGC-QF support to combat operations in Syria, see Uskowi, *Temperature Rising*, 77–96; Afshon Ostovar, *Vanguard of the Imam: Religion, Politics, and Iran's Revolutionary Guards* (New York: Oxford University Press, 2016), 204–29.

92. Uskowi, *Temperature Rising*, 82.

93. Interview with senior Jordanian and US officials, 2019. See also Phillip Smyth, *Lebanese Hezbollah's Islamic Resistance in Syria* (Washington, DC: Washington Institute for Near East Policy, April 26, 2018).

94. See, for example, Ярослав Карный-Розшук [Yaroslav Karny-Rozshuk], "А если взвесить все трезво?" [And if you weigh everything soberly?], Военно-промышленный курьер [Military-industrial courier], no. 23 (June 23, 2020); Максим Калашников [Maxim Kalashnikov], "Так нужна ли нам Сирия?" [So do we need Syria?], Военно-промышленный курьер [Military-industrial courier], no. 22 (June 16, 2020).

95. US Department of the Treasury, "Treasury Increases Pressure on Russian Financier," September 23, 2020; US Army, *Russian Private Military Companies: Their Use and How to Consider Them in Operations, Competition, and Conflict* (Fort Meade, MD: US Army, Asymmetric Warfare Group, April 2020).

96. McRaven, interview.

97. Seth G. Jones, Brian Katz, Catrina Doxsee, Eric McQueen, and Joe Moye, *Russia's Corporate Soldiers: The Global Expansion of Moscow's Private Military Companies* (Washington, DC: Center for Strategic and International Studies, 2021).

98. On the role of Russian special operations forces, see, for example, Александр Дворников [Alexander Dvornikov], Штабы для новых войн [Headquarters for new wars], Военно-промышленный курьер [Military-industrial courier], July 23, 2018.

99. Brian Katz, Seth G. Jones, Catrina Doxsee, and Nicholas Harrington, *Moscow's Mercenary Wars: The Expansion of Russian Private Military Companies* (Washington, DC: Center for Strategic and International Studies, 2020). Data updated to 2021.

100. David Petraeus, interview by the author, May 22, 2020.

101. See the comments by Gerasimov in "Векторы развития военной

стратегии" [Vectors of military strategy development], Красная звезда [Red star], March 4, 2019.

102. "Joint Statement by the Federal Bureau of Investigation (FBI), the Cybersecurity and Infrastructure Security Agency (CISA), the office of the Director of National Intelligence (ODNI), and the National Security Agency (NSA)," January 5, 2021.

103. United States of America v. Peter Rafael Dzibinski Debbins, District Court for the Eastern District of Virginia, Criminal no. 1:20-cr-193, August 20, 2020.

104. Владимир Путин [Vladimir Putin], Послание Президента Федеральному Собранию [Presidential Address to the Federal Assembly], Moscow, April 21, 2021.

105. Герасимов [Gerasimov], "Ценность науки в предвидении" [The value of science is in the foresight].

106. Nagata, interview.

CHAPTER 5: GUARDIAN OF THE REVOLUTION

1. Peter Baker, Ronen Bergman, David D. Kirkpatrick, Julian E. Barnes, and Alissa J. Rubin, "Seven Days in January: How Trump Pushed U.S. and Iran to the Brink of War," *New York Times*, January 11, 2020.

2. Baker et al., "Seven Days in January."

3. Baker et al., "Seven Days in January."

4. US Air Force, "MQ-9 Reaper," September 23, 2015; Gordon Lubold and Warren P. Strobel, "Secret U.S. Missile Aims to Kill Only Terrorists, Not Nearby Civilians," *Wall Street Journal*, May 9, 2019.

5. Colby Itkowitz and David A. Fahrenthold, "Trump Privately Told Donors New Details about Soleimani Airstrike at Mar-a-Lago Fundraiser," *Washington Post*, January 18, 2020; Adam Entous and Evan Osnos, "Qassem Suleimani and How Nations Decide to Kill," *New Yorker*, February 10, 2020.

6. Interviews with US government officials, 2020; Peter Beaumont, "Making of a Martyr: How Qassem Suleimani Was Hunted Down," *Guardian*, January 5, 2020.

7. US Department of Defense, "Statement by the Department of Defense," January 2, 2020.

8. Donald J. Trump (@realDonaldTrump), Twitter, January 3, 2020, 8:54 a.m.

9. Interview with US government officials, 2020.

10. Interview with US government official, 2020.

11. عباس میرزایی [Abbas Mirzaei], هجوم به تهاجم [Attack to invasion] (Tehran: Nashr-I Ya Zahra, 1395 [2016]), 11.

12. رازهای زندگی [Saeedeh Asadian-Seyyed Asad Rajabi], "سعیده اسدیان-سید اسد رجبی سردار ایرانی: حاج قاسم چگونه زندگی می‌کند [Secrets of the life of the Iranian general: How Qassem Soleimani lives], خبرگزاری فارس [Fars News], August 24, 2015.

13. "خاطرات – احمد،سلیمانی" [Soleimani, Ahmed—Memoirs], ساجد دفاع مقدس [Sajed Defae-e Moghaddas], April 8, 2007.

14. "خاطرات – احمد،سلیمانی" [Soleimani, Ahmed—Memoirs].

15. "خاطرات – احمد،سلیمانی" [Soleimani, Ahmed—Memoirs].

16. حاج قاسم : جستاری در خاطرات حاج قاسم [Ali Akbari Mazdabadi], علی اکبری مزدآبادی سلیمانی [Haj Qassem: A look at the memoirs of Haj Qassem Soleimani] (Tehran: Ya Zahra, 1394 [2015]); میرزایی [Mirzaei], هجوم به تهاجم [Attack to invasion], 11; "سردار قاسم سلیمانی :گمنامي: خواسته شهیدان ما بود" [Commander Qassem Soleimani: Anonymity was the wish of our martyrs], روزنامه جمهوري اسلامي [Jomhouri-ye Eslami], June 7, 2005; الهه بهشتی [Elahe Beheshti], دل دریایی: خاطرات سردار شهید محمد گرامی رئیس ستاد لشکر 41 ثارالله [A heart as wide as the sea: Memoirs of the martyred commander Mohammad Gerami, Forty-First Tharallah Division headquarters deputy] (Kerman, Iran: Lashkar-e 41 Sarallah, 1997), 23.

17. رجبی [Rajabi], "رازهای زندگی سردار ایرانی" [Secrets of the life of the Iranian general].

18. "سردار قاسم سلیمانی :گمنامي: خواسته شهیدان ما بود" [Commander Qassem Soleimani: Anonymity was the wish of our martyrs].

19. رجبی [Rajabi], "رازهای زندگی سردار ایرانی" [Secrets of the life of the Iranian general].

20. "سردار قاسم سلیمانی :گمنامي: خواسته شهیدان ما بود" [Commander Qassem Soleimani: Anonymity was the wish of our martyrs].

21. On the creation of the IRGC, see, for example, Afshon Ostovar, *Vanguard of the Imam: Religion, Politics, and Iran's Revolutionary Guards* (New York: Oxford University Press, 2016); Nader Uskowi, *Temperature Rising: Iran's Revolutionary Guards and Wars in the Middle East* (Lanham, MD: Rowman and Littlefield, 2019).

22. "Khomeyni Calls on Soldiers," Tehran Domestic Service in Persian, US Foreign Broadcast Information Service, February 14, 1979.

23. Ostovar, *Vanguard of the Imam*, 38; Uskowi, *Temperature Rising*.

24. Ali Alfoneh, "Iran's Secret Network: Major General Qassem Suleimani's Inner Circle," *Middle Eastern Outlook*, no. 2 (March 2011): 1.

25. See, for example, Juan Cole and Nikki Keddie, eds., *Sh'ism and Social Protest* (New Haven, CT: Yale University Press, 1986).

26. "سردار قاسم سليماني: گمنامي خواسته شهيدان ما بود" [Commander Qassem Solei-mani: Anonymity was the wish of our martyrs].

27. See, for example, سپاه پاسداران انقلاب اسلامی [Islamic Revolutionary Guard Corps], گذری بر دو سال جنگ [A glance at two years of war] (Tehran: Political Office, 1982).

28. See, for example, Efraim Karsh, *The Iran-Iraq War: A Military Analysis* (London: International Institute for Strategic Studies, 1987).

29. صف – خاطرات رزمندگان کرمان در عملیات کرخه [Ashraf Seif al-Dini], اشرف سیف‌الدینی نور [The line—Memoirs of Kerman fighters in Karkheh-ye Nour opera-tion] (Kerman: Vadi'at, 2008).

30. "تشریح سوابق فرمانده جدید نیروی قدس سپاه توسط سردار شریف" [IRGC spokesperson describes part of General Qaani's background, the new commander of the Quds Force], سپاه نیوز [Sepah news], January 5, 2020.

31. "درباره اسماعیل قاآنی" [About Ismail Qaani], خبرگزاری جمهوری اسلامی [Islamic Republic News Agency], January 3, 2020.

32. آغاز تا پایان: بررسی وقایع سیاسی - نظامی [Mohammad Durudiyan], حسین درودیان جنگ از زمینه سازی تهاجم عراق تا آتش بس [Beginning to end: A year-by-year analysis] (Tehran: Sepah Center for War Studies and Research, 1383 [2004/2005]), 50.

33. مزدآبادی [Mazdabadi], حاج قاسم : جستاری در خاطرات [Haj Qassem: A look at the memoirs]. On Soleimani's operations, also see علیرضا لطف‌الله زادگان [Ali-Reza Lotfollahzadegan], روزشمار جنگ ایران و عراق [Iran-Iraq War chronology] (Tehran: Sepah-e Pasdaran-e Enghelab-e Eslami, 2008), 49:262–72.

34. See, for example, میرزایی [Mirzaei], هجوم به تهاجم [Attack to invasion].

35. Dexter Filkins, "The Shadow Commander," *New Yorker*, September 23, 2013.

36. On OPERATION KARBALA 1, see مزدآبادی [Mazdabadi], جستاری : حاج قاسم [Haj Qassem: A look at the memoirs], 13; علی اکبر هاشمی رفسنجانی در خاطرات [Ali-Akbar Hashemi Rafsanjani], کارنامه و خاطرات هاشمی رفسنجانی، سال 1365 [Record and memoirs of Hashemi Rafsanjani 1986–87] (Tehran: Daftar-e Nashr-e Maaref-e Enghelab, 2009), 543.

37. روزشمار [Mehdi Ansari and Mahmoud Yazdanfam], محمود یزدانفام و مهدي انصاري جنگ ایران و عراق [Iran-Iraq War chronology] (Tehran: Sepah-e Pasdaran-e Enghelab-e Eslami, 2008), 51:644.

38. Interview with Afghan government official, 2020.

39. انصاری و یزدانفام [Ansari and Yazdanfam], روزشمار جنگ ایران و عراق [Iran-Iraq War chronology], 51:256, 607.

40. مرتضی آوینی[Morteza Aviny], "عملیات کربلای ۵" [Karbala V operation], 4shared, posted January 25, 2011, by omidhosseini80 (video, 14:54).

41. یحیي فوزي و علیرضا لطف‌الله زادگان [Yahya Fowzi and Ali-Reza Lotfollahzade-

gan], روزشمار جنگ ایران و عراق [Iran-Iraq War chronology] (Tehran: Sepah-e Pasdaran-e Enghelab-e Eslami, 2008), 43:284.

42. رجبی [Rajabi], "رازهای زندگی سردار ایرانی" [Secrets of the life of the Iranian general].

43. "عکس: آیت الله خامنه ای، شهید باکری، محسن رضایی، قاسم سلیمانی، رحیم صفوی در جبهه" [Photo: Ayatollah Khamenei, Martyr Bakeri, Mohsen Rezai, Qassem Soleimani, Rahim Safavi in the front], راسخون [Rasekhoon] (Tehran), January 10, 2011, http://www.rasekhoon.net.

44. کذری بر دو سال سپاه پاسداران انقلاب اسلامی [Islamic Revolutionary Guard Corps], جنگ [A glance at two years of war], 15.

45. Pierre Razoux, *The Iran-Iraq War*, trans. Nicholas Elliott (Cambridge, MA: Harvard University Press, 2015); David Crist, *The Twilight War: The Secret History of America's Thirty-Year Conflict with Iran* (New York: Penguin, 2020); Kenneth R. Timmerman, *The Death Lobby: How the West Armed Iraq* (New York: Houghton Mifflin, 1991).

46. The argument that the Iran-Iraq War was a proxy war supported by the United States is prevalent in IRGC histories of the war. See, for example, نقد و بررسی جنگ ایران و عراق: اجتناب محمد درودیان [Muhammad Durudiyan], ناپذیری جنگ [Critical study of the Iran-Iraq War: The inevitability of the war] (Tehran: Sipah-i Markaz-i Mutala'at va Tahghighat-I Jang, 2003–4), 198–201, 255–56, 283–85.

47. Williamson Murray and Kevin M. Woods, *The Iran-Iraq War: A Military and Strategic History* (New York: Cambridge University Press, 2014); Razoux, *Iran-Iraq War*.

48. Razoux, *Iran-Iraq War*, 574.

49. See, for example, Brandon A. Pinkley, *Guarding History: The Islamic Revolutionary Guard Corps and the Memory of the Iran-Iraq War*, Special Historical Study 12 (Washington, DC: Joint History Office, Office of the Chairman of the Joint Chiefs of Staff, 2018). Also see various IRGC histories, such as کتاب رویارویی استراتژی‌ها حسین اردستانی [Hossein Ardestani], جنگ عراق و ایران [Confrontation of strategies in the Iran-Iraq War] (Tehran: Sepah Center for Sacred Defense Documents and Research, 1388 [2009/2010]), 101–2; محمد درودیان [Durudiyan], آتش بس آغاز تا پایان [Armistice, beginning to end], 44.

50. "Iran: Complete Regulations of the Islamic Republic of Iran Armed Forces," Near East and South Asia Supplement, FBIS-NES-94-208-S, US Foreign Broadcast Information Service, October 27, 1994. Also see, for example, International Institute for Strategic Studies, "Tehran's Strategic Intent," chap. 1 in *Iran's Networks of Influence in the Middle East* (London: Routledge, 2020).

51. Ali Alfoneh, "Tehran's Shia Foreign Legion," Carnegie Endowment for International Peace, January 31, 2018.

52. مصاحبه با برادر مصلح [Interview with Brother Mosleh], پیام انقلاب [Payam-e enqelab], no. 138 (June 8, 1985): 73; Ostovar, *Vanguard of the Imam*, 117.

53. On the number of IRGC personnel in Lebanon, see Daniel Byman, *Deadly Connections: States That Sponsor Terrorism* (New York: Cambridge University Press, 2005), 82.

54. As IRGC brigadier general Ramazan Sharif remarked: "The Quds Force always endeavors to empower Muslims for the elimination of oppression, until, God willing, Jerusalem is taken back from occupation by the Zionists." "تشریح سوابق فرمانده جدید نیروی قدس سپاه توسط سردارشریف" [IRGC spokesperson describes part of General Qaani's background, the new commander of the Quds Force].

55. US Defense Intelligence Agency, *Iran Military Power: Ensuring Regime Survival and Securing Regional Dominance* (Washington, DC: US Defense Intelligence Agency, 2019), 57–63.

56. Quoted in Filkins, "Shadow Commander."

57. Ali Alfoneh, "Brigadier General Qassem Suleimani: A Biography," *Middle Eastern Outlook*, no. 1 (January 2011).

58. "درباره اسماعیل قاآنی" [About Ismail Qaani].

59. اویس روشندل [Oveys Roshandel], "سردار تحت تعقیب آمریکا و اسراییل + تصاویر" [The general wanted by the US and Israel + images], مشرق نیوز [Mashregh news], December 6, 2010.

60. کرامتی مرتضی [Mortaza Karamati], شجاعت‌ها و رشادت‌های سردار حاج سربازان سردار: قاسم سلیمانی و شهدای مدافع حرم [The soldiers of the commander: The bravery of General Qassem Soleimani and the martyred defenders of the sanctuary] (Qom, Iran: Sih Nuqtah, 1395 [2016/2017]). On Safavi, see "ناگفته های رحیم صفوی از 10 سال فرماندهی سپاه پاسداران" [Rahim Safavi's untold stories from ten years as revolutionary guards chief], مرکز اسناد انقلاب اسلامی [Islamic Revolution's Documents Center], January 11, 2010.

61. Joseph Votel, interview by the author, May 21, 2020.

CHAPTER 6: THE "SOLEIMANI STRUT"

1. See, for example, Alex Strick van Linschoten and Felix Kuehn, eds., *The Taliban Reader: War, Islam and Politics* (New York: Oxford University Press, 2018).

2. افغانستان، عصر مجاهدین و برآمدن طالبان [Tschanguiz Pahlavan], چنگیز پهلوان [Afghanistan—The era of the mujahideen and the rise of the Taliban]

(Tehran: Ghatreh, 1999). Also see, for example, US Embassy (Islamabad), "Afghanistan and Sectarian Violence Contribute to a Souring of Pakistan's Relations with Iran" (cable), March 13, 1997, released by the National Security Archive, George Washington University, Washington, DC.

3. US Embassy (Islamabad), "Afghanistan: [Excised] Describes Pakistan's Current Thinking" (cable), March 9, 1998, released by the National Security Archive, George Washington University, Washington, DC.

4. صادق زیباکلام [Sadegh Zibakalam], عکس های یادگاری با جامعه مدنی [Memorial photos with civil society] (Tehran: Entesharat-e Rowzaneh, 1999), 261.

5. Interview with foreign government official, 2020.

6. "Iran, Tajikistan Review Expansion of Defense Cooperation," Islamic Republic News Agency, January 21, 1999; Ali Soufan, "Qassem Soleimani and Iran's Unique Regional Strategy," *CTC Sentinel* 11, no. 10 (November 2018): 3.

7. The photograph comes from Anisa Shaheed, "Who Is Soleimani's Successor Ismail Khan?" *Tolo News* (Afghanistan), January 5, 2020.

8. Martin Chulov, "Qassem Suleimani: The Iranian general 'secretly running' Iraq," *Guardian*, July 28, 2011.

9. On Soleimani's relationship with his soldiers, see کرامتی مرتضی [Mortaza Karamati], سربازان سردار: شجاعت‌ها و رشادت‌های سردار حاج قاسم سلیمانی و شهدای مدافع حرم [The soldiers of the commander: The bravery of General Qasem Soleimani and the martyred defenders of the sanctuary] (Qom, Iran: Sih Nuqtah, 1395 [2016/2017]), 37–38.

10. سعیده اسدیان-سید اسد رجبی [Saeedeh Asadian-Seyyed Asad Rajabi], "رازهای زندگی سردار ایرانی: حاج قاسم چگونه زندگی می‌کند [Secrets of the life of the Iranian general: How Qassem Soleimani lives], خبرگزاری فارس [Fars News], August 24, 2015.

11. US Embassy (Islamabad), "Afghanistan: Taliban Seem to Have Less Funds and Supplies This Year, but the Problem Does Not Appear to Be That Acute" (cable), February 17, 1999, released by the National Security Archive, George Washington University, Washington, DC.

12. Interview with foreign government official present at the meeting, 2020.

13. Ryan Crocker, interview by the author, July 3, 2020.

14. Crocker, interview.

15. Crocker, interview.

16. Nader Uskowi, *Temperature Rising: Iran's Revolutionary Guards and Wars in the Middle East* (Lanham, MD: Rowman and Littlefield, 2019), 50.

17. James Dobbins, interview by the author, June 30, 2020.

18. Crocker, interview.

19. Crocker, interview.

20. Dexter Filkins, "The Shadow Commander," *New Yorker*, September 23, 2013.

21. George Tenet, *At the Center of the Storm: My Years at the CIA* (New York: HarperCollins, 2007), 244.

22. George W. Bush, *Decision Points* (New York: Crown, 2010), 233.

23. George W. Bush, "The President's State of the Union Address," United States Capitol, Washington, DC, January 29, 2002.

24. Dobbins, interview.

25. Crocker, interview; Ryan Crocker, email to the author, December 6, 2020.

26. Crocker, interview.

27. Bruce Riedel, "The Mysterious Relationship between Al-Qa'ida and Iran," *CTC Sentinel* 3, no. 7 (July 2010): 1–3.

28. Najwa bin Laden, Omar bin Laden, and Jean Sasson, *Growing Up Bin Laden: Osama's Wife and Son Take Us inside Their Secret World* (New York: St. Martin's Press, 2009), 294–95.

29. For an overview of al-Qaeda and Iran, see Seth G. Jones, "Al Qaeda in Iran: Why Tehran Is Accommodating the Terrorist Group," *Foreign Affairs*, January 29, 2012.

30. US Department of Justice, "Al Qaeda Spokesman Sulaiman Abu Ghayth Sentenced in Manhattan Federal Court to Life in Prison for Conspiring to Kill Americans, Providing Material Support to Terrorists," September 23, 2014.

31. On the deaths of Abu Muhammad al-Masri and Abu al-Khayr al-Masri, see Adam Goldman, Eric Schmitt, Farnaz Fassihi, and Ronen Bergman, "Al-Qaeda's No. 2, Accused in U.S. Embassy Attacks, Was Killed in Iran," *New York Times*, November 13, 2020.

32. Quoted by Andrew Nagorski, *The Greatest Battle* (New York: Simon & Schuster, 2007), 150–51.

33. Uskowi, *Temperature Rising*, 51–52.

34. Coalition Provisional Authority, "Presidential Update," May 29, 2003, CPA Archives (CD-ROM).

35. L. Paul Bremer, interview by the author, November 15, 2007.

36. Coalition Provisional Authority, Memo on Meeting between Ambassador Ryan Crocker and Abdul Aziz Hakim, June 9, 2003, CPA Archives (CD-ROM).

37. Julie Chappell to Ambassador Sawers, "Subject: Political Process; Call on Abdul Aziz al Hakim" (memo), June 20, 2003, CPA Archives (CD-ROM).

38. All sources here come from the CPA Archives (CD-ROM). John Sawers to Ambassador Bremer, "Subject: Visit to Tehran" (memo), July 31, 2003. On US concerns with Iran, also see Mike Gfoeller to Paul Bremer, "Subject: South Central Region: Progress, Opportunities, and Risks" (email), March 2, 2004; John F. Berry to the Administrator, "Subject: Weekly GC Update—Karbala" (info memo), January 31, 2004. Better border control arrangements came up repeatedly in CPA documents, including Steven W. Casteel to Deputy Administrator Jones, "Subject: Talking Points—Border Update; IPS Training (Egyptian Involvement); Jordan Academy" (info memo), March 17, 2004.

39. Uskowi, *Temperature Rising*, 52.

40. Norman Roule, interview by the author, June 26, 2020.

41. George W. Bush, "Press Conference by the President," White House, February 14, 2007.

42. Brian Castner, *The Long Walk: A Story of War and the Life that Follows* (New York: Doubleday, 2012).

43. The data were declassified by the US Department of Defense in 2015.

44. Stanley McChrystal, interview by the author, June 8, 2020; David Crist, *The Twilight War: The Secret History of America's Thirty-Year Conflict with Iran* (New York: Penguin, 2020), 521.

45. Charles Cleveland, interview by the author, May 15, 2020.

46. On Muqtada al-Sadr and Iran, see Uskowi, *Temperature Rising*, 53.

47. Joel D. Rayburn and Frank K. Sobchak, eds., *The U.S. Army in the Iraq War*, vol. 2, *Surge and Withdrawal, 2007–2011* (Carlisle, PA: Strategic Studies Institute, US Army War College Press, 2019), 66.

48. "ناگفته‌های جنگ ۳۳روزه در گفتگو با سرلشکر حاج قاسم سلیمانی" [Untold facts on Israel-Hezbollah War in an interview with Major General Qassem Soleimani], Khamenei.ir, October 1, 2019.

49. On Iran's Shia population, see the Central Intelligence Agency's *World Factbook*, 2020.

50. "ناگفته‌های جنگ ۳۳روزه" [Untold facts on Israel-Hezbollah War].

51. "ناگفته‌های جنگ ۳۳روزه" [Untold facts on Israel-Hezbollah War].

52. "ناگفته‌های جنگ ۳۳روزه" [Untold facts on Israel-Hezbollah War].

53. "ناگفته‌های جنگ ۳۳روزه" [Untold facts on Israel-Hezbollah War].

54. "خطاب السيد نصر الله في مهرجان الانتصار" [Mr. Nasrallah's speech at the victory festival], الأخبار [Al-Akhbar], September 23, 2006.

55. "Poll: Majority Wants Olmert Out," *Yediot Ahronoth*, August 25, 2006.

56. Caroline B. Glick, "The Path to the Next Lebanon War," *Jerusalem Post*, July 11, 2011.

57. Quoted in Michael Weiss, "Iran's Top Spy Is the Modern-Day Karla, John Le Carré's Villainous Mastermind," *Daily Beast*, January 3, 2020.

58. Stanley McChrystal, interview by the author, June 8, 2020.

59. Adam Entous and Evan Osnos, "Qassem Soleimani and How Nations Decide to Kill," *New Yorker*, February 10, 2020.

60. Entous and Osnos, "Qassem Soleimani and How Nations Decide to Kill."

61. Entous and Osnos, "Qassem Soleimani and How Nations Decide to Kill."

62. McChrystal, interview.

63. Michael R. Gordon and Bernard E. Trainor, *The Endgame: The Inside Story of the Struggle for Iraq, from George W. Bush to Barack Obama* (New York: Vintage, 2013), 322–23.

64. Crocker, interview.

65. Crocker, interview.

66. David Petraeus, interview by the author, May 22, 2020.

67. Petraeus, interview.

68. Filkins, "Shadow Commander."

69. Pierre Razoux, *The Iran-Iraq War*, trans. Nicholas Elliott (Cambridge, MA: Harvard University Press, 2015), 131–34, 211–15; Williamson Murray and Kevin M. Woods, *The Iran-Iraq War: A Military and Strategic History* (New York: Cambridge University Press, 2014), 177–86.

70. گذری بر دو سال [سپاه پاسداران انقلاب اسلامی][Islamic Revolutionary Guard Corps], جنگ [A glance at two years of war] (Tehran: Political Office, 1982); Murray and Woods, *Iran-Iraq War*, 178.

71. Razoux, *Iran-Iraq War*, 213.

72. [محمدیاسر رجبی][Mohammadiassar Rajabi], "کابوس آمریکایی‌ها" [The Americans' nightmare], مشرق نیوز [Mashregh news], November 6, 2011.

73. US Department of Justice, "Administration Takes Additional Steps to Hold the Government of Syria Accountable for Violent Repression against the Syrian People," May 18, 2011.

74. Barack Obama, "Remarks by the President on Ending the War in Iraq," White House, Office of the Press Secretary, October 21, 2011.

75. Ali Khedery, "Why We Stuck with Maliki—and Lost Iraq," *Washington Post*, July 3, 2014.

76. Michael Nagata, interview by the author, May 19, 2020.

77. Tim Arango, James Risen, Farnaz Fassihi, Ronen Bergman, and Murtaza Hussain, "The Iran Cables: Secret Documents Show How Tehran Wields Power in Iraq," *New York Times*, November 19, 2019.

78. Arango et al., "Iran Cables."

79. Arango et al., "Iran Cables."

80. Uskowi, *Temperature Rising*, 20–21, 72, 111, 208.

81. Rayburn and Sobchak, *U.S. Army in the Iraq War*, 2:639.

CHAPTER 7: THE MARTYR

1. Soleimani apparently arrived in Moscow on July 24, 2015, on Iran Air flight 5130 (operated by Aeroflot) from Tehran, and left Moscow on July 26 on Aeroflot flight 5120. See Jennifer Griffin and Lucas Tomlinson, "Exclusive: Quds Force Commander Soleimani Visited Moscow, Met Russian Leaders in Defiance of Sanctions," Fox News, August 6, 2015; Emanuele Ottolenghi, "Russia's Airline Aeroflot Carried Qassem Soleimani to Moscow and Back," Federation for the Defense of Democracies Policy Brief, August 17, 2015.

2. Interviews with US government officials, 2019 and 2020. Also see Laila Bassam and Tom Perry, "How Iranian General Plotted Out Syrian Assault in Moscow," Reuters, October 6, 2015.

3. Kareem Shaheen, "ISIS 'Controls 50% of Syria' After Seizing Historic City of Palmyra," *Guardian*, May 21, 2015.

4. Interviews with US government officials, 2019 and 2020. Also see Bassam and Perry, "How Iranian General Plotted Out Syrian Assault in Moscow."

5. Валерий Герасимов [Valery Gerasimov], "Ценность науки в предвидении: Новые вызовы требуют переосмыслить формы и способы ведения боевых действий" [The value of science is in the foresight: New challenges demand rethinking the forms and methods of carrying out combat operations], Военно-промышленный курьер [Military-industrial courier], no. 8 (February 26, 2013).

6. Keith A. Grant and Bernd Kaussler, "The Battle of Aleppo: External Patrons and the Victimization of Civilians in Civil War," *Small Wars and Insurgencies* 31, no. 1 (2020): 1–33.

7. "السيد نصرالله:بضياع سوريا تضيع فلسطين والقدس وغزة" [Mr. Nasrallah: With the loss of Syria, Palestine, Jerusalem and Gaza are lost], قناة العالم [Al-alam news], May 25, 2013.

8. Nader Uskowi, *Temperature Rising: Iran's Revolutionary Guards and Wars in the Middle East* (Lanham, MD: Rowman and Littlefield, 2019), 82.

9. Norman Roule, interview by the author, June 26, 2020.

10. Anton Lavrov, *The Russian Air Campaign in Syria: A Preliminary Analysis* (Arlington, VA: Center for Naval Analysis, June 2018).

11. Genevieve Casagrande, *Russian Airstrikes in Syria: September 30, 2015–September 19, 2016* (Washington, DC: Institute for the Study of War, October 2016); Tom Perry, Jack Stubbs, and Estelle Shirbon, "Russia and Turkey Trade Accusations over Syria," Reuters, February 3, 2016.

12. Tim Ripley, *Operation Aleppo: Russia's War in Syria* (Lancaster, England: Telic-Herrick Publications, 2018).

13. "Syria Army Captures Rebel-Held Hanano Area in Aleppo," Al Jazeera, November 27, 2016.

14. Ripley, *Operation Aleppo*.

15. Laila Bassam, "Wasteland Revealed after Battle for Aleppo's Old City," Reuters, December 9, 2016.

16. Genevieve Casagrande, *Russian Airstrikes in Syria: November 8–December 6, 2016* (Washington, DC: Institute for the Study of War, December 2016).

17. Laila Bassam and Lisa Barrington, "Syrian General Says Aleppo Offensive in Final Stages," Reuters, December 12, 2016.

18. Uskowi, *Temperature Rising*, 83.

19. Roule, interview.

20. See, for example, Amir Toumaj, "IRGC Qods Force Chief Spotted in Aleppo," *Long War Journal*, December 18, 2016; Heshmat Alavi, "Why Did Iran Publish Images of Their General Qasem Soleimani in Aleppo?" Al Arabiya, December 25, 2016; "حضور حاج قاسم سلیمانی در حلب" [IRGC Quds Haj Qassem Soleimani in Aleppo Syria], YouTube, posted December 26, 2016, by ali javid; "حضور حاج قاسم سلیمانی در حلب" [Iran IRGC Quds Haj Qassem Soleimani in Aleppo Syria], YouTube, posted December 4, 2016, by ali javid.

21. See "حضور حاج قاسم سلیمانی در حلب" [IRGC Quds Haj Qassem Soleimani in Aleppo Syria].

22. The Center for Strategic and International Studies (CSIS) translated the letter, which is found in Brecht Jonkers, "Iranian Courtesy: General Soleimani Apologizes to Albukamal House Owner," *Al-Masdar News*, November 25, 2017.

23. "رهبر معظم انقلاب اسلامی: مخالفت آمریکا با محور مقاومت در منطقه به نتیجه نخواهد رسید" [Supreme leader of the Islamic revolution: The US opposition to the axis of resistance in the region will not succeed], خبرگزاری مهر [Mehr News Agency], October 3, 2010.

24. Michael Morell, interview by the author, May 21, 2020.

25. Michael Vickers, interview by the author, May 19, 2020.

26. On Iranian corridors and routes, see, for example, Rex W. Tillerson, "Remarks on the Way Forward for the United States Regarding Syria"

(speech, Hoover Institute at Stanford University, January 17, 2018); Uskowi, *Temperature Rising*, 88.

27. Seth G. Jones, *Containing Tehran: Understanding Iran's Power and Exploiting Its Vulnerabilities* (Washington, DC: Center for Strategic and International Studies, 2020).

28. On Iran's regional interests, see, for example, حسن خدادادی [Hassan Khoda-dadi], "ثبات و امنیت و حفظ تمامیت ارضی ایران" [Stability and security and maintaining Iran's territorial integrity], پایگاه خبری تحلیلی بصیرت [Basirat news], June 16, 2019.

29. Interview with multiple individuals in the room during the briefing, 2020.

30. Donald Trump, "Remarks by President Trump on the Joint Comprehensive Plan of Action," White House, May 8, 2018.

31. Mike Pompeo, "After the Deal: A New Iran Strategy" (speech, Heritage Foundation, Washington, DC, May 21, 2018).

32. US Department of the Treasury, "Iran Sanctions," 2020.

33. International Monetary Fund, "Islamic Republic of Iran: At a Glance," June 2020.

34. "Iran Says It Continues to Surpass Enriched Uranium Limits," Radio Farda, August 13, 2019.

35. Tony Thomas, interview by the author, May 22, 2020.

36. Joel D. Rayburn and Frank K. Sobchak, eds., *The U.S. Army in the Iraq War*, vol. 2, *Surge and Withdrawal, 2007–2011* (Carlisle, PA: Strategic Studies Institute, US Army War College Press, 2019), 598.

37. Haider al-Abadi, interview by Charlie Rose, *The Charlie Rose Show*, January 26, 2015.

38. For an Iranian perspective on the Saudi war, see, for example, مهدی نوری [Mehdi Nouri], "کارنامه 4 سال جنگ یمن چه می گوید؟" [What does the record of the 4 years of the Yemeni war say?], پایگاه خبری تحلیلی بصیرت [Basirat news], March 25, 2019.

39. Michael Knights, "The Houthi War Machine: From Guerrilla War to State Capture," *CTC Sentinel* 11, no. 8 (2018): 15, 21.

40. United Nations Security Council, *Letter Dated 26 January 2018 from the Panel of Experts on Yemen Mandated by Security Council Resolution 2342 (2017) Addressed to the President of the Security Council*, S/2018/68 (New York: United Nations, January 16, 2018); Uskowi, *Temperature Rising*, 118–19; *Iran's Priorities in a Turbulent Middle East* (Brussels: International Crisis Group, April 13, 2018); Knights, "Houthi War Machine," 15–23.

41. Ali Soufan, "Qassem Soleimani and Iran's Unique Regional Strategy," *CTC Sentinel* 11, no. 10 (November 2018): 1–12.

42. Michael Nagata, interview by the author, May 19, 2020.

43. Vickers, interview.

44. United Nations Security Council, *Letter Dated 26 January 2018*, 29.

45. United Nations Security Council, *Letter Dated 26 January 2018*, 18.

46. Roule, interview.

47. Roule, interview.

48. On Saudi spending in Yemen, see "Saudi Downturn Deepens Yemen's Economic Despair," *Japan Times*, June 22, 2020. On the number of casualties and displaced people in Yemen, see Council on Foreign Relations, "War in Yemen," November 12, 2020.

49. Joseph Biden, "Remarks by President Biden on America's Place in the World," US Department of State Headquarters, Washington, DC, February 4, 2021.

50. Trump, "Remarks by President Trump on the Joint Comprehensive Plan of Action."

51. US Energy Information Administration, "Country Analysis Brief: Saudi Arabia," October 20, 2017.

52. Seth Frantzman, "Are Air Defense Systems Ready to Confront Drone Swarms?" *Defense News*, September 26, 2019.

53. "Shamoon: Destructive Threat Re-emerges with New Sting in Its Tail," Symantec Enterprise Blogs, *Threat Intelligence* (blog), December 14, 2018.

54. US Department of Justice, "Nine Iranians Charged with Conducting Massive Cyber Theft Campaign on Behalf of the Islamic Revolutionary Guard Corps," March 23, 2018.

55. James Lewis, interview by the author, June 3, 2020.

56. The *Financial Times* was the first to report the attack. See Mehul Srivastava, Najmeh Bozorgmehr, and Katrina Manson, "Israel-Iran Attacks: 'Cyber Winter Is Coming,'" *Financial Times*, May 31, 2020. Also see "Iranian Cyberattacks on Israeli Facilities Thwarted for a Year—Report," *Jerusalem Post*, June 7, 2020.

57. Tim Arango, James Risen, Farnaz Fassihi, Ronen Bergman, and Murtaza Hussain, "The Iran Cables: Secret Documents Show How Tehran Wields Power in Iraq," *New York Times*, November 19, 2019.

58. Arango, "Iran Cables."

59. Arango, "Iran Cables."

60. Qassem Soleimani (@sardar_haj_ghasemsoleimani), "Mr. Trump, the gambler! . . ." Instagram photo, July 30, 2018; emphasis added.

61. "Exclusive: Zarif Claims Soleimani Intervened in Diplomacy, Russia Wanted to Destroy JCPOA," *Iran International*, April 25, 2021; Farnaz Fassihi, "Iran's Foreign Minister, in Leaked Tape, Says Revolutionary

Guards Set Policies," *New York Times*, April 25, 2021; Kareem Fahim, "In Leaked Audio, Iran's Foreign Minister Laments Interference by Revolutionary Guard," *Washington Post*, April 26, 2021.

62. Quoted in Alissa J. Rubin, "Iraqis Rise against a Reviled Occupier: Iran," *New York Times*, November 4, 2019.

63. David Petraeus, interview by the author, May 22, 2020.

64. William McRaven, interview by the author, May 21, 2020.

65. "Iranian Campaign Touts IRGC Qods Force Commander Qassem Soleimani as 'Savior of Iraq,'" *MEMRI Special Dispatch*, no. 5877 (November 10, 2014).

66. The assessment of crowd size comes from satellite imagery analysis by Joseph S. Bermudez Jr. See Danika Newlee, Seth G. Jones, and Joseph S. Bermudez Jr., *Signposts of Struggle: Iran's Enduring Protest Movement* (Washington, DC: Center for Strategic and International Studies, January 2020).

67. Erin Cunningham, Sarah Dadouch, and Michael Birnbaum, "Soleimani's Funeral Procession in Iran Sees Massive Crowds and Calls for Revenge," *Washington Post*, January 6, 2020.

68. Nancy Gallagher, Ebrahim Mohseni, and Clay Ramsay, *Iranian Public Opinion under "Maximum Pressure"* (College Park, MD: Center for International and Security Studies, University of Maryland, October 2019), 36.

69. Gallagher et al., *Iranian Public Opinion under "Maximum Pressure,"* 38.

70. "Iran in Mourning, Vows Revenge for Qassem Soleimani's Killing," Al Jazeera, January 3, 2020.

71. Christopher Miller, interview by the author, October 1, 2020.

72. "درباره اسماعیل قاآنی" [About Ismail Qaani], خبرگزاری جمهوری اسلامی [Islamic Republic News Agency], January 3, 2020.

73. Avril Haines, *Annual Threat Assessment of the US Intelligence Community* (Washington, DC: Office of the Director of National Intelligence, April 9, 2021), 13.

74. Roule, interview.

75. "تصویر خاص از سردار قاآنی از سوریه در روزهای کرونایی" [Special image of Sardar Qaani from Syria in the days of corona], تابناک [Tabnak], September 11, 2020.

CHAPTER 8: THE ART OF WAR

1. "习近平在湖北省考察新冠肺炎疫情防控工作" [Xi Jinping visits Hubei province to investigate the prevention and control of the new coronavirus epidemic], 新华 [Xinhua], March 10, 2020.

2. Quoted in Yong Xiong and Nectar Gan, "This Chinese Doctor Tried to Save Lives, but Was Silenced. Now He Has Coronavirus," CNN, February 4, 2020.

3. Quoted in Cathy He, "Chinese Regime Muzzles Media Coverage amid Rampant Coronavirus Outbreak," *Epoch Times*, February 4, 2020.

4. The fabricated letter appeared on multiple accounts associated with Weibo, China's Twitter-like platform, such as "#罗斯福号航母舰长遭解职#美军吹哨人@美国驻华大使馆" [#Roosevelt Aircraft Carrier Captain-Dismissal# U.S. Navy Whistleblower @U.S. Embassy in China], 微博正文 [Weibo], April 4, 2020. It also appeared on Twitter, such as on the account of 自由广东电台 [Radio Free Guangdong] (@RF_Guangdong), Twitter, April 4, 2020, 12:17 p.m.

5. See, for example, Thomas Boghardt, "Operation INFEKTION: Soviet Bloc Intelligence and Its AIDS Disinformation Campaign," *Studies in Intelligence* 53, no. 4 (December 2009): 1–24; US Department of State, *Soviet Influence Activities: A Report on Active Measures and Propaganda, 1986–1987* (Washington, DC: US Department of State, August 1987), 33–43; US Department of State, *The U.S.S.R.'s AIDS Disinformation Campaign* (Washington, DC: US Department of State, July 1987).

6. Boghardt, "Operation INFEKTION," 14.

7. Mark Kelton, interview by the author, June 2, 2020.

8. 陳令申發 [Chen Lingshen], "開國上將張宗遜的子女今何在?" [Where are the children of founding general Zhang Zongxun today?], 每日頭條 [Daily headlines], June 21, 2017.

9. 百度 [Baidu], s.v. "张宗逊" [Zhang Zongxun], accessed January 31, 2021.

10. Bo Zhiyue, "Who Are China's 'Princelings'?" *Diplomat*, November 24, 2015; Bo Zhiyue, *China's Elite Politics: Governance and Democratization* (Singapore: World Scientific, 2010).

11. Minnie Chan, "General Zhang Youxia: Xi Jinping's 'Sworn Brother' Now His Deputy on China's Top Military Body," *South China Morning Post*, October 25, 2017.

12. 郑心仪 [Zheng Xinyi], "上将张又侠,在太空排兵布阵" [General Zhang Youxia, marching in space], 环球人物 [Global people], no. 18 (2016).

13. Mao Zedong, "On Correcting Mistaken Ideas in the Party," in *Selected Works of Mao Tse-tung* (Peking: Foreign Languages Press, 1967), 113.

14. "张又侠: 在纪念张廷发同志诞辰100周年座谈会上的讲话" [Zhang Youxia: Speech at the symposium to commemorate the 100th anniversary of Comrade Zhang Tingfa's birthday], 人民日报 [People's daily], April 11, 2018.

15. Cheng Li, "Zhang Youxia Biography," Brookings Institution, October 25, 2017.

16. "Zhang Youxia—Member of Political Bureau of CPC Central Committee," *China Daily*, October 26, 2017; James Mulvenon, "And Then There Were Seven: The New, Slimmed-Down Central Military Commission," *China Leadership Monitor*, no. 56 (Spring 2018).

17. Chan, "General Zhang Youxia."

18. David Petraeus, " 'The Art of War': As Relevant Now as When It Was Written," *Irish Times*, March 26, 2018.

19. Sun Tzu, *The Art of War*, trans. Samuel B. Griffith (New York: Oxford University Press, 1971), 67.

20. Sun, *Art of War*, 77.

21. Sun, *Art of War*, 147, 149.

22. See Zhang's references to Mao in "张又侠: 在纪念张廷发同志诞辰100周年座谈会上的讲话" [Zhang Youxia: Speech at the symposium to commemorate the 100th anniversary of Comrade Zhang Tingfa's birthday].

23. Mao Zedong, "On Protracted War," in *Selected Works of Mao Tse-tung*, 136–37.

24. Mao Zedong, *On Guerrilla Warfare*, trans. Samuel B. Griffith II (Urbana: University of Illinois Press, 2000), 46.

25. Mao, "On Protracted War," 140.

26. 毛澤東 [Mao Zedong], 毛澤東選集 [Selected works of Mao Zedong], 2nd ed. (Beijing: Renmin chubanshe, 1991), 3:1038–41; Taylor Fravel, *Active Defense: China's Military Strategy since 1949* (Princeton, NJ: Princeton University Press, 2019), 64–67.

27. See, for example, 中国人民解放军军语 [PLA dictionary of military terms] (Beijing: Military Science Press, 2011).

28. For an explanation of the CMC, see, for example, Fravel, *Active Defense*.

29. 彭德怀 [Peng Dehuai], 彭德怀军事文选 [Selected works of Peng Dehuai on military affairs] (Beijing: Zhongyang wenxian chubanshe, 1988), 601. Note that Peng Dehuai was a prominent Chinese Communist military leader, who served as China's defense minister from 1954 to 1959. Also see Fravel, *Active Defense*, 74.

30. Fravel, *Active Defense*, 72. Also see Taylor Fravel, "China's Changing Approach to Military Strategy: The Science of Military Strategy from 2001 to 2013," in *China's Evolving Military Strategy*, ed. Joe McReynolds (Washington, DC: Jamestown Foundation, 2017), 58–59.

31. Fravel, *Active Defense*, 107.

32. 周恩来 [Zhou Enlai], 周恩来军事文选 [Selected works of Zhou Enlai on military affairs] (Beijing: Renmin chubanshe, 1997), 4:426.

33. Franz-Stefan Gady, "War of the Dragons: Why North Korea Does Not Trust China," *Diplomat*, September 29, 2017.

34. Edward C. O'Dowd, *Chinese Military Strategy in the Third Indochina War* (New York: Routledge, 2007), 28–30; King C. Chen, *China's War with Vietnam, 1979: Issues, Decision, and Implications* (Stanford, CA: Hoover Institution Press, 1987), 88, 103.

35. 李文姬 [Li Wenji], "这几位中国现役将军 都曾战场杀敌" [These active-duty Chinese generals have killed the enemy on the battlefield], 法制晚报 [Legal evening news], August 28, 2017.

36. See, for example, Chinese and other accounts, such as 李 [Li], "这几位中国现役将军 都曾战场杀敌" [These active-duty Chinese generals have killed the enemy on the battlefield]; "Zhang Youxia—Member of Political Bureau," *China Daily*; Benjamin Kang Lim and Ben Blanchard, "China Combat Veteran, Close Ally of Xi, to Get Promotion: Sources," Reuters, October 17, 2017; Chan, "General Zhang Youxia."

37. Dennis Blasko, interview by the author, May 27, 2020.

38. See, for example, Fravel, *Active Defense*, 163–65; Gerald Segal, *Defending China* (New York: Oxford University Press, 1985), 211–27; Nayan Chanda, *Brother Enemy: The War after the War* (New York: Harcourt Brace Jovanovich, 1986); Chen, *China's War with Vietnam, 1979*; Steven J. Hood, *Dragons Entangled: Indochina and the China Vietnam War* (Armonk, NY: M. E. Sharpe, 1992); Bruce Elleman, *Modern Chinese Warfare, 1785–1989* (London: Routledge, 2001), 284–97.

39. Chen, *China's War with Vietnam, 1979*, 114.

40. 郑 [Zheng], "上将张又侠,在太空排兵布阵" [General Zhang Youxia, marching in space].

41. 郑 [Zheng], "上将张又侠,在太空排兵布阵" [General Zhang Youxia, marching in space]. Also see 李 [Li], "这几位中国现役将军 都曾战场杀敌" [These active-duty Chinese generals have killed the enemy on the battlefield].

42. Lim and Blanchard, "China Combat Veteran, Close Ally of Xi."

43. Andrew Scobell, David Lai, and Roy Kamphausen, eds., *Chinese Lessons from Other Peoples' Wars* (Carlisle, PA: Strategic Studies Institute, US Army War College, November 2011).

44. 江泽民 [Jiang Zemin], 江泽民国防和军队建设思想 [On national defense and army building] (Beijing: Jiefangjun chubanshe, 2002), 32. On Mao's inspiration from Stalin, see Yi Wang, " 'The Backward Will Be Beaten': Historical Lesson, Security, and Nationalism in China," *Journal of Contemporary China* 29, no. 126 (2020): 887–900.

45. 江泽民 [Jiang Zemin], 江泽民文选 [Selected works of Jiang Zemin] (Beijing: Renmin chubanshe, 2006), 1:285.

46. Fravel, *Active Defense*, 182.

47. Fravel, *Active Defense*, 223.

48. 黄斌 [Huang Bin, ed.], 科索沃战争研究 [A study of the Kosovo War] (Beijing: Jiefangjun chubanshe, 2000).

49. 江 [Jiang], 江泽民文选 [Selected works of Jiang Zemin], 3:578.

50. 乔杰 [Qiao Jie, ed.], 战役学教程 [Lectures on the science of campaigns] (Beijing: Junshi kexue, 2012), 30–31.

51. 百度 [Baidu], s.v. "洛阳英雄连" [Luoyang Hero Company], accessed January 31, 2021; "第十三集团军：山林猛虎" [The Thirteenth Group Army: Tiger in the Mountains], 人民日报 [People's daily], March 22, 2014.

52. Qiao Liang and Wang Xiangsui, *Unrestricted Warfare* (New York: Echo Point Books and Media, 1999), xix.

53. Qiao and Wang, *Unrestricted Warfare*, 27.

54. Qiao and Wang, *Unrestricted Warfare*, 33–34.

55. Qiao and Wang, *Unrestricted Warfare*, 182.

56. Taylor Fravel, interview by the author, May 21, 2020.

57. See, for example, M. Taylor Fravel, "China's Changing Approach to Military Strategy: The Science of Military Strategy from 2001 to 2013," in *China's Evolving Military Strategy*, ed. Joe McReynolds (Washington, DC: Jamestown Foundation, 2017), 42.

58. Fravel, *Active Defense*.

59. 彭光谦, 姚有志 [Peng Guangqian and Yao Youzhi, eds.], 战略学 [The science of military strategy] (Beijing: Junshi kexue, 2001), 189.

60. 彭, 姚 [Peng and Yao], 战略学 [The science of military strategy], 417.

61. 彭, 姚 [Peng and Yao], 战略学 [The science of military strategy], 327.

62. "上将张又侠：越自卫反击战一战成名" [General Zhang Youxia: Fame in the front line of the defensive counterattack against Vietnam], 环球人物 [Global people], August 13, 2014; "盘点解放军现役红二代将领：父子上将战功赫赫" [Inventory of the second-generation generals in active service of the PLA: Outstanding combat exploits of generals, fathers, and sons], 人民日报 [People's daily], December 22, 2014.

63. 张又侠 [Zhang Youxia], "伊拉克战争：对国际战略格局及我国安全环境的影响" [Iraq War: Impact on international strategic landscape and China's security environment], 国际展望 [World outlook], July 2003.

64. 张又侠, 王西欣 [Zhang Youxia and Wang Xixin], "在一体化训练实践中推进中国特色军事变革" [Promoting military transformation with Chinese characteristics through integrated training practices], 解放军报 [PLA daily], May 25, 2004.

65. See, for example, "牢牢把握国防和军队建设的重要指导方针" [Firmly grasp the important guidelines for national defense and army building], 解放军报 [PLA daily], January 1, 2006. For good discussions of "informatization," see Fravel, *Active Defense*, 218–19; Joe McReynolds and James Mulvenon, "The Role of Informatization in the People's Liberation Army under Hu Jintao," in *Assessing the People's Liberation Army in the Hu Jintao Era*, ed. Roy Kamphausen, David Lai, and Travis Tanner (Carlisle, PA: Strategic Studies Institute, US Army War College, 2014), 207–56.

66. 张, 王 [Zhang and Wang], "在一体化训练实践中推进中国特色军事变革" [Promoting military transformation with Chinese characteristics through integrated training practices].

CHAPTER 9: THREE WARFARES

1. "The Chinese Mata Hari Who Seduced Los Angeles and the FBI," *Sydney Morning Herald*, April 13, 2003.

2. US Department of Justice, Office of the Inspector General, *A Review of the FBI's Handling and Oversight of FBI Asset Katrina Leung: Unclassified Executive Summary* (Washington, DC: US Department of Justice, Office of the Inspector General, May 2006), 4.

3. US Department of Justice, Office of the Inspector General, *Review of the FBI's Handling and Oversight*, 1–6.

4. United States v. Katrina Leung, United States District Court for the Central District of California, no. CR 03-428-FMC, February 2003.

5. United States v. Katrina Leung; FBI Affidavit in Support of Criminal Complaint (United States v. Katrina Leung), 2003.

6. FBI Affidavit in Support of Criminal Complaint (United States v. James J. Smith), 2003.

7. Mark Kelton, interview by the author, June 2, 2020.

8. Sun Tzu, *The Art of War*, trans. Samuel B. Griffith (New York: Oxford University Press, 1971), 149.

9. James M. Olson, *To Catch a Spy: The Art of Counterintelligence* (Washington, DC: Georgetown University Press, 2019), 12.

10. Kenneth DeGraffenreid, ed., *The Cox Report: The Unanimous and Bipartisan Report of the House Select Committee on U.S. National Security and Military Commercial Concerns with the People's Republic of China* (Washington, DC: Regnery, 1999).

11. Quoted in David Wise, *Tiger Trap: America's Secret Spy War with China*

(New York: Houghton Mifflin, 2011), 10–11. For a discussion on the scope and impact of Chinese intelligence operations, see Peter Mattis, "A Guide to Chinese Intelligence Operations," War on the Rocks, August 15, 2015.

12. On Chinese lessons from the war in Iraq, see, for example, 张又侠 [Zhang Youxia], "伊拉克战争:对国际战略格局及我国安全环境的影响" [Iraq War: Impact on international strategic landscape and China's security environment], 国际展望 [World outlook], July 2003; 乔杰 [Qiao Jie, ed.], 战役学教程 [Lectures on the science of campaigns] (Beijing: Junshi kexue, 2012), 30–31; 郝唯学, 蒋杰 [Hao Weixue and Jiang Jie], "中国人民解放军心理战理论的历史发展及特点" [The history and characteristics of PLA's psychological warfare theory], 军事历史研究 [Military historical research] 4 (2008): 67. On broader Chinese lessons from the US invasion of Iraq and other wars, see Andrew Scobell, David Lai, and Roy Kamphausen, eds., *Chinese Lessons from Other Peoples' Wars* (Carlisle, PA: Strategic Studies Institute, US Army War College, November 2011).

13. "新修订的'中国人民解放军政治工作条例'颁行" [The revised "PLA political work regulations" are promulgated], 中新网 [China News Service], December 15, 2003; "中共中央关于颁布'中国人民解放军政治工作条例'的通知" [The circular of the CCP Central Committee on "Chinese People's Liberation Army political work regulations"], 中国共产党新闻网 [News of the Communist Party of China], December 15, 2003.

14. See, for example, 姜玉坤, 阎永峰 [Mei Yushen and Yan Yongfeng], "沈阳军区某集团军拉开'三战'序幕" [A certain group army of the Shenyang military region pulls back the curtain on the "three warfares"], 中国青年报 [China youth daily], July 17, 2004; 侯宝成 [Hou Baocheng], "政治工作为什么要加强对'三战'的研究" [Why political work should step up the study of the "three warfares"], 解放军报 [PLA daily], July 29, 2004.

15. Mao Zedong, "On Correcting Mistaken Ideas in the Party," in *Selected Works of Mao Tse-tung* (Peking: Foreign Language Press, 1965), 1:106. For a good explanation, see Peter Mattis, "China's 'Three Warfares' in Perspectives," War on the Rocks, January 30, 2018.

16. 侯 [Hou], "政治工作为什么要加强对'三战'的研究" [Why political work should step up the study of the "three warfares"].

17. 王幸生著 [Wang Xingsheng, ed.], 军队政治工作学 [The science of military political work] (Beijing: Junshi kexue, 2011), 267.

18. Larry M. Wortzel, *The Chinese People's Liberation Army and Information*

Warfare (Carlisle, PA: Strategic Studies Institute, US Army War College, March 2014).

19. 武怀堂, 左军占 [Wu Huaitang and Zuo Junzhan, eds.], 心理战实用知识 [The practical knowledge of psychological warfare] (Beijing: Junshi kexue, 2006); 郝, 蒋 [Hao and Jiang], "中国人民解放军心理战理论的历史发展及特点" [The history and characteristics of PLA's psychological warfare theory]; 陈辉 [Chen Hui], "中国军队开展舆论战, 心理战, 法律战研 究和训练" [China's military conducts research and training on public opinion warfare, psychological warfare, and legal warfare], 新华 [Xinhua], June 21, 2004. Also see, for example, Wortzel, *Chinese People's Liberation Army and Information Warfare.*

20. Yu Guohua, "NDU Officer on Weaker Force Achieving Victory in Local War," *China Military Science*, May 20, 1996. Quoted in Mark A. Stokes, "The Chinese Joint Aerospace Campaign: Strategy, Doctrine, and Force Modernization," in *China's Revolution in Doctrinal Affairs: Emerging Trends in the Operational Art of the Chinese People's Liberation Army*, ed. James Mulvenon and David Finkelstein (Alexandria, VA: CNA Corporation, December 2005), 273.

21. 彭光谦, 姚有志 [Peng Guangqian and Yao Youzhi, eds.], 战略学 [The science of military strategy] (Beijing: Junshi kexue, 2001), 79.

22. 刘继贤, 刘铮主编 [Liu Jixian and Liu Zheng, eds.], 新军事变革与军事法制建设 [The new revolution in military affairs and building a military legal system] (Beijing: PLA Press, 2005). See also 郑申侠, 刘源主编 [Zheng Shenxia and Liu Yuan, eds.], 国防和军队建设贯彻落实科学发展观学习提要 [Study materials for completely building the military and national defense] (Beijing: PLA Press, 2006), 192–94.

23. Sun, *Art of War*, 66.

24. 程寶山 [Cheng Baoshan, ed.], 舆论战心理战法律战基本问题 [The fundamental issues of public opinion warfare, psychological warfare, and legal warfare] (Beijing: Junshi kexue, 2004), 2–3, 205.

25. 张又侠, 石香元, 许勇 [Zhang Youxia, Shi Xiangyuan, and Xu Yong], "主权控制战—现实军事斗争拟可采用的一种作战形式" [War of sovereignty control: A practical kind of warfare that can be tried in preparation for war], 军事学术 [Military art] 29, no. 11 (2002): 3–6.

26. University of Chicago, "Statement on the Confucius Institute at the University of Chicago," September 25, 2014.

27. 刘仰 [Liu Yang], "怕孔子学院？美国的自信去哪了" [Afraid of the Confucius Institute? Where is American self-confidence?], 人民日报 [People's daily], June 20, 2014.

28. "Confucius Teaches Cultures," *China Daily*, June 25, 2014; Elizabeth

Redden, "Debate Renews over Confucius Institutes," *Inside Higher Education*, July 24, 2014.

29. "Petition to the Committee of the Council," various University of Chicago professors, 2014.

30. Elizabeth Redden, "Rejecting Confucius Funding," *Inside Higher Education*, April 29, 2014.

31. "Petition to the Committee of the Council."

32. Elizabeth Redden, "Censorship at China Studies Meeting," *Inside Higher Education*, August 6, 2014; Marshall Sahlins, "China U.," *Nation*, October 20, 2013.

33. "Petition to the Committee of the Council."

34. Sahlins, "China U."

35. Kelton, interview.

36. Olson, *To Catch a Spy*, 7.

37. "Confucius Teaches Cultures," *China Daily*. This direct response to a letter from the American Association of University Professors was representative of China's response to criticisms of its Confucius Institutes.

38. 刘 [Liu], "怕孔子学院？美国的自信去哪了" [Afraid of the Confucius Institute? Where is American self-confidence?].

39. National Association of Scholars, "How Many Confucius Institutes Are in the United States?" January 19, 2021.

40. See, for example, "Confucius Teaches Cultures," *China Daily*; 刘 [Liu], "怕孔子学院？美国的自信去哪了" [Afraid of the Confucius Institute? Where is American self-confidence?].

41. See, for example, the statement by the American Association of University Professors: "On Partnership with Foreign Governments: The Case of Confucius Institutes," June 2014.

42. National Association of Scholars, "How Many Confucius Institutes Are in the United States?" January 19, 2021.

43. Anne-Marie Brady, *Magic Weapons: China's Political Influence Activities under Xi Jinping* (Washington, DC: Wilson Center, September 2017); Jonas Parello-Plesner and Belinda Li, *The Chinese Communist Party's Foreign Interference Operations: How the U.S. and Other Democracies Should Respond* (Washington, DC: Hudson Institute, June 2018); Alexander Bowe and US-China Economic and Security Review Commission, *China's Overseas United Front Work: Background and Implications for the United States* (Washington, DC: US-China Economic and Security Review Commission, August 24, 2018).

44. On the relations between Zhang and Xi, see, for example, 杨念军 [Yang Nianjun], "习近平大姐建议让张又侠再干五年？" [Xi Jinping's elder sis-

ter suggests that Zhang Youxia serve another five years?], 外参 [WAI-CAN], March 3, 2017.

45. "上将张又侠：对越自卫反击战一战成名" [General Zhang Youxia: Fame in the front line of the defensive counterattack against Vietnam], 环球人物 [Global people], August 13, 2014.

46. Dennis Blasko, interview by the author, May 27, 2020.

47. 张又侠, 邱建 [Zhang Youxia and Qiu Jian], "加强部队党的建设核心是确保党对军队绝对领导" [Key to stepping up party building in military units is ensuring the party's absolute leadership over the military], 解放军报 [PLA daily], February 20, 2003.

48. 张又侠, 黄献中 [Zhang Youxia and Huang Xianzhong], "做学习实践科学发展观的好战士好青年—向新一代青年士兵楷模向南林学习" [Learning and practicing scientific concepts of development as a good soldier and young man—Learning from Xiang Nanlin, a model of a new generation of young soldiers], 求是 [Qiushi], no. 11 (2008).

49. Minnie Chan, "General Zhang Youxia: Xi Jinping's 'Sworn Brother' Now His Deputy on China's Top Military Body," *South China Morning Post*, October 25, 2017.

50. Timothy R. Heath, Kristen Gunness, and Cortez Cooper, *The PLA and China's Rejuvenation: National Security and Military Strategies, Deterrence Concepts, and Combat Capabilities* (Santa Monica, CA: RAND, 2016), 9.

51. People's Republic of China, *China's National Defense in 2010* (Beijing: Information Office of the State Council, March 2011).

52. 江鑫嫻 [Jiang Xinxian], "海陸空 '五虎將' 隨梁光烈出訪" [The "five high ranking tigers" of the army, navy, and air force accompany Liang Guanglie on a foreign trip], 文汇报 [Wen wei po], May 7, 2012.

53. 褚文 [Chu Wen], "张又侠等试用美制步枪 惊叹比95步枪强多了[视频]" [Zhang Youxia and others try US-made rifle and marvel that it is much stronger than the QBZ-95 (video)], 多維新聞 [Duowei news], July 9, 2018.

54. "Adversarial training enriches PLA's combat experience," 新华 [Xinhua], January 2, 2010.

55. "沈阳军区司令员张又侠解读新时期军事训练新革命" [Commander Zhang Youxia of the Shenyang military region interprets the new revolution in military training in the new period], 人民日报 [People's daily], November 20, 2009.

56. "强化政治自觉，下决心根治'和平病'" [Strengthen political awareness and resolve to eradicate "peace disease"], 中国军网 [China military network], July 2, 2018; 倪文鑫 [Ni Wenxin], "实战化训练必须聚焦明天的战场—军区空军实战化训练对联合训练的启示" [Training made

realistic to actual war must focus on tomorrow's battlefield: What military region air force's training made realistic to actual war can tell us about joint training], 人民前线 [People's front], October 25, 2013, 4.

57. 寿晓松 [Shou Xiaosong, ed.], 战略学 [The science of military strategy] (Beijing: Junshi kexue, 2013), 101.

58. On China's desire to create a world-class military, see, for example, 习近平 [Xi Jinping], "决胜全面建成小康社会夺取新时代中国特色社会主义伟大胜利—在中国共产党第十九次全国代表大会上的报告" [Secure a decisive victory in building a moderately prosperous society in all respects and strive for the great success of socialism with Chinese characteristics for a new era: Report at the 19th National Congress of the Communist Party of China], 新华 [Xinhua], October 18, 2017.

59. 寿 [Shou], 战略学 [The science of military strategy], 79.

60. 钱晓虎, 扶满 [Qian Xiaohu and Fu Man], "常万全房峰辉张阳赵克石张又侠吴胜利马晓天魏凤和分别参加审议" [Chang Wanquan, Fang Fenghui, Zhang Yang, Zhao Keshi, Zhang Youxia, Wu Shengli, Ma Xiaotian, Wei Fenghe participate in review], 中国军网 [China military network], March 8, 2017.

61. 习近平 [Xi Jinping], "习近平：积极树立亚洲安全观 共创安全合作新局面" [Xi Jinping: New Asian security concept for new progress in security cooperation] (speech, Conference on Interaction and Confidence Building Measures in Asia [CICA], Shanghai, May 21, 2014).

62. Mike Green, interview by the author, May 21, 2020.

CHAPTER 10: THE GREAT WALL OF SAND

1. David R. Stilwell, "The South China Sea, Southeast Asia's Patrimony, and Everybody's Own Backyard" (remarks, Center for Strategic and International Studies, Washington, DC, July 14, 2020). Also see "How Much Trade Transits the South China Sea?" Center for Strategic and International Studies, August 2, 2017.

2. The data come from Jeremy Bender, "These 8 Narrow Chokepoints Are Critical to the World's Oil Trade," *Business Insider*, April 1, 2015.

3. See, for example, Zhang's comments on the *Haikou*, a Chinese Type 052C destroyer. 尹航 [Yin Hang], "海军海口舰先进事迹报告会在京举行" [Report on advanced deeds of naval *Haikou* ship delivered in Beijing], 中国军网 [China military network], July 31, 2018; 陈欣 [Chen Xin], "海军海口舰先进事迹报告会举行" [Naval *Haikou* ship advanced deeds report meeting held], 央广网 [CCTV], July 31, 2018.

4. 中国的军事战略 [China's military strategy] (Beijing: Guowuyuan xinwen bangongshi, 2015).

5. Michael Morell, interview by the author, May 21, 2020.

6. On Zhang's view of sovereignty, see 张又侠, 石香元, 许勇 [Zhang Youxia, Shi Xiangyuan, and Xu Yong], "主权控制战—现实军事斗争拟可采用的一种作战形式" [War of sovereignty control: A practical kind of warfare that can be tried in preparation for war], 军事学术 [Military art] 29, no. 11 (2002): 3–6.

7. Минобороны России [Russian Ministry of Defense] (@mod_russia), Twitter, September 4, 2019, 6:54 a.m.

8. David E. Sanger and Rick Gladstone, "Piling Sand in a Disputed Sea, China Literally Gains Ground," *New York Times*, April 8, 2015.

9. Michael Vickers, interview by the author, May 19, 2020.

10. "China Tests 'Magic Island Maker,'" *Maritime Executive*, November 4, 2017.

11. Adam Entous, Gordon Lubold, and Julian Barnes, "U.S. Military Proposes Challenge to China Sea Claims," *Wall Street Journal*, May 12, 2015.

12. Interviews with multiple US defense officials, 2020; US Office of the Secretary of Defense, *Military and Security Developments Involving the People's Republic of China 2019: Annual Report to Congress* (Washington, DC: US Department of Defense, 2019), ii.

13. 战立鹏 [Zhan Lipeng], "毛泽东人民海军建设思想及启示" [Contemporary lessons from Mao Zedong thought on building the People's Navy], 军事历史 [Military history], no. 3 (2009): 20.

14. Harry B. Harris Jr., Speech at the Australian Strategic Policy Institute (Canberra, Australia, March 31, 2015).

15. Quoted in Hannah Beech, "China's Sea Control Is a Done Deal, 'Short of War with the U.S.,'" *New York Times*, September 20, 2018.

16. "中国之声：减少对南中国海的恐慌" [China Voice: Drop fearmongering over South China Sea], 新华 [Xinhua], April 16, 2015. Also see "菲律宾间歇对华撒泼 以为获美支持就赢得全世界" [The Philippines sporadically stirs trouble with China, believing that the support of the U.S. will win the world], 人民日报 [People's daily], April 15, 2015.

17. 张, 石, 许 [Zhang, Shi, and Xu], "主权控制战—现实军事斗争拟可采用的一种作战形式" [War of sovereignty control: A practical kind of warfare that can be tried in war preparation].

18. On the ruling, see Press Release, The South China Sea Arbitration (The Republic of the Philippines v. the People's Republic of China), Permanent Court of Arbitration, The Hague, July 12, 2016.

19. "中华人民共和国外交部关于应菲律宾共和国请求建立的南海仲裁案仲裁庭所作裁决的声明" [Statement of the Ministry of Foreign

Affairs of the People's Republic of China on the award of the arbitration tribunal of the South China Sea arbitration case established at the request of the Republic of the Philippines], 中华人民共和国外交部 [Ministry of Foreign Affairs of the People's Republic of China], July 12, 2016.

20. Interview with US Navy commander, 2020.

21. Lukas Lenart, Security Bulletin S2-045, Apache Struts 2 Wiki, March 7, 2017.

22. US Department of Homeland Security, United States Computer Emergency Readiness Team, "Apache Software Foundation Releases Security Updates," March 8, 2017.

23. "全军实战化军事训练座谈会代表发 言摘登" [Excerpts from the representative of the military training seminar on actual combat], 解放军报 [PLA daily], August 7, 2016; "高津任战略支援部队司令员" [Gao Jin becomes strategic support force commander], 新浪 [Sina], January 1, 2016.

24. On the concept of strategic frontiers, see 周碧松 [Zhou Bisong], 战略边疆 [Strategic frontiers] (Beijing: Long March Press, 2015).

25. Catherine Wong, "China's Hong Kong Garrison 'Ready to Safeguard National Security' in the City," *South China Morning Post*, May 26, 2020.

26. United States of America v. Wu Zhiyong, Wang Qian, Xu Ke, Liu Lei, United States District Court for the Northern District of Georgia, Atlanta Division, Criminal Indictment, January 28, 2020.

27. US Department of Justice, "Chinese Military Personnel Charged with Computer Fraud, Economic Espionage and Wire Fraud for Hacking into Credit Reporting Agency Equifax," February 10, 2020; emphasis added.

28. See, for example, David E. Sanger, *The Perfect Weapon: War, Sabotage, and Fear in the Cyber Age* (New York: Crown, 2018), 111–17; Damian Paletta, "US Intelligence Chief James Clapper Suggests China behind OPM Breach," *Wall Street Journal*, June 25, 2015.

29. James M. Olson, *To Catch a Spy: The Art of Counterintelligence* (Washington, DC: Georgetown University Press, 2019), 3.

30. 记者梅世雄, 梅常伟 [Mei Shixiong and Mei Changwei], "张又侠在看望慰问驻京部队时强调 深入贯彻习近平强军思想 不断开创部队建设新局面" [Zhang Youxia emphasizes deep implementation of Xi Jinping thought on strengthening the military and continuing to promote a new situation in army building when visiting troops stationed in Beijing], 新华 [Xinhua], January 22, 2020; "张又侠：领导干部要自觉抵御各种'糖衣炮弹' 诱惑" [Zhang Youxia: Leading cadres must consciously resist various temptations of "sugar-coated shells"], 解放军报 [PLA daily], November 14, 2015; 邹维荣, 宗兆盾 [Zou Weirong and Zong Zhao-

dun], "张又侠：坚决打好反腐倡廉建设纵深仗" [Zhang Youxia: Fight resolutely in the battle against corruption to build a clean government], 解放军报 [PLA daily], July 2, 2015.

31. Minnie Chan, "General Zhang Youxia: Xi Jinping's 'Sworn Brother' Now His Deputy on China's Top Military Body," *South China Morning Post*, October 25, 2017.

32. 张晓祺, 张利文, 宗兆盾 [Zhang Xiaoqi, Zhang Liwen, and Zong Zhaodun], "在新起点上推动武器装备建设科学发展" [Promoting the scientific development of weaponry construction at a new starting point], 解放军报 [PLA daily], December 10, 2012.

33. "张又侠：在纪念张廷发同志诞辰100周年座谈会上的讲话" [Zhang Youxia: Speech at the symposium to commemorate the 100th anniversary of Comrade Zhang Tingfa's birthday], 人民日报 [People's daily], April 11, 2018.

34. US Department of Justice, "Chinese Military Personnel Charged."

35. US Office of the Secretary of Defense, *Military and Security Developments*, 48.

36. 梅常伟 [Mei Changwei], "张又侠魏凤和分别与伊朗国防部长会见会谈" [Zhang Youxia and Wei Fenghe meet and talk, respectively, with Iranian defense minister], 新华 [Xinhua], September 7, 2018.

37. See, for example, "习近平在印度尼西亚国会的演讲" [Xi Jinping's speech at the Indonesian Parliament], 新华 [Xinhua], October 3, 2013.

38. Richard A. Gabriel, *The Great Armies of Antiquity* (Westport, CT: Praeger, 2002), 9.

39. Terence N. D'Altroy, *The Incas*, 2nd ed. (New York: Wiley, 2015), 5.

40. Jonathan E. Hillman, *The Emperor's New Road: China and the Project of the Century* (New Haven, CT: Yale University Press, 2020).

41. "习近平在印度尼西亚国会的演讲" [Xi Jinping's speech at the Indonesian Parliament].

42. Morgan Stanley, "Inside China's Plan to Create a Modern Silk Road," March 14, 2018.

43. On the amount of Chinese investment in Serbia, see Vuk Vuksanovic, "Light Touch, Tight Grip: China's Influence and the Corrosion of Serbian Democracy," War on the Rocks, September 24, 2019.

44. "塞尔维亚总统武契奇会见张又侠" [Serbian president Vučić meets with Zhang Youxia], 新华 [Xinhua], September 8, 2019.

45. Masanori Tobita, "Coronavirus in Djibouti Increases Risk of China Debt Trap," *Nikkei Asia*, April 26, 2020.

46. Hillman, *Emperor's New Road*.

47. Agatha Kratz, Daniel H. Rosen, and Matthew Mingey, "Booster or

Brake? COVID and the Belt and Road Initiative," Rhodium Group, April 15, 2020; Agatha Kratz, Allen Feng, and Logan Wright, "New Data on the 'Debt Trap' Question," Rhodium Group, April 29, 2019; Benn Steil and Benjamin Della Rocca, "Belt and Road Tracker," Council on Foreign Relations, May 8, 2019.

48. Shi Jiangtao, "Chinese Ambassador Accused of Threatening German Car Industry If Huawei Is Frozen Out," *South China Morning Post*, December 15, 2019.

49. On German reactions, see, for example, Katrin Bennhold and Jack Ewing, "In Huawei Battle, China Threatens Germany 'Where It Hurts': Automakers," *New York Times*, January 16, 2020.

50. US Office of the Secretary of Defense, *Military and Security Developments*, i.

51. US Defense Intelligence Agency, *China Military Power: Modernizing a Force to Fight and Win* (Washington, DC: US Defense Intelligence Agency, 2019), 34.

52. On Zhang's discussions with Pakistan leaders, see, for example, China Ministry of Defense, "Senior Chinese, Pakistani Military Officials Meet," July 29, 2019.

53. Interview with US government official, 2020.

54. Hillman, *Emperor's New Road*, 125–49.

55. Joseph Votel, interview by the author, May 21, 2020.

56. Tony Thomas, interview by the author, May 22, 2020.

57. Sean O'Connor and Nicholas Armstrong, *Directed by Hollywood, Edited by China: How China's Censorship and Influence Affect Films Worldwide* (Washington, DC: US-China Economic and Security Review Commission, October 28, 2015).

58. William P. Barr, Remarks on China Policy (Gerald R. Ford Presidential Museum, Grand Rapids, MI, July 16, 2020).

59. Quoted in Edward Wong, " 'Doctor Strange' Writer Explains Casting of Tilda Swinton as Tibetan," *New York Times*, April 26, 2016.

60. Daryl Morey (@dmorey), Twitter, October 4, 2019. Morey later deleted the tweet.

61. Consulate-General of the People's Republic of China in Houston, "Chinese Consulate General Spokesperson's Remarks on the Erroneous Comments on Hong Kong by General Manager of the Houston Rockets," October 6, 2019.

62. Ben Cohen and James T. Areddy, "One Year after China Banned the NBA, Basketball Returns to Chinese TV," *Wall Street Journal*, October 9, 2020. On financial losses for the NBA, also see Ben Cohen,

"China Standoff Cost the NBA 'Hundreds of Millions,'" *Wall Street Journal*, February 16, 2020.

63. Quoted in Colin Ward-Henninger, "NBA Commissioner Adam Silver Says Chinese Government Asked Him to Fire Rockets GM Daryl Morey after Tweet," CBS Sports, October 17, 2019.

64. US Department of State, "Briefing with Senior U.S. Government Officials on the Closure of the Chinese Consulate in Houston, Texas," July 24, 2020.

65. Dustin Volz, "Data Sharing in China Sets Debate at Airbnb," *Wall Street Journal*, November 21, 2020.

66. Airbnb, Inc. filing with the United States Securities and Exchange Commission, Form S-1 Registration Statement under the Securities Act of 1933, Registration no. 333, November 16, 2020.

67. On the shrinking number of Confucius Institutes, see National Association of Scholars, "How Many Confucius Institutes Are in the United States?" January 19, 2021.

68. Spencer Buell, "The Indicted Harvard Professor's Other Double Life: Pumpkins," *Boston Magazine*, February 4, 2020.

69. FBI Affidavit in Support of Application for Criminal Complaint against Charles Lieber, January 21, 2020.

70. "Senior Chinese Military Official Stresses Sci-Tech Progress for Strong Military," Xinhua, January 3, 2020.

71. Mark Kelton, interview by the author, June 2, 2020.

72. FBI Affidavit against Charles Lieber.

73. Kari Bingen, interview by the author, May 29, 2020.

74. US Department of Justice, "MIT Professor Indicted on Charges Relating to Grant Fraud," January 20, 2021.

75. Federal Bureau of Investigation, "FBI Special Agent in Charge Joseph R. Bonavolonta's Remarks at Press Conference Announcing Arrest of MIT Professor Gang Chen," January 14, 2021.

76. 习近平 [Xi Jinping], "决胜全面建成小康社会夺取新时代中国特色社会主义伟大胜利—在中国共产党第十九次全国代表大会上的报告" [Secure a decisive victory in building a moderately prosperous society in all respects and strive for the great success of socialism with Chinese characteristics for a new era: Report at the 19th National Congress of the Communist Party of China], 新华 [Xinhua], October 18, 2017.

77. Lei Zhao, "Xi Unveils Beidou Full-Scale Coverage," *China Daily*, August 1, 2020.

78. "国务院印发'中国制造2025'" [The state council issued "Made in China 2025"], 新华 [Xinhua], May 19, 2015; "中国制造2025瞄准十大重点领

域 (政策解读)" [Made in China 2025 targets ten key areas (policy interpretation)], 人民日报 [People's daily], May 20, 2015.

79. 新时代中国国防 [China's national defense in the new era] (Beijing: Guowuyuan xinwen bangongshi, 2019).

80. Минобороны России [Russian Ministry of Defense] (@mod_russia), Twitter, September 4, 2019, 6:54 a.m.

81. 王子晖 [Wang Zihui], "'斗争'！习近平这篇讲话大有深意" ["Struggle"! Xi Jinping's speech was very meaningful], 新华 [Xinhua], September 4, 2019. Also see Zhou Xin and Sarah Zheng, "Xi Jinping Rallies China for Decades-Long 'Struggle' to Rise in Global Order, amid Escalating US Trade War," *South China Morning Post*, September 5, 2019.

82. "Xi Meets Representatives to Military Conference on Ideological, Political Education," *People's Daily*, December 5, 2020.

CHAPTER 11: COUNTERING THE WOLF WARRIORS

1. Michael Morell, interview by the author, May 21, 2020.

2. See, for example, 李云龙 [Li Yunlong], "'美式民主' 神话的终结" (国际论坛) ["American Democracy"—The End of the Myth], 人民日报 [People's daily], January 13, 2021; 张健 [Zhang Jian], "政治乱象的背后：美式价值观的衰落" [Behind the Political Chaos: The Decline of American Values], 光明日报 [Guangming daily], January 12, 2021.

3. Rob Cain, "China's 'Wolf Warrior 2' Becomes 2nd Film in History to Reach $800M in a Single Territory," *Forbes*, August 27, 2017.

4. Игорь Панарин [Igor Panarin], Информационная война и коммуникации [Information war and communications] (Moscow: Goryachaya Liniya-Telekom, 2015), 118.

5. Панарин [Panarin], Информационная война и коммуникации [Information war and communications], 116.

6. Сергей Чекинов и Сергей Богданов [Sergey Chekinov and Sergey Bogdanov], "Влияние непрямых действий на характер современной войны" [The influence of indirect actions on the character of contemporary war], Военная мысль [Military thought] 6 (2011): 7, 10.

7. Michael Vickers, interview by the author, May 19, 2020.

8. Robert Gates, interview by the author, June 17, 2020.

9. On the Chinese practice of blocking internet sites and digital platforms, see Peter C. Oleson, "Chinese Offensive Intelligence Operations," *Intelligencer* 26, no. 1 (Fall 2020): 9–17.

10. China jailed at least fifty people in 2019 and 2020 for criticizing the gov-

ernment on foreign social media platforms. Chun Han Wong, "China Jails Twitter Users to Stifle Critics," *Wall Street Journal*, January 30, 2021.

11. David Petraeus, interview by the author, May 22, 2020.

12. Ronald Reagan, "Remarks at the Annual Convention of the National Association of Evangelicals in Orlando, Florida," March 8, 1983.

13. Morell, interview.

14. Stanley McChrystal, interview by the author, June 8, 2020.

15. "U.S. Relations with the USSR," National Security Decision Directive no. 75, January 17, 1983, Executive Secretariat, NSC: Records [NSDDs], NSDD 75 [U.S. Relations with the USSR], Box 91287, Ronald Reagan Presidential Library, Simi Valley, CA.

16. "U.S. Relations with the USSR," National Security Decision Directive no. 75.

17. Preamble to the Constitution of the United States of America.

18. Abraham Lincoln, "Gettysburg Address," November 19, 1863.

19. "人民锐评：世界见证美式"双标"大型翻车现场" [People's daily editorial commentary: The world watches as the American "double-standard" collides in real-time], 人民日报 [People's daily], January 8, 2021.

20. Gates, interview.

21. See, for example, John J. Mearsheimer, *The Great Delusion: Liberal Dreams and International Realities* (New Haven, CT: Yale University Press, 2018).

22. "George Kennan's 'Long Telegram,'" February 2, 1946, History and Public Policy Program Digital Archive, National Archives and Records Administration, Department of State Records (Record Group 59), Central Decimal File, 1945–1949, 861.00/2-2246, reprinted in US Department of State, ed., *Foreign Relations of the United States, 1946*, vol 6., *Eastern Europe; The Soviet Union* (Washington, DC: US Government Printing Office, 1969), 696–709.

23. This paragraph and other parts of this section were informed, to a great extent, by my coauthored article in the *Wall Street Journal*: Jude Blanchette and Seth G. Jones, "The U.S. Is Losing the Information War with China," *Wall Street Journal*, June 20, 2020.

24. Taylor Fravel, interview by the author, May 21, 2020.

25. Liang Xia, *A Discourse Analysis of News Translation in China* (New York: Routledge, 2019).

26. "国家测绘局2009年度预算执行情况和其他财政收支情况审计结果" [Auditing results of the 2009 annual budget implementation and other financial revenues and expenditures of the State Bureau of Survey-

ing and Mapping], 中华人民共和国审计署 [People's Republic of China Audit Office], June 23, 2010.

27. IBIS World, "Language Instruction in the U.S., Market Size 2001–2026," 2020.

28. "George Kennan's 'Long Telegram.'"

29. McChrystal, interview.

30. Stuart Bradin, interview by the author, May 18, 2020.

31. Mark Kelton, interview by the author, June 2, 2020.

32. Gates, interview.

33. William McRaven, interview by the author, May 21, 2020.

34. Kathleen Hicks and Alice Hunt Friend, *By Other Means, Part I: Campaigning in the Gray Zone* (Lanham, MD: Rowman and Littlefield, 2019), 2.

35. On the US overreliance on conventional warfare, see, for example, Sean McFate, *The New Rules of War: Victory in the Age of Durable Disorder* (New York: HarperCollins, 2019).

36. The unclassified version of the *National Defense Strategy* included a brief reference to North Korean "unconventional" weapons, but virtually nothing about irregular warfare or related issues, such as political, hybrid, or asymmetric warfare. US Department of Defense, *Summary of the 2018 National Defense Strategy of the United States of America* (Washington, DC: US Department of Defense, 2018).

37. US Department of Defense, *Summary of the Irregular Warfare Annex to the National Defense Strategy* (Washington, DC: US Department of Defense, 2020).

38. "Secretary of Defense Esper Tells U.S. Naval War College Students His Focus Is Great-Power Competition," US Naval War College, August 28, 2019.

39. Devon L. Suits, "Esper: Army to Focus on Recruiting, Training, Modernization to Prepare for Future Conflict," *Army News Service*, May 2, 2018; emphasis added.

40. Interview with US Department of Defense official, 2020. I corroborated this account with two others in the room during the briefing.

41. Interview with US Department of Defense official, 2020. I corroborated this account with two others in the room during the briefing.

42. Gerald F. Seib, "China Hawk Pushes for U.S. Action," *Wall Street Journal*, May 12, 2020.

43. Michael Nagata, interview by the author, May 19, 2020.

44. Mark Mitchell, interview by the author, May 20, 2020.

45. Nagata, interview.

46. Christopher Miller, interview by the author, October 1, 2020.

47. George Washington to John Trumbull, June 25, 1799, in George Washington, *The Papers of George Washington*, Retirement Series, vol. 4, *April–December 1799*, ed. W. W. Abbot (Charlottesville: University Press of Virginia, 1999), 159.

48. See the comments by Gerasimov in "Векторы развития военной стратегии" [Vectors of military strategy development], Красная звезда [Red star], March 4, 2019.

49. The US Defense Department's fiscal year 2019 budget was $685 billion (though the total defense budget was $716 billion, which included overseas contingency operations [OCO] and emergency funding), and the US State Department's fiscal year 2019 budget was $54.376 billion. See US Department of Defense, *Fiscal Year 2020 Budget Request* (Washington, DC: Office of the Under Secretary of Defense [Comptroller]/CFO, March 2019); Todd Harrison and Seamus P. Daniels, *What Does the Bipartisan Budget Act of 2019 Mean for Defense?* (Washington, DC: Center for Strategic and International Studies, August 4, 2019); US Department of State, *Foreign Operations and Related Programs: FY2019 Budget and Appropriations* (Washington, DC: Congressional Research Service, March 12, 2019).

50. US General Accounting Office, *U.S. Information Agency: Options for Addressing Possible Budget Reductions* (Washington, DC: General Accounting Office, 1996), 18–19.

51. Morell, interview.

52. 记者梅世雄, 梅常伟 [Mei Shixiong and Mei Changwei], "张又侠在看望慰问驻京部队时强调 深入贯彻习近平强军思想 不断开创部队建设新局面" [Zhang Youxia emphasizes deep implementation of Xi Jinping thought on strengthening the military and continuing to promote a new situation in army building when visiting troops stationed in Beijing], 新华 [Xinhua], January 22, 2020; "张又侠：领导干部要自觉抵御各种 '糖衣炮弹' 诱惑" [Zhang Youxia: Leading cadres must consciously resist various temptations of "sugar-coated shells"], 解放军报 [PLA daily], November 14, 2015; 邹维荣, 宗兆盾 [Zou Weirong and Zong Zhaodun], "张又侠：坚决打好反腐倡廉建设纵深仗" [Zhang Youxia: Fight resolutely in the battle against corruption to build a clean government], 解放军报 [PLA daily], July 2, 2015.

53. See, for example, Joan Tilouine, "A Addis-Abeba, le siège de l'Union Africaine espionné par Pékin," *Le Monde*, January 26, 2018.

54. Michael Hayden, interview by the author, May 18, 2020.

55. Ladislav Bittman, *The KGB and Soviet Disinformation: An Insider's View* (Washington, DC: Pergamon-Brassey's, 1985); Ladislav Bittman (for-

mer deputy chief of the Disinformation Department of the Czechoslo-vak Intelligence Service), statement, in *Soviet Covert Action (the Forgery Offensive): Hearings before the Subcommittee on Oversight of the Permanent Select Committee on Intelligence, House of Representatives, Ninety-Sixth Congress, Second Session, February 6, 19, 1980* (Washington, DC: US Government Printing Office, 1980); Stanislav Levchenko (former KGB major), statement, in *Soviet Active Measures: Hearings before the Permanent Select Committee on Intelligence, House of Representatives, Ninety-Seventh Congress, Second Session, July 13, 14, 1982* (Washington, DC: US Government Printing Office, 1982). Also see Ilya Dzhirkvelov, *Secret Servant: My Life with the KGB and the Soviet Elite* (New York: Harper & Row, 1987).

56. George P. Shultz to the President, "Subject: USG-Soviet Relations—Where Do We Want to Be and How Do We Get There?" (memo), March 3, 1983, Soviet Union-Sensitive File-1983, Rac Box 3, Robert McFarlane file, Ronald Reagan Presidential Library, Simi Valley, CA.

57. Steve Sestanovich to Robert C. McFarlane, "Subject: East-West Paper for Shultz Meeting" (memo), August 6, 1984, USSR (8/6/84), Box 25A, Executive Secretariat, NSC: Country File: Records, Ronald Reagan Presidential Library, Simi Valley, CA.

58. See, for example, Charles T. Cleveland, *The American Way of Irregular Warfare: An Analytical Memoir* (Santa Monica, CA: RAND, 2020).

59. McChrystal, interview.

60. Joseph Votel, interview by the author, May 21, 2020.

61. See, for example, Michael J. Mazarr and Ashley L. Rhoades, *Testing the Value of the Postwar International Order* (Santa Monica, CA: RAND, 2018); Charles L. Glaser, "A Flawed Framework: Why the Liberal International Order Concept Is Misguided," *International Security* 43, no. 4 (Spring 2019): 51–87.

62. HSBC, "Six Things You May Not Know about Chinese Millennials," 2018.

63. Arnold Rampersad, ed., *The Collected Poems of Langston Hughes* (New York: Vintage, 1995), 189.

IMAGE CREDITS

INDEX

HOW THREE KEY FIGURES IN MOSCOW, BEIJING, AND TEHRAN BUILT RUTHLESS IRREGULAR WARFARE CAMPAIGNS THAT ARE ERODING AMERICAN POWER.

Defense expert Seth G. Jones argues that the United States is woefully unprepared for the future of global competition. While America has focused on building fighter jets, missiles, and conventional deterrence systems, Russia, Iran, and China have increasingly adopted irregular and hybrid tactics to undermine American power and seize territory without directly confronting the United States.

Offering an "unparalleled look at how Beijing, Moscow, and Tehran are competing with the United States" (General Michael Hayden, former CIA director), Jones profiles the principal builders of Moscow, Beijing, and Tehran's military strategies—Russian chief of staff Valery Gerasimov; the deceased Iranian major general Qassem Soleimani; and vice chairman of China's Central Military Commission Zhang Youxia. Drawing on interviews with dozens of US military, diplomatic, and intelligence officials, and hundreds of documents translated from Russian, Farsi, and Mandarin, *Three Dangerous Men* details the key steps the United States must take to completely rethink how it engages in competition before it is too late.

> "A brilliantly conceived exposé of modern conflict through the lives of three warrior-innovators. . . . An invaluable book."
> —**Thomas Rid, Johns Hopkins University,** author of *Active Measures*

> "A must-read for anyone seeking to understand the present-day challenges facing the United States and our allies and partners around the world."
> —**General David Petraeus, former CIA director**

SETH G. JONES is the senior vice president, Harold Brown Chair, and director of the International Security Program at the Center for Strategic and International Studies (CSIS), as well as the author of *A Covert Action*, *In the Graveyard of Empires*, and *Hunting in the Shadows*. He lives outside of Washington, DC.

POLITICAL SCIENCE

ISBN 978-1-324-05056-8

Cover design: Jaya Miceli
Cover photograph: Peter Dazeley / The Image Bank / Getty Images
Author photograph: Suzanne M. Jones

NORTON
WWNORTON.COM | @WWNORTON